Bankruptcy and Divorce:
A Practical Guide for the Family Lawyer

Bankruptcy and Divorce:
A Practical Guide for the Family Lawyer

THIRD EDITION

Matthew Barker, Insolvency Partner, Clarke Willmott LLP,
Southampton and a Licensed Insolvency Practitioner

Simon Calhaem, Barrister, 29 Bedford Row Chambers, London

Jonathan Middleton, Solicitor and Deputy Registrar in Bankruptcy

Gareth Schofield, Family Partner, Clarke Willmott LLP, Bristol

 **Family Law**

Published by Family Law
a publishing imprint of
Jordan Publishing Limited
21 St Thomas Street
Bristol BS1 6JS

British Library Cataloguing-in-Publication Data

A catalogue record for this book is available from the British Library.

ISBN 978 1 84661 206 0

Typeset by Letterpart Ltd, Reigate, Surrey

Printed in Great Britain by CPI Antony Rowe, Chippenham, Wiltshire

FOREWORD BY LORD JUSTICE WILSON

Family practitioners become edgy if asked to address the impact of the bankruptcy of a spouse (let us say the husband) on proceedings for ancillary relief or on other financial issues following divorce. Eyes tend to glaze; brows to pucker; even lower lips to tremble. The bankruptcy – practitioners will recognise – is a very serious development; there are clear rules on the subject, but of which they harbour only a dim awareness; their failure to advise the wife – or indeed the husband – accurately on the likely legal consequences of rival courses of action may prove gravely prejudicial to their client; indeed the whole subject has for them the unpleasant whiff of a potential negligence action.

I confess that, when I was in practice, I tended to phone a friend for education about bankruptcy issues. Yes, it was as unprofessional as that; but the limitation period has expired. If only this book had then been in print. Its first edition, under the title "Debt and Insolvency on Family Breakdown", was published in 1994; and there was a second edition in 2003. But the book now in your hands is a thorough revamp, as is reflected by the change of title. It is written specifically for family lawyers but speaks with the authority of two top insolvency practitioners as well as of two top family practitioners.

Family judges as well as practitioners need to know the score: (a) when the husband has gone bankrupt prior to the wife's issue of proceedings for ancillary proceedings; (b) when he goes bankrupt during them; and (c) when it is foreseeable that he will go bankrupt soon after their conclusion. This book, which I have read in proof, could not, I think, address these scenarios more clearly.

But, of course, questions go wider than to discern when and how to proceed against *the other spouse*. The non-bankrupt spouse has to decide how to deal with *the trustee*. With him, battle has often to be joined by way of the assertion of a substantial equitable interest in the home and/or of objection to his demand for sale of it. In the former respect the authors valiantly strive to navigate us around the law up to and including *Stack v Dowden*; in the latter they explain an important provision (s 283A) inserted into the Insolvency Act 1986 by the Enterprise Act 2002.

Helpfully the authors also include a chapter on the wife's susceptibility to enforcement against her of the charge upon her interest in the home which, so unwisely, she executed by way of security for such of the husband's business debts as, whether or not actually bankrupt, he cannot now repay. The foundation of the jurisprudence is *Etridge* and, instead of reading 374 paragraphs of the speeches, we should now read Chapter 7 of this book.

It is an honour to be asked to write this foreword. I will be using this book and warmly commend its use to my fellow family lawyers.

Nicholas Wilson
3 March 2010

PREFACE

Since the second edition of this work the world has ridden the boom and now is paying the price. Levels of personal insolvency have soared, with family practitioners having to deal with these issues on day to day basis within their usual caseload, which is stressful enough at the best of times. This edition is intended to give the family practitioner a head start in understanding those issues in a way which is both approachable and also informative.

As ever thanks go to Jordans for their support and patience in putting this latest edition together as the deadlines have come and gone. In addition grateful thanks must go to all those who wrote for previous editions of this book, and whose hard work lives on in many of the chapters.

Matthew Barker
Simon Calhaem
Jonathan Middleton
Gareth Schofield
March 2010

CONTENTS

TABLE OF CASES

References are to paragraph numbers.

TABLE OF STATUTES

References are to paragraph numbers.

TABLE OF STATUTORY INSTRUMENTS

References are to paragraph numbers.

TABLE OF ABBREVIATIONS

CCR	County Court Rules 1981
COA 1979	Charging Orders Act 1979
CPR	Civil Procedure Rules 1998
ECtHR	European Court of Human Rights
EU	European Union
FLA 1996	Family Law Act 1996
IA 1986	Insolvency Act 1986
IA 2000	Insolvency Act 2000
IHT	Inheritance Tax
IVA	individual voluntary arrangement
LPA 1925	Law of Property Act 1925
LRA 2002	Land Registration Act 2002
MCA 1973	Matrimonial Causes Act 1973
RSC	Rules of the Supreme Court 1965
TLATA 1996	Trusts of Land and Appointment of Trustee Act 1996
WRPA 1999	Welfare Reform and Pensions Act 1999

Chapter 1

PRACTICAL CONSIDERATIONS

OVERVIEW

1.1   This chapter is intended to set out the practical considerations that should be borne in mind when negotiating with a trustee in bankruptcy where he has an interest in the family home. The chapter touches on various technical issues that are considered in much more detail elsewhere in the book.

1.2   As a generality, where a bankruptcy estate has more than a minimal asset value, the Official Receiver will ensure that an insolvency practitioner is appointed to be trustee in bankruptcy of the estate of the bankrupt. In some cases, a bankruptcy estate with property interests will however remain with the Official Receiver.

1.3   The likelihood therefore is that a solicitor representing a bankrupt, the bankrupt's spouse or other family members, will find himself dealing with an insolvency practitioner, rather than the Official Receiver.

1.4   The trustee will be a licensed insolvency practitioner, who will take the appointment in his own name. He will most likely be a partner in a firm of accountants, although day-to-day administration of the case will probably be handled by a member of staff.

1.5   The trustee is a regulated professional. He is also an officer of the court. Moreover, a sample of his casework is audited by his regulator and his actions have to be objectively justifiable to his regulator and creditors.

1.6   The trustee owes a duty to the bankrupt's creditors. He must act in what he considers to be their best interests. As he acts in a fiduciary capacity, he must do what he believes is objectively correct in accordance with best practice and with what his regulator will require.

1.7   In practical terms, what this means is that the trustee is obliged to pursue avenues of investigation and to pursue assets, where it is reasonable for him to do so. It also means that the trustee cannot unilaterally walk away from assets or legal claims and rights where he considers that creditors or his regulator could criticise him for doing so.

1.8   The trustee will be practical and commercial when looking to realise assets. In almost all bankruptcies, the only significant capital asset will be an interest in the family home, which is usually occupied by family members and in which, usually, the bankrupt's spouse has an interest. So, the trustee will be concerned to ensure that he is able to realise his interest in the property. The trustee's starting position will be to negotiate and he will almost certainly have written to the bankrupt and the bankrupt's spouse setting out what he considers to be his interest and asking them to agree terms as to how it can be realised. Whilst the trustee will have a degree of empathy for the bankrupt's family, he will not compromise his position, merely through a sense of sympathy.

1.9   Ideally, the trustee will want to avoid litigation and will want to negotiate settlement, but if that is not possible, he will have no difficulty in pursuing his interest in a property or other claims through the courts. If so, he will instruct lawyers to act on his behalf.

1.10   It is always worth remembering that for the trustee, litigation is simply part of his job. Moreover, it is probable that his solicitors and counsel will be prepared to act on a CFA as a matter of course. This means that if the trustee obtains a costs order against the wife, she will not only have to pay his base legal costs, but also an uplift on those costs, at the level agreed between the trustee and his solicitors. For the bankrupt and their family, it will be an extremely stressful exercise and they will have to fund their own legal costs. Public Funding is rarely available.

1.11   Some bankrupts (and their families) upon occasion take the view that the trustee in some way acts for or represents the bankrupt. This is not the case. The level of duty that the trustee could be said to owe a bankrupt is limited and only materially arises in relatively unusual circumstances, such as a case where there will be a surplus to be repaid to the bankrupt, once the assets have been realised and the costs of the bankruptcy and creditors paid in full.

1.12   As a final point, some bankrupts and their family decide that a tactical strategy of making multiple complaints to the trustee's regulator will be a useful bargaining chip in trying to persuade him to withdraw from a claim (or indeed a case). All that this will do is increase costs and make negotiations more heated. Even if there were to be a settlement, the regulator would still have to deal with the complaint so this aspect would fall outside the control of the parties. The trustee will be well aware of this. It is not a wise strategy.

CREDITORS

1.13   The overriding duty which will be in the forefront of the trustee's mind will be to act in the best interests of creditors. In short, he is required to realise assets in a timely manner and for the best price obtainable in the circumstances, for the benefit of creditors. Inevitably, this process will result in the trustee expending costs and incurring expenses. It has been held that even if all of the realisations from assets will go to pay the costs of the bankruptcy (which include the trustee's costs), that is no reason for the trustee not to proceed to realise those assets.

1.14 Once the costs of the bankruptcy are paid, the trustee will pay a dividend to creditors. Crown preference for certain arrears of PAYE, NIC and VAT has now fallen away and the Crown now ranks in the general body of unsecured creditors.

1.15 The trustee does not need to pay all creditors in full. All he has to do is to pay creditors out, pro rata, in accordance with their claims, from the realisations that have come into the estate.

1.16 Once there is a discharge from bankruptcy, then the bankrupt is discharged from the debts which rank for dividend against the bankruptcy estate. The definition of a 'debt' for such purposes is very broadly drawn and includes almost all categories of liability, but not payments due under Family Court orders (although it does include costs orders and lump sum orders for the purpose of dividends but not release), student loans and other limited categories of liability.

1.17 Usually, a bankruptcy order (if it is the first bankruptcy order made against the debtor) will be automatically discharged on the first anniversary of the making of the bankruptcy order. It is possible for the Official Receiver to grant early discharge of the bankruptcy order, although this may cease soon as a consultation paper to repeal this has been issued. Recently, early discharge has become less common. Moreover, if a bankrupt is un-cooperative, the trustee or the Official Receiver can apply to court to suspend the automatic discharge of the bankruptcy order, until the bankrupt does co-operate. Also, the Official Receiver may apply to court to put a bankruptcy restriction order in place, which will mean that the bankruptcy is discharged in the usual way, but the former bankrupt is still subject to certain restrictions.

1.18 The discharge of the bankrupt does not affect the vesting of assets in the trustee. The only circumstances where assets re-vest are in relation to the family home under s 283A of the 1986 Act. All other assets in which the trustee has an interest will continue to be vested in him, until realised.

1.19 The trustee will take creditors' views into account to a certain extent, but he will act in accordance with the professional advice given to him and his opinion as to what is best for creditors, in all the circumstances. As such, if a particular creditor desires the trustee to undertake a disproportionate level of investigation or pursue claims which are not meritorious, the trustee will not do so. If an interested party is dissatisfied by the trustee's decision in this regard, that party will need to establish that the trustee is acting in a way in which no reasonable trustee would act, if he is to persuade the court to interfere with or reverse the trustee's decision.

DOING A DEAL WITH THE TRUSTEE

1.20 In most bankruptcies, the only significant asset which vests in the trustee will be an interest in the family home.

1.21 Chapter 4 considers this in detail and those points will not be rehearsed here. The point is that the court will determine interests in property applying trust principles, not the usual principles applied in the Family Court.

1.22 The trustee is a commercial animal. He will always look to settle rather than litigate, to realise his interest in an asset (typically, the family home), but he will go to court if the bankrupt/wife refuse to engage with him or if they cannot put forward an acceptable offer to enable him to realise his interest in an asset.

1.23 Whilst some bankrupts and or their wives/families take the approach that they want to 'fight' the trustee 'as a matter of principle', objectively, one would have thought that the overriding intention of the bankrupt and/or the wife is to save the family home, if possible, or, if that is unrealistic, to get it sold for the best price, so that the wife, if she has an interest in it, can recover the maximum amount out of it, possibly (amongst other things) by negotiating that she should be given credit for costs savings.

1.24 The courts have generally been reluctant to accept human rights based arguments where a trustee is seeking to realise a property and whilst the 'exceptional circumstances' argument will apply in certain limited cases (usually related to very poor health), the courts generally order that the trustee's right to possession and sale of the property will be suspended for a period. It would be rare for such an application to result in the trustee being denied his interest in the property altogether. The family therefore needs to be advised to be pragmatic and put aside emotional attachments to the home, otherwise, the costs of litigating the matter can quickly outweigh any benefit achieved through litigation.

1.25 So, the family of a bankrupt will usually be faced with several options:

(1) Settle with the trustee on terms to buy out his interest in the property;

(2) Apply to annul the bankruptcy order on the ground of payment in full;

(3) Agree to voluntarily sell;

(4) Do nothing – in which event the trustee will apply for an order for possession and sale, provided that his interest in the property is worth enough to make that worthwhile.

1.26 In all cases, it is crucial to engage with the trustee on a sensible basis and address the issue quickly. Delay just costs money, particularly where the strategy decided upon is to annul the bankruptcy order on the ground of payment in full (see below).

1.27 If the value of the trustee's interest in the equity in the house is significantly greater than the bankruptcy debts and costs, then annulment may be a better route.

COMMERCIALITY – AGREEING THE TRUSTEE'S INTEREST IN THE FAMILY HOME

1.28 The trustee will evaluate what he considers to be his interest in the property and will usually write to the bankrupt and his spouse (and any other co-owners) setting this out and inviting offers to buy out his interest in the property. Frequently, those letters are ignored and, in order to move the matter forward, the trustee will instruct lawyers to negotiate and issue proceedings if negotiations do not result in a satisfactory outcome. There is nothing to stop the wife in making the first approach to the trustee, if she is keen to resolve the matter quickly.

1.29 The starting point for the trustee will be the value of the property. He will be guided in this by advice from an agent. The trustee will ideally want access to the property for his agent to provide a valuation, although if this is not forthcoming, the trustee is likely to rely upon a drive by valuation. If the wife intends challenging the trustee's valuation, she will need to obtain her own valuation(s) to do so. If she opposes the valuation on the basis that the condition of the property is poor, then it would be sensible to allow the trustee's agent access to view the property and report back.

1.30 The trustee will look to agree value, for the purpose of reaching settlement. If this is not possible, then the question of value will be determined by the court, using expert opinion.

1.31 Next, the outstanding mortgage will be deducted, giving a gross equity figure. The trustee's opening position will be that unless there is a written trust recording the parties' equitable interest in a jointly owned property in a different proportion, this is to be split 50/50 between the husband and wife owners.

1.32 Chapter 4 considers in detail considerations around adjustments in equity and these will not be rehearsed in this chapter. However, the practical point is that if the wife runs arguments departing from the 50/50 principle, those arguments must be evidenced and the costs of running such arguments will eat into the sums available for distribution.

1.33   Once each party's equity figure is established, it is possible to apply discounts to the trustee's interest, to reflect the costs savings that will be achieved by reaching settlement rather than applying to court for an order for sale and the costs of sale.

1.34   The costs deductions could be calculated at half of a selling agent's commission (at a standard commission rate) and half the conveyancing costs. The trustee *may* concede some deduction in respect of the costs that he would incur in taking possession of the property, but that is by no means certain.

1.35   If a wife is to claim that the equity is to be adjusted in her favour, then she will have to evidence that claim. The trustee will find great difficulty in justifying accepting unevidenced claims and if the question is placed before the court, it will be for the wife to prove her allegations. Hence, it would be sensible for the wife to provide full early disclosure of her claim to the trustee, in order to avoid having the issue litigated.

1.36   The trustee also may claim occupation rent as against the wife. Historically, it was thought that occupation rent could only net down to nil a claim by the wife to have equity adjusted in her favour. However, recent case law has established that a trustee's claim for occupation rent can outweigh any claim by the wife and actually adjust matters in favour of the trustee. An award of occupation rent is a discretionary matter for the court, but it may be well for the wife to consider, if making an unevidenced or poorly evidenced claim to equity adjustment, when faced with a counter argument for occupation rent, to consider settling as she could lose heavily in court with her having to pay the trustee's costs.

1.37   The trustee will be looking to settle on payment of a lump sum to him by the wife/family. He will only consider a short deferment on the basis that the source of funds is readily available (such as a third party property being re-mortgaged where it is clear that this will definitely happen in a short timescale). Long-term periodic payments will not be attractive to him.

ANNULMENT

1.38   A bankruptcy order can be annulled on two grounds. First, on the ground that the order ought not to have been made and secondly on the ground that the creditors and costs of the bankruptcy have been paid or secured for in full to the satisfaction of the court.

1.39   If a bankruptcy order is annulled, then the legal position is that it is as if the bankruptcy order had never been made. The assets will automatically re-vest in the bankrupt, although the actions of the trustee will still stand.

1.40   The first head generally is taken to cover circumstances where there is a procedural irregularity in the making of the bankruptcy order. For example, the bankrupt was not properly served with the papers. It is frequently the case that HM Revenue & Customs obtain bankruptcy orders against individuals based on determinations rather than tax liabilities based on returns. HM Revenue & Customs are entitled to demand tax on this basis and even if the returns are subsequently submitted, and it transpires that there was no liability to tax, that does not mean that the bankruptcy order ought not to have been made.

1.41 If an application is made under this head, the main respondent is the petitioning creditor, not the trustee or the Official Receiver and it is not for the trustee or the Official Receiver to make the application. It is most usually made by the bankrupt or his spouse or former spouse (particularly where a spouse or former spouse considers that the bankruptcy is a device to avoid ancillary relief). The trustee or the Official Receiver would not expect to be involved in the application, save to ensure that the costs and expenses are paid. As to who pays those costs is within the discretion of the court, but if the application is successful, the usual order would be for the petitioning creditor to pay.

1.42 As a generality, the court would expect such an application to be issued shortly after the making of the bankruptcy order. As to whether the court will annul the making of a bankruptcy order under the first head is always within the discretion of the court and any person issuing an application under the first head needs to bear in mind that if he has delayed making the application for a number of years, he will need to explain that to the court. Also, it may be that even if his application is successful, the court may order that he has to pay the trustee's costs of dealing with the annulment.

1.43 It may be that the bankrupt and his family should consider making an annulment application under the second head. This may be the case if the amount required to pay creditors in full, plus interest (at the statutory rate of 8% per annum (or a higher contractual rate if the creditor is entitled to that)) and the costs of the bankruptcy is significantly less than the trustee's interest in the property. If the family is able to raise such a sum, then it may be a cheaper option to make an application for annulment under the second head.

1.44 The costs that will have to be paid will include the petitioning creditors' costs, the Official Receiver's fee and the trustee's costs and disbursements (including his legal costs). The level of the Official Receiver's fee is set by statutory instrument and cannot realistically be challenged. If the bankrupt wishes to challenge the petitioning creditor's costs, then it is for the bankrupt to deal direct with the petitioning creditor in that regard. The trustee's concern will merely be to ensure that those costs are paid.

1.45 If the annulment application is to be funded out of realisations from the estate, then such realisations will be paid into the Insolvency Services Account and will attract statutory charges (unless the bankruptcy order was made prior to 1 April 2004 in which case the Secretary of State's fees applied to the sums paid into the Insolvency Services Account will not apply). If the annulment application is to be funded from third party monies, then these should not be paid into the Insolvency Services Account and such charges will not be levied.

1.46 The trustee's costs are always subject to the ultimate approval of the court and it is open to a bankrupt (or a creditor) to ask the court to review those costs. In some cases, a trustee's costs have been significantly reduced by the court, in others, the court has largely approved the costs. The practical point is that any application to challenge a trustee's costs is a protracted and expensive exercise. The bankrupt is best advised to appreciate that the court will almost certainly order that a significant proportion of those costs must be paid and it may well be the case that the cost of the application will outweigh any saving following assessment. It should be noted that challenge 'as a principle' for the sake of challenge is unlikely to produce an ultimately satisfactory outcome. Any challenge must bear in mind the proportionality of the costs under challenge and the costs that will be incurred in dealing with the challenge.

1.47 The trustee will also have incurred certain disbursements, for example in insuring and valuing the property. It is highly unlikely that these are practically capable of challenge.

1.48 So, if the bankrupt issues an annulment application under head 2, the more that he argues with the trustee and the more that matters are delayed, the greater the level of costs that may be incurred. As the bankrupt will have to arrange for those costs to be paid, it is in his best interests to be open and co-operative with his trustee and provide the trustee with the information that he requests.

1.49 If a bankrupt (or his wife) intends seeking an annulment under the second head, then it is in their best interests to engage fully and openly with the trustee and explain the plan and the timescale and how funding is to be obtained. The bankrupt is best advised to ask the trustee for an estimated outcome statement, showing what is required to obtain an annulment and once funding is available to immediate issue the application. The trustee and the Official Receiver are both respondent and must both be served with the application, although it is unusual for the Official Receiver to play any active part in the proceedings, if an external trustee has been appointed.

1.50 Creditors are entitled to be paid in full and to be paid statutory interest at 8% (or the higher contractual rate, if the creditor asks for it, which is very rare). It may be possible for the bankrupt to persuade creditors to forego their right to interest (or indeed some capital). If the applicant wishes to attempt this, it is for him to contact creditors, not the trustee. The applicant should do this in writing and advise creditors of their right to be paid in full, with interest. If a creditor agrees to forego interest or capital, then confirmation of that needs to be obtained in writing from the creditor and the creditor needs to confirm in writing to the trustee that its proof of debt is adjusted accordingly.

The applicant should exhibit all such correspondence to his annulment application and send copies to the trustee.

1.51 If the bankrupt wishes the trustee to undertake the exercise of liaising with creditors and challenging their claims, then the bankrupt must accept that he will ultimately have to bear the increased costs of the trustee doing so. In these circumstances, if a bankrupt objects to the level of a creditor's claim, it is far better for the bankrupt to deal direct with the creditor, rather than getting the trustee to do this, as the bankrupt, with knowledge of the dispute, is far better placed to make his points.

1.52 For the application to be successful, the applicant must raise sufficient monies to enable creditors and costs to be paid in full (or at agreed lower amounts). If such a sum cannot be raised, then the application is unlikely to be successful. The strict letter of the law requires that before the application is heard, creditors must be paid or secured for to the satisfaction of the court. However, on some occasions, an order can be obtained if the applicant is in funds to pay creditors immediately following the making of the order.

1.53 The trustee's involvement is to oversee the arrangements to make sure that the proposed annulment is feasible and that creditors are properly informed of their rights. The trustee also submits a report to the court on the annulment proposal, which comments on the proposal and the creditors and assets in the bankruptcy. The trustee will also bring such other matters to the attention of the court as he thinks fit, including the level of co-operation or otherwise of the bankrupt. The trustee's report will be neutral and will be used to guide the court. It is important to advise the bankrupt that annulment is always within the discretion of the court (unless the annulment is sought following the approval of an individual voluntary arrangement), so if his conduct is very poor, the court may still not annul the order (although this is unlikely).

1.54 On occasion, a bankrupt will issue an application under the second head, alleging that as he should not have been made bankrupt, he disputes all creditors and all costs and therefore has to pay nothing. The best advice to such a bankrupt is that he should proceed on the basis of a more sensible application that actually addresses the creditors and costs issues.

WHEN TO SELL UP

1.55 Once the extent of the trustee's interest has been evaluated, the bankrupt and his family can see whether a deal with the trustee to buy out his interest or to achieve an annulment under the second head is possible. If so, then best advice is to move ahead as quickly as possible.

1.56 It has historically been possible for bankrupt's to re-mortgage their homes to raise enough to pay the trustee out. Whilst initially attractive, as it enables the family to retain the home, they need to be confident that payment terms can be met. If not, this may simply eat up the wife's equity in the home and if subsequently repossessed by the new mortgagee, the family will not have a lump sum to put down as a deposit for a new property.

1.57   Therefore, if the family cannot afford to keep the home, then the best advice is to sell voluntarily and seek to agree with the trustee how much each is to recover out of the proceeds of sale and try to negotiate with the trustee that his share bears the costs of sale.

THE SALE

1.58   If a trustee is to sell his interest in the property, either by way of a sale back to the bankrupt or his wife or to a third party through a conveyancing transaction, neither transaction will be a 'standard' conveyance.

1.59   If the property is in the joint names of the bankrupt and a third party, then the bankrupt and the third party will continue as legal owners, holding the property on trust for the trustee and third party. The trustee's interest therefore is in equity alone.

1.60   If the legal title in the property is to be transferred, unless the trustee has obtained an Order for Sale, it will be the legal owners who will sign the Form TR1. The trustee is only able to join in the sale to convey his equitable interest.

1.61   So, if the wife 'does a deal' with the trustee, he can provide her with an assignment of his equitable interest in the property. Following that, the bankrupt and the wife will hold the property on trust for the wife alone.

1.62   If the bankrupt is the sole legal owner of the property, then the trustee can apply to the Land Registry to have the property transferred into his name. He can then convey the property.

1.63   In any trustee sale, the trustee will not use standard documents and he will be concerned to ensure that he conveys giving no warranties or representations and will want to exclude his personal liability. Moreover, the trustee will have very little information concerning the contents of the property and will therefore be unable to give full answers to pre-contract enquiries (and even if he can provide some responses, he will not warrant them).

Chapter 2

BANKRUPTCY AND INDIVIDUAL VOLUNTARY ARRANGEMENTS

INTRODUCTION

2.1   The purpose of this chapter is to provide a brief guide to bankruptcy and individual voluntary arrangements which will put in context the remainder of this book.

INSOLVENCY LAW

Bankruptcy

2.2   On 29 December 1986 the new bankruptcy code contained in the Insolvency Act 1986 (IA 1986) came into force. It applies to bankruptcy petitions presented on or after that date. This is what is called 'the new law'. The Bankruptcy Act 1914 still applies to cases where the petition was presented before 29 December 1986 and indeed to any proceedings where the receiving order or adjudication order was made before that date. This is called 'the old law' or 'the former law'. With the passage of time, it is unlikely that there are many old law bankruptcies still proceeding so this book concerns itself primarily with the new law. Having said that, however, it is appropriate to refer briefly to the old law as certain authorities to which reference will be made in this book are old law authorities. In this regard, it is important to know that under the old law there was a two-stage process before a debtor became a bankrupt.

2.3   The first stage was the order made on the bankruptcy petition which was called the receiving order. This constituted the Official Receiver as a receiver and manager of the debtor's property but it was only when the adjudication order was made that the debtor became bankrupt. Under the new law, both of these consequences flow from the making of the bankruptcy order. It should be noted that under the old law on the adjudication order the property of the bankrupt vested in the trustee in bankruptcy. The position under the new law is that vesting occurs when the appointment of a trustee in bankruptcy other than the Official Receiver is certified or, if no meeting of creditors is held, when the Official Receiver so notifies the court, in which case the Official Receiver acts as the trustee in bankruptcy.[1] It should be noted that the Official Receiver is now likely to act as the trustee in bankruptcy in the vast majority of small cases.

2.4   Bankruptcy arises where a bankruptcy order has been made and, in this jurisdiction, applies only to individuals. Insolvency, on the other hand, does not have a precise meaning and is applied to both individuals and companies. It is, however, very often used where liabilities exceed assets or where someone is unable to pay their debts as they fall due. The fact that an individual is insolvent does not mean that he or she is bankrupt.

Corporate insolvency

2.5   Different terms are used in corporate insolvency, which is beyond the scope of this book.[2] Liquidation, which is either compulsory, ie by court order, or voluntary, ie by resolution of the company's members, is a corporate equivalent of bankruptcy. It is also known as 'winding up', for example the order for compulsory liquidation is known as a 'winding-up order'. Other insolvency procedures that may arise in a corporate context are:

(a)   administration, which imposes a moratorium against enforcement mechanisms to assist with rescue or a better result for creditors or to make a distribution;

(b)   administrative receivership, which is primarily a mechanism for the realisation of security held by a debenture holder, but is likely to become less frequent as a result of s 72A of the IA 1986 which with certain exceptions prohibits the appointment of an administrative receiver by the holder of a qualifying floating charge entered into on or after 15 September 2003.

Voluntary arrangements

2.6   It is also possible for both an individual and a company, as well as a partnership, to have a voluntary arrangement. Voluntary arrangements are the least structured of all formal insolvency procedures under the IA 1986. In broad terms, a voluntary arrangement is either a composition in satisfaction of debts, ie where the creditors agree to accept something less than 100p in the £, or a scheme of arrangement of the debtor's affairs which is more wide ranging than a simple composition. Although there are certain restrictions in relation to voluntary arrangements, these are not substantial and the debtor has a clean sheet of paper on which to draft the proposal. Briefly, the debtor needs to put forward a reasoned proposal which demonstrates clearly that the creditors are going to be better off by accepting it than by petitioning for liquidation or bankruptcy.

---

[1]   See **3.4**.
[2]   See, for example *Loose on Liquidators*, 6th Ed (2010), Jordans.

2.7   There are important differences between the provisions governing corporate and individual voluntary arrangements but the procedure for an individual voluntary arrangement is described briefly at **2.19** et seq. Reference will also be made below at **2.31** to what are called fast track voluntary arrangements.

2.8   Reference will also be made below to insolvent partnerships.[3]

BANKRUPTCY PROCEDURE

Jurisdiction

2.9   There are two usual types of petition for a bankruptcy order: a creditor's petition and a debtor's petition. Figures 1 and 2 in Appendix 1 demonstrate both procedures.

2.10   Before dealing with these procedures it is necessary to refer to Council Regulation (EC) No 1346/2000 of 29 May 2000 which came into force in this jurisdiction on 31 May 2002. Although largely concerned with jurisdictional questions affecting the European Union (EU), it is important as it affects the extent of vesting of assets in a trustee in bankruptcy in a case to which the Regulation applies. It should be noted that it applies to all EU countries excluding Denmark. There is also an exclusion for insurance undertakings and credit institutions.

2.11   It is only if the centre of the debtor's main interests is in England or Wales that what are called 'main proceedings' can be opened here. If 'main proceedings' are opened one of the consequences is that the debtor's assets, whether in this jurisdiction or outside it, will vest in a trustee in bankruptcy. Whilst this is generally true, difficulties can still arise in relation to rights in rem over assets situated in a state the subject of the said Regulation. It is not proposed to consider this in detail nor indeed in relation to other countries where assets may be situated which on general principles would fall within the bankruptcy.

2.12   If the centre of main interests is in another EU state apart from Denmark, there will be jurisdiction to open proceedings in England and Wales in respect of the debtor only if the debtor has an 'establishment' in the UK, and in that instance the proceedings will be limited to assets in the UK. This is an exception to the general principle of universality which applies in bankruptcy generally.

2.13   It should be noted that even if there is an establishment in this jurisdiction, proceedings can only be opened if one or other of the following conditions are satisfied:

---

[3]   At **2.45**.

(1)   if main insolvency proceedings cannot be opened because of conditions laid down by the state having the centre of main interests;

(2)   where the proceedings are issued by a creditor who has his domicile, habitual residence or registered office in this jurisdiction or whose claim arises from the operation of the establishment here.

Creditor's petition

2.14   In respect of a creditor's petition, there are two grounds on which it can be presented. The first is that the debtor has failed to comply with a statutory demand for payment. The second is that there is an unsatisfied execution on a judgment debt. With the benefit of either of these grounds, a creditor can present and serve a bankruptcy petition. It is at the hearing of the bankruptcy petition that a bankruptcy order may be made. However, it should be noted that, by virtue of s 284 of the IA 1986, any disposition made by the debtor in the period beginning with the day of presentation of the bankruptcy petition and ending with the vesting of the bankrupt's property in a trustee in bankruptcy is void unless validated by the court.

2.15   Further, at any time when proceedings on a bankruptcy petition are pending or when a person has been adjudged bankrupt, the court may stay any action, execution or legal process against the property or person of the debtor or bankrupt.[4] The court to which reference has been made is the bankruptcy court but there are additional powers for any court in this regard in s 285(2) of the IA 1986.

2.16   Once a bankruptcy order has been made, a creditor with a provable debt will not have any remedy against the property or person of the bankrupt in respect of that debt, nor can such a creditor commence any action or other legal proceedings against the bankrupt save with the leave of the court.[5] Again, this is a reference to the bankruptcy court. The effect of discharge, which is the normal 'end' to a bankruptcy, is referred to at **2.41** et seq and in chapter 6.

Debtor's petition

2.17   In the case of a debtor's petition, the only ground which can be relied upon is that the debtor is unable to pay his debts. The debtor's petition and his statement of affairs are then presented to the court and, subject to what is said below about small bankruptcies, the court will in most cases make a bankruptcy order immediately. The application of s 284 of the IA 1986 referred to above will, therefore, be minimal. There is also very little opportunity for a third party to intervene prior to the bankruptcy order being made but it is possible for the issue of abuse of process or the like to be considered on an

---

4   IA 1986, s 285(1).
5   Ibid, s 285(3).

application to annul the bankruptcy order on the ground that it ought not to have been made and this is referred to in more detail in chapters 1 and 6.

2.18 It should be noted that where the debtor has debts below the small bankruptcy level of £20,000, has assets of £2,000 and has not been bankrupted nor made a composition with his creditors nor a scheme of arrangement within 5 years, the court is, however, obliged to consider the possibility of a voluntary arrangement as an alternative to bankruptcy. The manner in which this is dealt with is set out in ss 273 and 274 of the IA 1986 and differs from the normal procedure considered immediately below. It should however be noted that there is at present a consultation exercise being undertaken as to whether the court should continue to deal with debtors petitions at least in relation to the making of a bankruptcy order – see *Reforming Debtor Petition Bankruptcy and Early Discharge from Bankruptcy* a consultation document issued in November 2009.

INDIVIDUAL VOLUNTARY ARRANGEMENT

IVA procedure

2.19 A debtor may seek to avoid bankruptcy by entering into an individual voluntary arrangement (IVA) with his creditors. The procedure for an IVA is prescribed by the IA 1986 and the Insolvency Rules 1986. As a result of the implementation of the Insolvency Act 2000 (IA 2000), there are now two main routes available for obtaining an IVA. In addition there are also fast track voluntary arrangements which are referred to below at **2.31**.

2.20 The first option, which is likely to be preferred where there is no significant creditor pressure, involves the court only to the extent that various documents have to be filed in court. The debtor will need to find an insolvency practitioner to act and with his assistance prepares the proposal, which goes to creditors. The insolvency practitioner, who at this stage is called the nominee, prepares and files in court a report indicating that the debtor's proposal has a reasonable prospect of being approved and implemented and that a meeting of creditors should be called. The nominee will then summon the meeting of creditors and, for the proposal to be approved, a majority in excess of 75% in value of creditors present in person or by proxy and voting on the proposal is required. If it is approved, the voluntary arrangement will then be implemented under the control of the supervisor, who is likely to be the same person as the nominee. It will be necessary for the chairman of the meeting (usually the nominee) to file with the court a report concerning the meeting.

2.21 The alternative route will involve the debtor in seeking the protection of the court from significant creditor pressure. Again, the first step is to involve a licensed insolvency practitioner who is prepared to act in relation to the debtor's proposal to his creditors. Assuming the insolvency practitioner is prepared to act, the debtor applies to the bankruptcy court for an interim order. The interim order has the effect of putting a moratorium on proceedings against the debtor.

2.22   The exact terms of the moratorium are contained in s 252(2) of the IA 1986. The effect of the application for the interim order is contained in s 254 of the IA 1986.

2.23   The insolvency practitioner, who is again known as the nominee, files with the court a report setting out whether or not the debtor's proposal has a reasonable prospect of being approved and implemented. If the nominee's report is in favour of the proposal being put to the creditors, the court extends the interim order to enable the creditors' meeting to take place. The nominee then summons the meeting of the creditors who decide whether to accept the proposal or reject it (a majority in excess of 75% in value of creditors present in person or by proxy and voting on the proposal is again required). The nominee, who is usually the chairman of the meeting, files a report with the court setting out the decision of the meeting. If the voluntary arrangement is approved, it is then implemented under the control of the supervisor. A flowchart in respect of this second route is included as Figure 3 in Appendix 1 below.

IVAs and financial provision for spouses

2.24   In the context of family breakdown, one point that a family practitioner needs to be aware of is that, unless there is agreement about the financial provision for a spouse or former spouse or the court has determined the same, it will be difficult for the debtor to put forward a clear proposal to his creditors because the position of the spouse or former spouse will represent an unknown and unpredictable liability. The creditors will, therefore, find it difficult to be convinced that they will be better off by agreeing to the proposal. It should not be assumed that the Standard Conditions for IVAs produced by the Association of Business Recovery Professionals or for that matter the IVA Forum address adequately the position of a spouse or former spouse. Specific provisions will be required.

2.25   Useful guidance on this topic can be obtained from the looseleaf work *Individual Voluntary Arrangements* (Jordan Publishing) edited by Stephen Lawson, Paul French and Giles Frampton. In particular it deals with the position in the light of two decisions – *Re Bradley-Hole*[6] and *Re A Debtor; JP v a Debtor*.[7] In summary, the following points can usefully be made.

(1)   The nominee should give the former spouse notice if there is any possibility whatsoever of the former spouse being a creditor.

(2)   Quantifiable claims such as those relevant in *Re Bradley-Hole* (in particular arrears of maintenance and costs where the order is made prior to the relevant date) are provable and the former spouse is entitled to vote. If the former spouse is not notified the position in this regard is set out in s 260(2A) of the IA 1986 which provides that in the event of non-payment

---

[6]   [1995] 1 WLR 1097.
[7]   [1999] BPIR 206.

of the sum due under the arrangement and the arrangement not having ended prematurely the debtor remains liable to pay the amount due under the arrangement. It should also be noted that the time for challenging the arrangement under s 262 of the IA 1986 is extended in the case of non-notification.

(3) The special position of the former spouse also needs to be reflected in the terms of the voluntary arrangement and, if it is not, the former spouse would be entitled to apply under s 262 of the IA 1986 to set aside the voluntary arrangement on the ground that it is unfairly prejudicial. The special position of the former spouse derives from the fact that, in bankruptcy, the former spouse would have retained the right by virtue of s 281(5)(b) to enforce the matrimonial debt notwithstanding the statutory release of a bankrupt from debts upon his discharge.

THE OFFICIAL RECEIVER

2.26 On the making of a bankruptcy order, the Official Receiver assumes control and protects the bankrupt's estate. There is no longer any obligation for the Official Receiver to investigate a case but this arises at the discretion of the Official Receiver.

2.27 Within 21 days from the bankruptcy order on a creditor's petition, the bankrupt has to submit a statement of affairs in the prescribed form to the Official Receiver.

2.28 The Official Receiver is required to send to all creditors a report relating to the bankruptcy proceedings at least once after the making of the bankruptcy order. Where a statement of affairs has been lodged, the Official Receiver must send a summary together with any observations to the creditors, unless he has already reported to them and has formed the view that the statement discloses no further matters which ought to be brought to the attention of the creditors.

2.29 Unless the court appoints a trustee in bankruptcy, the Official Receiver must decide whether to summon a general meeting of the bankrupt's creditors for the purpose of appointing a trustee in bankruptcy as soon as practicable within 12 weeks of the making of the bankruptcy order. If the Official Receiver decides against summoning a meeting, he must, within the 12-week period, so notify the court and every creditor known to the Official Receiver or identified in the bankrupt's statement of affairs. From the date on which the court receives such notification, the Official Receiver becomes the trustee in bankruptcy and the bankrupt's property vests in him. This is no longer an unusual event.

2.30 If a creditors' meeting is to be held, this must be done within 4 months from the date of the bankruptcy order. The meeting deals primarily with two issues: the appointment of a licensed insolvency practitioner to be trustee in bankruptcy and the establishment of a creditors' committee. The trustee's appointment is certified by the chairman of the meeting, which certificate is then sent to the Official Receiver, if he is not the chairman, who endorses it and files it in court. The trustee's appointment is effective from the date on which the appointment is certified and it is only at this time that vesting of the bankrupt's property will occur.

2.31   There are various other functions which the Official Receiver performs, but the most usual contact with him will be in the period before appointment of a trustee or as trustee if no licensed insolvency practitioner is appointed unless of course steps are taken for a fast track voluntary arrangement when there will be contact on this topic. Whilst such an arrangement might be unlikely where there has been a family breakdown it is appropriate to give some idea of what is involved. It only arises where there is a debtor who is an undischarged bankrupt who does not need the protection of an interim order. Basically the debtor prepares a proposal which is submitted to the Official Receiver who must then decide whether he agrees to act as nominee. If he decides to act the Official Receiver submits the proposal to all known creditors inviting them to approve or reject it by a certain date. The proposal may be approved by a majority in excess of 75% in value submitting their vote. Once approved the arrangement is implemented as a standard IVA. However it should be emphasized that this sort of procedure is only likely to be used in cases involving straightforward disposals of assets and/or the collection of regular payments. If the case is complicated this will not be the case.

TRUSTEE IN BANKRUPTCY

2.32   The official name of the trustee is 'The Trustee of the Estate of [name of bankrupt], a bankrupt' but he is also known as the trustee in bankruptcy of the particular bankrupt. The main function of the trustee is to get in and realise the bankrupt's estate and then distribute it in accordance with the provisions of the IA 1986 and the Insolvency Rules 1986.

2.33   The assets of the bankrupt vest in the trustee automatically upon the appointment of the trustee. Reference here should be made to the effect of the Council Regulation set out in **2.10** et seq. This aspect of bankruptcy law is considered further in chapter 3. The assets in the bankrupt's estate are, after payment of the expenses of the bankruptcy, distributed amongst the creditors in respect of bankruptcy debts which have been proved. A bankruptcy debt is, subject to certain exceptions, any debt or liability to which the bankrupt is subject at the commencement of the bankruptcy.

2.34   Two relevant exceptions for family practitioners are, 'any obligation (other than an obligation to pay a lump sum or to pay costs) arising under an order made in family proceedings or under a maintenance calculation under the Child Support Act 1991'. 'Family proceedings' are defined in s 281(8) of the IA 1986 as being family proceedings within the meaning of the Magistrates'

Courts Act 1980 and any proceedings which would be such proceedings but for s 65(1)(ii) of that Act, and also family proceedings within the meaning of Part V of the Matrimonial and Family Proceedings Act 1984. In the light of the above it will be seen that lump sums and costs are provable but as will be seen in **2.41** below these debts are unlikely to be released on discharge. Sums due under a separation agreement would not, however, fall within this exception and so would be provable, although consideration may have to be given to s 329 of the IA 1986 which provides for deferment of 'credit provided' by a bankrupt's spouse until other creditors are paid in full. One further relevant question, whilst on the subject of bankruptcy debts, is whether an undertaking given to a court to pay a sum or sums of money is a bankruptcy debt. Is it 'an order made in family proceedings'? This is discussed in chapter 6.

2.35 If the trustee in bankruptcy needs to commence proceedings in relation to his functions, these are likely to be commenced in the court in which the bankruptcy order was made or the court to which the proceedings were transferred after the making of the bankruptcy order. In broad terms, jurisdiction is conferred on: (a) the High Court in relation to proceedings which are allocated to the London insolvency district; and (b) the relevant county court in relation to proceedings which are allocated to the insolvency district of that court. The trustee in bankruptcy will not be minded to proceed elsewhere unless the claim is straightforward, for example debt collecting, or he is obliged to proceed in a court other than the bankruptcy court.

RESTRICTIONS AND DISQUALIFICATIONS

2.36 The main restrictions upon an undischarged bankrupt or where there is a bankruptcy restriction order or undertaking in force under Sch 4A to the IA 1986 are that:

(1)   he cannot obtain credit of £500 or more without disclosing his status;

(2)   he cannot trade in a name other than that in which he was an adjudged bankrupt;

(3)   he cannot be a director or take part in the management of a company.

2.37 There are also various disqualifications which affect undischarged bankrupts in certain professions and, in particular, solicitors, estate agents and insolvency practitioners. However, it should be noted that the impact of the making of a bankruptcy order is not always straightforward as, for example, in the case of a solicitor, it is possible to seek permission from the Solicitors Regulation Authority to be issued with a practising certificate albeit subject to conditions. The disqualifications in respect of members of both Houses of Parliament and members of local authorities have been removed for undischarged bankrupts but replaced by similar provisions where there is a bankruptcy restriction order or undertaking. However such orders or undertakings which can last between 2 and 15 years are intended to be applicable to the minority of cases where there has been some misconduct. There is no prohibition against having a bank account. This is really a matter for the bankrupt and the bank in question to discuss. Reference can usefully be made to the Insolvency Service website – *www.insolvency.gov.uk* – which has a leaflet explaining about bank accounts.

ANNULMENT

2.38   As its name suggests, annulment cancels the bankruptcy order and puts the bankrupt back to his original situation. It has to be distinguished from discharge which is considered at **2.41** et seq.

2.39   Leaving on one side annulment where an IVA has been approved there are two principal grounds for annulment:

(1)   the bankruptcy order ought not to have been made;

(2)   the bankruptcy debts have been paid in full.

2.40   If the bankruptcy is annulled, the bankrupt's estate which remains vests again in the former bankrupt.

DISCHARGE FROM BANKRUPTCY

2.41   Automatic discharge is available in most cases after one year or indeed earlier if the Official Receiver certifies that as being appropriate. As to the possibility of a discharge within 1 year, it should be noted that at the time of writing there is a consultation process being undertaken as to whether this should be retained or not. In relation to this abbreviated period before discharge it should be noted that it is important for the trustee in bankruptcy to have instituted any application for an income payments order before discharge although the order and indeed any income payments agreement can still last for three years. Whilst this deals with the general position it should be noted that it is possible for the trustee in bankruptcy or the Official Receiver to apply to suspend discharge but only where the bankrupt has failed or is failing with his obligations.

2.42   The effect of discharge is to release the bankrupt from the bankruptcy debts and, subject to any bankruptcy restriction order or undertaking, remove the restrictions and disqualifications upon the bankrupt. Such release and removal are of particular importance to the family practitioner in the context of financial provision. It should be noted that there are certain exceptions to the release obtained from discharge and, in particular, the discharge will not release any order made in family proceedings. This includes a lump sum and costs. It is, however, possible to apply to the bankruptcy court to obtain a release from orders made in family proceedings. There have been no reported cases concerning any such application. It is, therefore, difficult to predict the circumstances in which an order would be made. An additional exception to the release referred to above is a maintenance assessment under the Child Support Act 1991.

2.43 One effect which discharge does not have is the revesting of the bankrupt's property in the bankrupt. This includes the bankrupt's estate at the time of the bankruptcy order and also 'after-acquired property', which means property acquired between the bankruptcy order and the discharge, which has been the subject of a claim by the trustee under s 307 of the IA 1986. Bearing in mind that there is no revesting on discharge, a spouse or co-owner will need to think seriously, even in cases of negative equity, of making a proposal to acquire the trustee in bankruptcy's interest so that if there is a rise in property prices this will enure to the benefit of the spouse or co-owner rather than the trustee in bankruptcy. The strategy in this regard will, however, need to be considered in the light of the changes made to IA 1986 by the Enterprise Act 2002, and this is discussed further in chapter 5. In particular, whilst there is no revesting on discharge, there will be revesting if the trustee does not take steps to realise the home. In particular the trustee has only a three year window from the date of the bankruptcy order to take one of the steps set out in s 283A of the IA 1986 after which time the property revests. It should also be noted that even if there is an application to the court to realise such property it will be dismissed in low value cases as explained in s 313A of the IA 1986 so that in this situation there is bound to be revesting. An alternative is for the trustee to obtain a charging order under s 313 of the IA 1986, in which event the property does revest in the bankrupt but subject to the charge although such an order could not be obtained in a low value case. An advantage for a bankrupt in respect of such a charging order is that he would obtain the benefit of any increase in value of the property after the date of the order.

2.44 It should be noted that the power of the trustee to claim 'after-acquired property' is not available in respect of property acquired after discharge.

INSOLVENT PARTNERSHIPS

2.45 The Insolvent Partnerships Order 1994, although an improvement on its predecessor, is complex and it is likely to be encountered in a limited number of cases. However, it is worth making the following points.

(1) It is possible to bankrupt partners individually outside the scope of the Insolvent Partnerships Order 1994, in which case the position will be no different from any other bankruptcy.

(2) Under the Insolvent Partnerships Order 1994, it is necessary to draw a distinction between the partnership and the partners. In the case of the partnership it is treated as an unregistered company and is wound up

accordingly. It is, however, possible to petition for bankruptcy orders against an individual partner or partners in addition to obtaining a winding-up order against the partnership itself. It is in the context of such bankruptcy orders that a family practitioner is likely to encounter the Insolvent Partnerships Order 1994. The position will not be significantly different from that under other bankruptcy orders, although it should be noted that, where partnership assets are insufficient to pay the creditors in full, the unpaid partnership creditors will be entitled to rank pari passu with the separate creditors of each individual bankrupt partner.

(3)   It is now possible under the Insolvent Partnerships Order 1994 to have what is known as a partnership voluntary arrangement in relation to a partnership. This operates in a similar manner to a company voluntary arrangement.

(4)   It is also now possible to have an administration order made in respect of a partnership. An alternative may be to use the statutory moratorium in the IA 2000 which has been extended to partnerships.

(5)   In the case of LLPs, these are generally treated as companies.

RULE CHANGES

2.46   Although not yet in force it should be noted that the above may be affected by the Legislative Reform (Insolvency) (Miscellaneous Provisions) Order 2009 and the Insolvency (Amendment) (No 3) Rules 2009 which are due to come into force in April 2010. The changes are minor, in so far as they relate to the subject matter of this book, but they will still need to be checked.

DOES AN IVA AFFECT THE POSSIBLE CLAIMS UNDER ANCILLARY RELIEF OR ENTITLEMENTS UNDER AN IVA?

2.47   Just at the time of going to press the decision of HHJ Pelling QC in *CMEC v Mark Beesley and Darren Whyman*[8] deals with a point which is novel. In that case 94% of Mr Whyman's debts were arrears of child maintenance under a CSA assessment. He entered into an IVA where his creditors would get £0.27p. The mother was aware of the proposal but did not attend the meeting at which the proposal was approved. Had she done so, she would have been able to defeat the proposal as the majority creditor.

2.48   CMEC (who brought the case) argued the mother's case that she was not a creditor so therefore was not entitled to vote at the creditors meeting, and was

---

[8]   [2010] EWHC 485 (Ch).

not bound by the IVA terms. In the alternative, they sought to revoke the proposal on the basis that the IVA was unfairly prejudicial to her. By analogy in bankruptcy proceedings arrears of maintenance are not provable and survive discharge.

2.49 The judge held that the mother was a creditor (which is perhaps odd – see bankruptcy point above) but that the IVA was unfairly prejudicial to her and should be revoked.

2.50 This case reinforces the need for the practitioner to take care to ensure that if an IVA is being considered the wife client who has any debts at that point under a matrimonial order must make her views known before the IVA is established. The finding on unfair prejudice may give comfort where the IVA has already taken place without her knowledge. The case is very specific to its own facts but appears to make it clear that the mother cannot rely upon claiming unfair prejudice after the event, so the advice must be to attend and vote at an IVA creditors' meeting of which she receives notice.

Chapter 3

ASSETS VESTING IN THE TRUSTEE

WHAT IS VESTING?

3.1   Upon the appointment of a trustee of the estate of a bankrupt, the assets owned by the bankrupt, with certain very limited exceptions, will automatically vest in the trustee by operation of law. In effect, this automatically transfers ownership of those assets from the bankrupt to the trustee. Certain assets may require the formality of legal transfer, but that will not prevent the trustee from claiming those assets from the date of his appointment.

The need to define the bankrupt's estate

3.2   When advising a bankrupt, their spouse, or indeed any other person with an interest in the family assets, it is important to identify the assets comprising the bankrupt's estate over which the trustee will gain control upon his appointment or to which the trustee may make a claim, for example if he is successful in setting aside a transaction. Once the relevant assets have been identified, the practitioner will know which assets are out of his client's reach for the purposes of ancillary financial relief claims, and which assets may be liable to attract the attention of a trustee in current or future bankruptcy proceedings, even if those assets have previously passed into the hands of the bankrupt's spouse. In short, unless an asset falls within limited classes of asset which are clearly excluded (see below), then it is sensible for the adviser to assume that all other assets will fall into the bankruptcy estate.

The process of vesting

3.3   The process of vesting of assets within England and Wales does not usually involve the signing of any document such as a conveyance, assignment or transfer and it may not, therefore, be apparent upon the face of that asset that ownership has passed from the original owner. If the practitioner believes that there is any prospect of bankruptcy he should ensure that a bankruptcy search is carried out to identify whether a bankruptcy petition has been presented. If that has not occurred, it may be prudent to pursue practical enquiries to identify whether bankruptcy is likely to occur in the foreseeable future, or whether a bankruptcy order has actually been made.

3.4   The vesting of the bankrupt's estate in his trustee occurs upon the appointment of a trustee other than the Official Receiver taking effect or, in the case of the Official Receiver, upon his becoming trustee.[1] The Official Receiver will become trustee if no external trustee is appointed. In any event, either an external insolvency practitioner or the Official Receiver will be appointed trustee within a maximum period of 4 months of the making of the bankruptcy order. The Official Receiver takes custody and control of the bankrupt's property pending appointment of the trustee, unless the trustee was appointed immediately upon the making of the bankruptcy order under s 292 of the IA 1986, which is only likely to take place upon a bankruptcy petition, following a failed IVA, where the supervisor of the IVA seeks his own appointment as trustee.

3.5   During the period between the presentation of a bankruptcy petition, and the appointment of the trustee, any disposition of property or payment of money by the debtor will be void unless approved by the court, either at the time or subsequently. This is so even if the property would not have formed part of the bankrupt's estate under s 283 of the IA 1986, such as tools of the bankrupt's trade.[2] Protection is, however, provided by s 284(4) of the Act to third parties, being bona fide purchasers for value without notice of the petition. A wife to whom property has been transferred in part satisfaction of her ancillary financial relief claims is unlikely to receive the automatic protection of s 284(4) and would have to seek ratification of the transaction from the court.

THE BANKRUPT'S ESTATE

Definition

3.6   The bankrupt's estate comprises all property belonging to, or vested in, the bankrupt at the commencement of the bankruptcy, ie the date of the bankruptcy order,[3] together with any property which by virtue of any of the remainder of s 283 is treated as falling within s 283(1)(a). 'Property' is defined by s 436 of the IA 1986 as including:

> 'Money, goods, things in action, land and every description of property wherever situated and also obligations and every description of interest, whether present or future or vested or contingent, arising out of, or incidental to, property.'

3.7   In most instances it will not be difficult to determine whether a particular property item is or is not part of the bankrupt's estate. However, various types of asset have attracted judicial consideration.

---

[1]   IA 1986, s 306.
[2]   IA 1986, s 284.
[3]   Ibid, s 283(1)(a).

Life assurance and pensions

3.8   The bankrupt's interest in life assurance may fall within his estate. Whether the trustee chooses to realise that interest, by assignment or surrender so far as the terms of the policy permit, will depend primarily on its value.

3.9   Where life assurance is effected for the benefit of the bankrupt's immediate family (ie wife and children), a trust is created whereby the policy does not form part of the bankrupt's estate so long as his wife and children remain alive. The trustee may, however, seek to claim that the insurance policy constitutes a transaction at an undervalue which, accordingly, should be set aside.

3.10   In *Cork v Rawlins*,[4] the Court of Appeal held that money payable under an insurance policy, the payment of which was accelerated as a result of the insured's permanent disablement, fell into the insured's estate on his bankruptcy and was divisible between his creditors as no part of the sum payable related to pain and suffering. This position can be compared to the decision in *Ord v Upton*,[5] where part of the claim related to compensation for pain and suffering, where the bankrupt did retain some equitable interest.

3.11   The treatment of pensions in bankruptcy is now governed by the Pensions Act 1995 and ss 11–16 of the Welfare Reform and Pensions Act 1999 (WRPA 1999).

3.12   The operation of the WRPA 1999 has rendered the line of authority from *Re Landau*[6] to *Krasner v Dennison, Lesser v Lawrence*,[7] *Jones v Patel*,[8] *Rowe v Sanders*,[9] which dealt with the vesting of pension benefits in trustees for bankruptcy, of relevance only to those situations in which the bankruptcy petition was issued before 29 May 2000. This line of cases will be relevant in few bankruptcies now.

3.13   The effect of ancillary relief is dealt with in chapter 6 below.

Solicitors' files

3.14   It would appear that all papers and correspondence in a solicitor's file which belong to the bankrupt, as distinct from the solicitor,[10] are included in the bankrupt's property. Therefore, even papers and documents which are privileged from disclosure in any proceedings should be delivered up to the trustee by virtue of s 312 of the IA 1986. However, a court might exempt the

---

4   [2001] 4 All ER 50.
5   [2000] Ch 352.
6   [1997] 3 WLR 225.
7   [2001] Ch 76.
8   [2001] BPIR 919, CA.
9   [2002] EWCA Civ 242, CA.
10   See the *Guide to the Professional Conduct of Solicitors*, 8th edn (1999), Chap 16, p 329.

bankrupt from the obligation to hand over privileged communications unrelated to the bankrupt's property or financial affairs, such as papers relating to a divorce suit. Ancillary financial relief pleadings and accompanying paperwork are highly unlikely to be exempted from disclosure. The trustee's powers to compel disclosure confer greater powers than simply the ability to obtain those documents comprised within a solicitors' file that belong to a trustee. The trustee can compel a solicitor to deliver up his files of papers, in its entirety, under IA 86, s 366. A solicitor cannot exercise a lien over his file of papers, as against a trustee in respect of unpaid bills by the bankrupt. However, the solicitor can exercise a lien, in relation to documents which give title to property and are held as such.

3.15 The decision of Gibson J in *Re Konigsberg (A Bankrupt)*[11] is of relevance on this point. Here, the wife of a bankrupt was denied legal professional privilege as against her husband's trustee in bankruptcy in relation to certain papers on their joint solicitor's files. It was held that the husband and wife who had instructed the solicitor jointly could not maintain privilege against each other and that the trustee was treated as standing in the shoes of the bankrupt for the purpose of privilege in proceedings against the wife. This decision was considered in the case of *Worrell (Trustee) v Woods*[12] where the Federal Court of Australia rejected the trustees in bankruptcy's application for a former legal adviser to the bankrupt to produce documents in his possession in relation to a number of matters including an application pursuant to the Domestic Relationships Act 1994. In *Worrell*, the FCA found it competent and proper for the former legal adviser to assert a claim to legal professional privilege against producing the documents sought by the trustees. Whether English law will move in this direction remains to be seen, but the impact of the Human Rights Act 1998 will need to be addressed.

3.16 In this regard, the point has been considered by the European Court of Human Rights (ECtHR) in *Foxley v United Kingdom*[13] where the trustee in bankruptcy had obtained an order that all postal packages addressed to the bankrupt be redirected to her. The ECtHR held that there had been a violation of Art 8 of the European Convention for the Protection of Human Rights and Fundamental Freedoms 1950 (European Convention on Human Rights) (right to respect for private and family life) as regards the interception of the bankrupt's correspondence covered by legal professional privilege during the period of the redirection required by the order. However, in *Smedley v Brittain*,[14] the trustee's use of mail re-direction was upheld. As to whether or not a re-direction of post is appropriate and would be upheld by the court entirely depends upon the facts of each bankruptcy.

3.17 Although a solicitor would not appear to have any obligation to inform a client of any requirement to hand over papers, it would be advisable to do so,

---

[11] [1989] 1 WLR 1257.
[12] [1999] FCA 242.
[13] (2001) 31 EHRR 25.
[14] [2008] BPIR 219.

particularly in order to give the client an opportunity to make an application to the court under s 303(1) of the IA 1986 when the information contained in the paperwork is of a sensitive and personal nature. If the client objects, then the solicitor needs to explain that to the trustee. If the solicitor simply ignores the request and refuses to deliver up the files, then it is likely that if the trustee obtains an order for delivery up, the solicitor will have to pay the trustee's costs. However, if the solicitor informs the trustee that due to instructions from his client, he cannot deliver up the files, but the solicitor will not object if the trustee applies to court for an order for delivery up, then the solicitor may not, however, be ordered to pay the costs of an application against him for disclosure of information and documents under s 366 of the IA 1986.

Personal papers

3.18 In the widely publicised case of *Haig v Aitken*,[15] Rattee J refused the trustee's application for the bankrupt's private and personal correspondence to form part of the estate, finding that it fell outside the definition of property for the purposes of IA 1986, s 283. The effect of the Human Rights Act 1998 was also seen in this case. The judge referred to Art 8 of the European Convention on Human Rights (the right to respect for private and family life) in support of his finding that the bankrupt's private and personal correspondence should not form part of the estate.

'Things in action'

3.19 'Things in action' which are personal in nature, such as personal actions for negligence resulting in personal injury, assault, false imprisonment and damage to personal reputation do not vest in the trustee, whereas actions of a non-personal nature, such as actions for negligence causing injury to property, do. Causes of action vest in the trustee at the date of appointment.[16] As a generality, personal injury compensation cannot be claimed by the trustee for the bankruptcy estate (*Lang v McKenna*[17] and *Rahall v McLennan*[18]). This has been subsequently questionned in *Re Bell*,[19] where the court held that claims for personal injury, leading to damages to assets of economic value may be regarded as property (and hence claimed by the trustee to some extent).

3.20 Claims for 'personal injury' frequently contain elements which relate to the bankrupt's person and other elements which relate to economic loss, ie, contain hybrid claims, some of which fall inside the estate and some of which fall outside. The Court of Appeal has given consideration to the vesting of a hybrid claim for personal injury and injury to property in *Ord v Upton*.[20] The Court of Appeal held that the capacity of a human being to earn a living is a

---

[15]   [2000] 3 All ER 80.
[16]   *Heath v Tang* [1993] 1 WLR 1421.
[17]   [1996] BPIR 419.
[18]   [2000] BPIR 140.
[19]   [1998] BPIR 36.
[20]   [2000] BPIR 104.

'capital asset' and 'property right', the value of which is realisable for the benefit of his creditors. It followed that compensation for an individual's loss of such assets and rights would also vest in the trustee 'subject to retention for maintenance' (which is a phrase, the precise meaning of which, has been the subject of further debate). In *Ord v Upton*, the court concluded that the entire claim was vested in the trustee, but the trustee held any proceeds of the action relating to the personal element on trust by the trustee for the bankrupt.

3.21   The vesting of causes of action, which are of such a hybrid nature, were further considered in *Mulkerrins v Pricewaterhouse Coopers*.[21] The facts of the case are somewhat unusual but merit consideration if the vesting of this type of asset is in issue. In particular, the House of Lords considered the hybrid approach taken in *Ord v Upton* but did not reach a final conclusion on the issue. In *Mulkerrins* it is noteworthy that none of the counsel involved were able to explain what 'subject to retention for maintenance' might mean. In *Grady v Prison Service*, the Court of Appeal held that damages for unfair dismissal was held to be personal, and did not therefore vest in the trustee. The issue of 'hybrid claim' has been further considered in *Kaberry v Freethcartwright* where the court commented that a personal injury claim was vested in the trustee.

3.22   In *Khan v Trident Safeguards Limited*, the Court of Appeal held that a bankrupt could 're-characterise' claims alleging racial discrimination by restricting the remedy sought to a declaration and compensation for injured feelings, thereby removing such claims from the category of 'hybrid claims' which would vest in and be pursued by the trustee. The right to seek a new business tenancy was considered to be 'property' and hence vest in the trustee (*Saini v Petroform Ltd*[22]). Interestingly, the right of a bankrupt to receive royalties from the Performing Rights Society vested in the trustee (*Performing Rights Society v Rowland*[23]) and the right of a lawyer to receive professional fees under a conditional fee agreement fell into the estate (*Royal Bank of Canada and Burlingham Associates v Chetty*[24]). The only conclusion that one can reach is that the line between personal claims, which fall outside the estate, and property claims, which the trustee can claim, is unclear, with each case being looked at on its individual merits.

3.23   It would appear that the rights, which a party may have to pursue claims for ancillary relief under the MCA 1973, are deemed to be of a personal nature and do not, therefore, vest in the trustee. In *D(J) v D(S)*,[25] it was said that one must be 'extraordinarily cautious' in extending the meaning of 'causes of action' to applications for financial relief in the Family Division, as they are essentially personal in nature and derive from no source other than the matrimonial legislation.

---

[21]   [2002] BPIR 582.
[22]   [1997] BPIR 515.
[23]   [1998] BPIR 128.
[24]   [1997] BPIR 137.
[25]   [1973] 1 All ER 349.

3.24 There is a significant body of case-law which deals with the assignment of a cause of action back to a bankrupt. It is very often the case that the bankrupt is the only one who is prepared to pursue a claim, and the Official Receiver or trustee enters into an arrangement with the bankrupt such that he or she will pay a proportion of the net proceeds of the action to the Official Receiver or trustee for distribution amongst the creditors. Care has to be exercised in relation to assignments, and various problems have been addressed in the cases of *Haq v Singh*,[26] *Phillips v Spon Smith*[27] and *Francis v National Mutual Life Association of Australasia Limited*.[28]

3.25 Generally, rights of action are vested in the trustee. This can create technical issues where the right which the bankrupt wishes to pursue is that which is the foundation of the petition debt and the bankrupt wishes to appeal the bankruptcy order itself, hence challenging the debt (see *Heath v Tang*). The right to pursue an appeal may or may not vest in the trustee. The question has been debated before the courts on a number of occasions.

Property subject to an order in ancillary relief proceedings

3.26 The relationship between bankruptcy and ancillary relief proceedings is considered fully in chapter 6. The decision in *Harper v O'Reilly and Harper*[29] is, however, of relevance to the issue of vesting in the context of ancillary relief proceedings. In May 1995, an order was made on the wife's application for ancillary relief whereby the family home which was owned jointly with the husband in equal shares was to be sold and the net proceeds of sale were to be paid to the wife. In December 1995, before the property was sold, a bankruptcy order was made against the husband. The wife contended that the whole of the husband's beneficial interest in the property vested in her from the date of the ancillary relief order so that the husband's interest did not form part of the bankrupt's estate within IA 1986, s 283(1). The trustee contended that the transfer or extinguishment of the husband's interest could not occur except on completion of the sale of the property and that the husband's interest formed part of the bankrupt's estate within IA 1986, s 283(1) and vested in the trustee under IA 1986, s 306. The wife's application succeeded and it was found that the order for sale with payment of the entire proceeds to the wife had the immediate effect of transferring the beneficial interest to her.

3.27 The decision in *Harper v O'Reilly and Harper* initially differed from that in *Mountney v Treharne: Re Stewart Richard Mountney*.[30] In this case, Burnton J dismissed Mrs Mountney's appeal against the district judge's decision that a property transfer order in matrimonial proceedings did not give rise to a constructive trust or any other proprietary right enforceable by a wife against the supervening interest of her husband's trustee in bankruptcy. The decision of

---

[26] [2001] BPIR 1002.
[27] [2001] BPIR 326.
[28] [2001] BPIR 480.
[29] [1997] 2 FLR 816.
[30] [2002] BPIR 556, ChD; [2002] 2 FLR 930, CA.

Parker J in *Beer v Higham*[31] was upheld. The Court of Appeal's judgment on Mrs Mountney's appeal overturned that decision. Mrs Mountney's appeal was successful and the Court of Appeal held that a property transfer order in matrimonial proceedings had the effect of conferring a proprietary right, enforceable by a wife against the supervening interest of her husband's trustee in bankruptcy, at the moment when that order took effect, namely on the making of the decree absolute, even though no transfer had been executed. The point is that in this case, the ancillary relief order had been made and become unconditional before the presentation of the bankruptcy petition against the husband. *Beer v Higham* was wrongly decided. The decision was accepted on its facts in *Treharne and Sands v Forrestor*[32] but distinguished there because of the operation of s 284 of the IA 1986 which invalidated a disposition between presentation of the bankruptcy petition and the appointment of a trustee. Section 284 of the IA 1986 had not been an issue in *Mountney v Treharne.*

3.28   The issue has been considered by the Court of Appeal in *Hill v Haines*, which is considered in detail in chapter 6.

Assets held on trust

3.29   In *Re Coath*[33] the district judge held that assets held on trust by the supervisor of an IVA were excluded from the estate vesting in the trustee in bankruptcy by virtue of s 283(3)(a) of the IA 1986. The precise terms of the IVA need to be considered in each case, as the IVA trusts may or may not terminate upon the making of a bankruptcy order. If the trusts are not expressed to terminate, then they will continue.

Statutory tenancies

3.30   Various statutory tenancies are now excluded from the bankrupt's estate by the terms of s 283(3A) of the IA 1986. Reference can be made to *City of London Corporation v Bown*[34] and *Re Vedmay Ltd*[35] as to the relevant background.

Assets outside the jurisdiction

3.31   The definition of assets which vest in the trustee also includes assets owned by the bankrupt which are held outside the jurisdiction of the court.[36] The trustee's initial position is likely to be that all assets, wherever situated, will fall within the bankruptcy estate. The effect of Council Regulation (EC) No 1346/2000 (see **2.10**) should, however, be considered. Issues in relation to where the bankrupt's centre of main interest lies are relevant. This is a complex

---

[31]   [1997] BPIR 349.
[32]   [2003] EWHC 2784 (Ch), [2004] 1 FLR 1173.
[33]   [2000] BPIR 981.
[34]   (1990) 22 HLR 32.
[35]   (1994) 26 HLR 70.
[36]   [2001] 2 All ER 75.

question, which is frequently debated. The difficulties attaching to overseas property were considered in *Pollard v Ashurst*[37] where the Court of Appeal dismissed the bankrupts' appeal against an order for sale of a Portuguese villa. In relation to overseas assets, whether an asset vests in the trustee will depend upon how that jurisdiction treats assets (for example, in Florida, the family home falls outside the bankruptcy estate) and whether or not that jurisdiction is a signatory to the European Convention. Each asset has to be looked at in turn.

The bankrupt's home

3.32 This is dealt with in detail in chapter 4. The Enterprise Act 2002 introduces s 283A of the IA 86, which was intended to deal with the perceived unfairness that arose where a bankruptcy order had been made many years before, where the family home had simply not been dealt with and when a trustee appointed many years later looked to realise it. Section 283A relates to a dwellinghouse, which was the principal residence of the bankrupt, the bankrupt's spouse or civil partner or a former spouse or former civil partner of the bankrupt. This provides that at the end of three years, the trustee's interest in the property shall automatically re-vest in the bankrupt, unless the trustee takes steps to realise the property as set out in sub-s (3) of s 283A. It is possible for the three-year period to be extended or curtailed by court order and the time may not start to run if the bankrupt does not inform the trustee of his interest in the property.

Items which the bankrupt requires for his personal use

3.33 The bankrupt's personal use must arise either by virtue of his employment[38] or to satisfy his basic household needs and those of his family.[39] The provisions of s 283(2)(a) and (b) are subject to the provision of s 305 which gives the trustee the right to claim property which is excluded from the bankrupt's estate by virtue of s 283(2), but which can reasonably be replaced by similar items of a lesser value, thus producing a surplus for the estate.

Property held by the bankrupt on trust for any other person

3.34 Where there is a trust of property for a third party, the beneficial interests in the trust property continue to subsist and cannot be taken by the trustee for the creditor's benefit, for example, solicitor's client account money,[40] and beneficial interests in the estate of a deceased person of which the bankrupt is executor.

3.35 However, if the bankrupt has a direct beneficial interest, it will vest in the trustee. The exact extent of the interest of the trustee will depend upon the

---

[37] [2001] Ch 595.
[38] IA 1986, s 283(2)(a).
[39] Ibid, s 283(2)(b).
[40] *Re A Solicitor (1951 M No 234)* [1952] Ch 328.

terms of the trust. If it is genuinely a discretionary trust, where the bankrupt has no absolute right to any interest under it, then it may be that the trustee does not have an enforceable interest. In short, the trustee can be in no better position as a beneficiary than the bankrupt might be. In addition, where the bankrupt was a settlor, and the settlement was not for value, the trustee may be able to attack the transaction upon the grounds that it was a transaction at an undervalue under s 339 of the IA 86,[41] or a transaction at an undervalue, one of the purposes of which was to place assets beyond the reach of creditors under s 423 of the IA 86.

The family home

3.36   In the majority of cases, the asset held by the bankrupt which will be the most likely subject of a dispute between the trustee and a third party, will be the family home. This topic is covered fully in chapter 4.

Chattels

3.37   Section 283(2)(b) of the IA 1986 excludes from the bankrupt's estate 'such clothing, bedding, furniture, household equipment and provisions as are necessary for satisfying the basic domestic needs of the bankrupt and his family'. There is no longer any cash value limit on such items and, therefore, the ordinary contents of the home are unlikely to be claimed by the trustee. However, where the realisable value of such an asset exceeds the cost of a reasonable replacement, the trustee may claim that property for the bankrupt's estate.[42] Basic household items will generally have a minimal second-hand value and so will be unlikely to be subject to a claim by the trustee under s 308(1). Antique furniture, or an expensive motor car, may attract the interest of the trustee. The trustee may have the exempt property and a replacement item valued and would secure the 'excluded' asset, replacing it with a cheaper alternative. This is only likely to be relevant where the difference in value is very material.

3.38   The issue of the exclusion of the bankrupt's 'tools, books, vehicles and other items of equipment as are necessary to the bankrupt for use personally by him in his employment, business or vocation'[43] was considered by the Court of Appeal in *Pike v Cork Gully*.[44] Here, a horse box was found not to vest in the trustee as it was a vehicle which was necessary for the bankrupt's business, but an issue remained as to whether a less expensive replacement would be appropriate for the bankrupt to use. This issue was to be returned to the county court if agreement could not be reached between the bankrupt and the trustee.

---

[41]   IA 1986, s 339.
[42]   IA 1986, s 308(1).
[43]   IA 1986, s 283(2).
[44]   [1997] BPIR 723.

Contracts with the bankrupt

3.39 The basic principle is that the benefit of a contract made by a bankrupt is property in itself which passes to the trustee.[45]

3.40 The principle is subject to a number of exceptions. The benefit of a contract for the skill and labour of the bankrupt does not pass to the trustee[46] but reference should be made to **3.54** et seq covering income payments orders. Where the goods subject to the contract are subject to rights of lien, stoppage in transit and resale, the trustee's powers over those goods may be substantially limited, as they may be subject to the rights of third parties.

3.41 If a vendor in a conveyancing transaction goes bankrupt between exchange of contracts and conveyance, the vendor's trustee can compel the purchaser to pay the price and take a conveyance of the property. Equally, the purchaser can compel the trustee to complete. The trustee is unlikely to object to this, provided he is satisfied that the property is being sold for market value. It is crucial to carry out a bankruptcy search in respect of a vendor either when buying or selling, so as to ensure that bankruptcy proceedings have not been commenced. When acting for a vendor, who is subject to bankruptcy proceedings, it is crucial that the solicitor accounts to the trustee, rather than the bankrupt, for the proceeds of sale.

3.42 If a vendor is aware that a bankruptcy petition has been presented against a prospective purchaser, he should not complete with him, even if contracts have been exchanged. In such a situation, the payment by the bankrupt purchaser could be recovered by his trustee.

3.43 When a person who is subsequently adjudged bankrupt is party to a contract, the fact of the bankruptcy itself does not necessarily put an end to the contract. If the bankrupt is an employer, then the making of the bankruptcy order will amount to a repudiatory breach of the employees' contracts and if accepted will terminate them. Other contracts may contain terms which will automatically terminate the contract upon bankruptcy or entitle the other party to terminate. In practice, many contracts will simply continue and the bankrupt will continue to perform them. The trustee is only likely to be interested if there is value that he can unlock from a contract for the bankruptcy estate. Where a contract is considered by the trustee to be unprofitable, he may disclaim the contract by virtue of ss 315–321 of the IA 1986 as discussed further below. At common law the general rule, as laid down in *Brooke v Hewitt*,[47] was that the bankruptcy of a party to a contract did not terminate that contract. Section 345 redresses the balance, at least so far as the other contracting party is concerned. The other party can now apply to the court to have the contractual obligations discharged. The court's power under

---

[45] *Morris v Morgan* [1998] BPIR 764.
[46] *Lucas v Moncrieff* [1905] 21 TLR 683.
[47] (1796) 3 Ves 253.

s 345 is discretionary and allows for compensation payments to be ordered to be paid by either party. It cannot, however, be invoked by the trustee.

Conclusion

3.44   The definition of property is, therefore, so wide that it would be unwise to assume that an asset does not form part of the bankrupt's estate unless it is abundantly clear that it comes within the statutory exceptions, as discussed below. In some cases, especially in relation to claims and causes of action, which may contain both personal and proprietorial elements, the question is a complex one which may not be easy to answer.

Disclaimed property

3.45   Just as the trustee can take control of property owned by the bankrupt which is in excess of his personal needs, so can he disclaim such property which is 'onerous'. Onerous property is defined by s 315(2)(a) and (b) of the IA 1986 as being (a) any unprofitable contract, or (b) any other property in the bankrupt's estate which is unsaleable, or not readily saleable, or is such that it may give rise to a liability to pay money or perform any other onerous act.

3.46   The disclaimer is by written notice and operates so as to determine all rights, interests and liabilities of the bankrupt and his estate in such property and discharges the trustee from all personal liability in respect of it as from the commencement of the trusteeship. The disclaimer does not, however, affect the rights and liabilities of any other person except to the extent necessary to release the bankrupt, his estate, or the trustee.[48] The House of Lords' decision in *Hindcastle Ltd v Barbara Attenborough Associates Limited*[49] provides authority for this contention. Here, the disclaimer of a lease by a liquidator did not operate to determine the liability under the lease of the original lessee or of his surety. Section 315(3) of the IA 1986 does not preclude the court from making a vesting order under IA 1986, s 320(3) which directly or indirectly benefits the bankrupt's estate.[50] Property which has been claimed for the estate under s 307 (after-acquired property[51]) or s 308 (personal property of the bankrupt exceeding reasonable replacement value) cannot be disclaimed without leave of the court.[52]

3.47   Any person interested in property can, by written application, compel the trustee to elect, within 28 days from the service of the application, whether or not to disclaim under s 315. The trustee is deemed to adopt any contract/asset which he does not disclaim and loses the right to disclaim it.[53]

---

[48]   IA 1986, s 315(3).
[49]   [1997] AC 70.
[50]   *Lee v Lee* [1998] 1 FLR 1018.
[51]   See **3.48** et seq.
[52]   IA 1986, s 315(4).
[53]   Ibid, s 316.

After-acquired property

3.48   The bankrupt is under a duty throughout the term of his bankruptcy to give notice to the trustee of any property acquired by him or which devolves upon him.[54] Such after acquired property would include an inheritance. In *Re the Estate of Bertha Hemmings (Deceased)*,[55] the court held that the right to receive an inheritance, even thought the administration of the estate was not completed pre-discharge, still vested in the trustee as a 'thing in action'. Notice of after-acquired property must be given within 21 days of acquiring the property, and the bankrupt must not dispose of the property without the trustee's consent within 42 days of serving the notice of acquisition.[56] Such property does not automatically vest in the trustee. If the trustee wishes to claim it for the estate, he must do so by serving notice upon the bankrupt within 42 days after the trustee first became aware of the acquisition of the property.[57] The property falls into the estate at the time when the bankrupt acquired it and the notice, therefore, has retrospective effect.[58] If the period of 42 days has elapsed, leave of the court is required to serve a notice.[59] A notice cannot be served in respect of exempt property under s 283, or property excluded by any other statute or property acquired after discharge, except where the discharge is made conditional upon payment or transfer of future money or property.[60] The issue of after-acquired property and the definition of 'income' which does not vest in the trustee is addressed in the decision of Evans-Lombe J in *Supperstone v Lloyd's Names Association Working Party and Others*[61] and is also considered in *Re X*.[62]

3.49   Where a third party has obtained after acquired property bona fide for value and without notice of the bankruptcy, the trustee will have no claim against that person, whether or not the trustee has served a section 309 notice.

3.50   If, however, the recipient of such property had notice of the bankruptcy, or had not purchased the property for value, a notice may be served upon him by the trustee under s 309 of the IA 1986. Under such circumstances, if the recipient of the notice has performed his side of the bargain, he will not have a provable debt and, at most, can only hope for relief under the rule in *Re Condon, ex parte James*[63] which operates to prevent trustees in bankruptcy from standing on their strict legal rights, in bad faith.

3.51   Where a third party is proposing to make a monetary payment or transfer of assets to a person who is known or suspected to be the subject of

---

[54]   Ibid, s 333(2).
[55]   [2008] EWHC 8565 (Ch), [2009] BPIR 50.
[56]   Insolvency Rules 1986, r 6.200.
[57]   IA 1986, ss 307 and 309.
[58]   Ibid, s 307.
[59]   Ibid, s 309(1).
[60]   Ibid, s 307(2)(a)–(c).
[61]   [1999] BPIR 832.
[62]   [1996] BPIR 494.
[63]   (1874) 9 Ch App 609.

bankruptcy proceedings, he should do so with caution. Such a situation may arise upon the resolution of financial matters following divorce proceedings, or when a personal representative is called upon to distribute assets of a deceased's estate. There is a risk that the paying party may become a party to, or liable for, any misconduct by the bankrupt if the bankrupt does not declare the receipt of such money or assets to the trustee in accordance with s 333(2) of the IA 1986. A bankruptcy search made immediately prior to the intended disposition would clarify the position. It is, therefore, suggested that, at the very least, a search be made if there is any reason to suspect that the intended recipient may be the subject of bankruptcy proceedings.

Preferences and transactions at an undervalue

3.52   As well as identifying those assets which vest in him upon the making of a bankruptcy order, or when acquired by the bankrupt at a later date, the trustee will also consider whether the bankrupt has been involved in any transactions which are capable of being attacked as having been entered into as a transaction at an undervalue under the provisions of s 339 of the IA 1986 or which constitute a preference under s 340 or a which may constitute a transaction at an undervalue the purpose of which is to place assets beyond the reach of creditors (s 423 of the IA 86). If the trustee is able to establish that transactions falling within the provisions of s 339 or s 340 or s 423 have taken place, it is open to him to apply to the court for an order restoring the position to what it would have been if the bankrupt had not entered into the transaction. The discretion of the court is very broad in considering what order it should make on such applications.

3.53   The making of such an order could have extremely serious consequences for a spouse or former spouse of a bankrupt. It is, therefore, imperative that the family law practitioner identifies transactions which could fall within the provisions of ss 339, 340 and 423 in order that such steps as are available may be taken to avoid the transaction falling within those provisions and to give the client the appropriate advice if the possibility remains that those provisions will apply in the future. Where the trustee is seeking to enforce the provisions of ss 339, 340 and 423, the family law practitioner should be aware of the ways in which an application by the trustee under these provisions may be resisted. This important subject is discussed in greater detail in chapter 6.

Income of the bankrupt

Income payments order

3.54   Although the bankrupt is entitled to keep his earnings as they do not vest in the trustee, the trustee may make an application to the court for an income payments order under s 310 of the IA 1986. Alternatively, the trustee and the bankrupt can agree that the bankrupt is to pay a certain level of income to the bankruptcy estate by way of an income payments agreement (under s 310A of the IA 86). The bankrupt's income for these purposes includes every payment in the nature of income which is from time to time made to him, or to which from time to time he becomes entitled, including any payment in respect of the carrying on of any business or in respect of any office or employment.[64] There is, therefore no distinction between personal earnings and the profits of a business. The decision of Evans-Lombe J in *Supperstone v Lloyd's Names Association Working Party and Others*[65] provides consideration of the definition of income. In this case, it was held that even if a fee payment is a 'one off', it would still constitute income 'from time to time' under s 310, as income for these purposes did not mean periodical or regular payments but simply payments 'at any time' during the relevant period. In *Kilvert v Flackett*[66] it was held that a tax-free lump sum payable under a pension scheme fell within the definition of income in IA 1986, s 310(7), but see the discussion of vesting of pensions generally at **3.8** et seq.

3.55 Where an income payments order is made, the income of the bankrupt must not be reduced below what is 'necessary for meeting the reasonable domestic needs of the bankrupt and his family'. The word 'reasonable' within this definition can be contrasted with the use of the word 'basic' in the context of the domestic needs of the bankrupt and his family for clothing, bedding, furniture, etc as defined in s 283(2) of the IA 1986. This section may make it possible to argue that a higher level of income should be allowed to the bankrupt and his family when compared with the standard of furniture, etc that he is allowed to retain. A flavour of the broad range of discretion available to the court in this area is indicated by the decision in *Re Rayatt*.[67] Here, the monthly income of the bankrupt's household was £2,003 and £844 was spent on school fees. On the particular facts of the case, an income payments order was discharged to permit the children of the family to remain in private education. The discharge of an income payments order as a short-term expedient was also considered in *Malcolm v Official Receiver*.[68] The same criteria will be applied by the Official Receiver or the trustee when negotiating an income payments agreement. It is always open to the bankrupt and the trustee to vary the amount payable under an income payments agreement or income payments order as the bankrupt's circumstances change. Curiously, it remains unclear as to whether maintenance payments to a spouse would be included in the calculation of what income is required by the bankrupt.

3.56 The obiter comments of Singer J in *Re X (A Bankrupt)*[69] are of relevance to the relationship between an income payments order and a Child Support Agency assessment. Singer J accepted the submission that, as a matter of practice, a Child Support Agency assessment would be taken into account in the exercise of the court's discretion when considering an income payments

---

[64]   IA 1986, s 310(7).
[65]   [1999] BPIR 832.
[66]   [1998] 2 FLR 806.
[67]   [1998] 2 FLR 264.
[68]   [1999] BPIR 97.
[69]   [1996] BPIR 494.

order, and no income payments order would be made which would deprive the child of the benefit of such assessment.

3.57   As a generality, an income payments agreement or an income payments order will last for 3 years from its inception. It is always possible for the court to discharge an income payments order early. It is worth noting that an income payments order or income payments agreement can only be entered into whilst the bankruptcy order remains un-discharged. At present, a first bankruptcy order is automatically discharged on the anniversary of the order. It is possible for the automatic discharge provisions to be suspended, although this will only occur by the making of a court order. An application will only be made if the bankrupt is un-cooperative with the trustee or Official Receiver, although this is becoming less common. It is proposed that the early discharge provisions that currently apply with be repealed shortly.

The needs of the family

3.58   The word 'family' is defined in s 385 of the IA 1986 as meaning dependants living with the bankrupt. It would therefore appear that maintenance paid to an estranged or divorced wife of a bankrupt, whether for herself or the children of the family, may not be included when assessing the bankrupt's need for income, however arguments based upon *Re X (A Bankrupt)*[70] may be successful in the light of the wording of s 310(1) which confers a general discretion on the court.

The procedure for an income payments order

3.59   The bankrupt must be given at least 28 days' notice of a hearing of an application for an income payments order, together with a copy of the application and a short statement of grounds. The trustee must also explain that, unless at least 7 days before the hearing the bankrupt notifies the trustee and the court that he consents to the order, he must attend.[71]

3.60   An income payments order must, in respect of any payment of income to which it is to apply, either: (a) require the bankrupt to pay the trustee an amount equal to so much of that payment as is claimed by the order; or (b) require the person making the payment to pay so much of it as is so claimed to the trustee, instead of to the bankrupt.[72]

---

[70]   See **3.56**.
[71]   Insolvency Rules 1986, r 6.189.
[72]   IA 1986, s 310(3).

Chapter 4

OWNERSHIP OF THE FAMILY HOME

INTRODUCTION

4.1   In ancillary relief proceedings it is not usually necessary to ascertain the parties' respective legal interests in the family home, as the court has the power to make such orders adjusting their interests as it deems appropriate. In bankruptcy proceedings, the court has no such power and can only determine, rather than adjust the parties' interests.

4.2   It is only the bankrupt's interest in the family home that is available to his trustee for realisation and distribution to the creditors. Both the trustee and the bankrupt's wife need therefore to determine their interest in the home. Often, unfortunately, it will only be at this late stage that thought will be given to the exact beneficial ownership of the property.

Start point

4.3   The current law determining rights of ownership remains complex, inconsistent and difficult to apply notwithstanding the attempt of the House of Lords in *Stack v Dowden*[1] to clarify the position. It is acknowledged that the law is unsatisfactory in this area, and there have been two attempts to reform it, the first by the 2002 Law Commission Discussion Paper Sharing Homes, and the second by their report of 2007, the recommendations from which the government chose not to pursue. It is widely felt that the House of Lords have not provided the certainty they hoped to achieve in *Stack v Dowden*; see for instance *Jones v Kernott*.[2]

4.4   So the basic start point is land law. Under s 53(1)(a) of the LPA 1925 a deed is required to create or to convey a legal estate. However, under s 53(2) of the LPA 1925 and s 2(5) of the Law of Property (Miscellaneous Provisions) Act 1989, this does not affect the operation of the equitable doctrines of resulting, implied or constructive trusts, or of proprietary estoppel, where written evidence is not necessarily a requirement to substantiate a claim for a beneficial interest in a property. Such a claim relates to a share in the sale proceeds of the property in question.

---

[1]   [2007] UKHL 17.
[2]   [2009] EWHC 1713 (Ch), [2009] BPIR 1380.

4.5   The basic principle is that whilst the legal estate may be clear from the title, it is not necessarily conclusive and does not prevent a contrary intention being shown as to the beneficial interest which overrides the legal title, provided there is no express declaration as to how the beneficial interest is held.[3]

4.6   This is a complex area of law and complete text books have been written on this subject alone. The intention of this chapter is to give an overview of the subject. It is fair to say that the trustee's approach will be to assume that the legal title defines the beneficial interest in most cases. For more on this point and their approach see chapter 1. Great care needs to be taken to ensure that if the client wife wishes to run a complicated argument to justify a beneficial interest, the argument is a cost effective one to pursue. The trustee will be entitled to take his own advice and this will be a legitimate cost in the bankruptcy proceedings which is likely to erode the benefits of any success.

4.7   There will be two types of case: those where the house is in the bankrupt's sole name and those where the property is in joint names. In summary:

House in joint names

4.8   If the house is in joint names it is relatively simple for the court to conclude that each party should have a beneficial interest in the property. However, it obviously cannot be assumed that just because the parties hold the legal title as joint tenants, they hold the beneficial title jointly. If the property is beneficially owned as tenants in common with clear confirmation of how the sale proceeds are to be split, they will be divided according to that provision. If the property is beneficially owned as joint tenants, the start point on severance will be a 50/50 division if there is no clear evidence on the face of the deeds or with the Land Registry of a contrary intention, but it will be open to either owner or a third party to argue differently; see also *HSBC Bank plc v Dyche and Anor* for a different view.[4]

4.9   From *Re Gorman*,[5] provided it is clear that the property is held on trust for the two trustees, with no possibility of third party ownership, then the right of one party under survivorship means that they will be held to own the beneficial interest equally. Note that in *Re Gorman* the transfer was unsigned. However, on the difficulties that are encountered where the transfer is not clearly executed, see *Robinson v Robinson*,[6] *Harwood v Harwood*,[7] *Huntingford v Hobbs*[8] and *Stack v Dowden*.[9] *Huntingford* also considers the situation where there is no express declaration of beneficial interests, but simply a declaration

---

[3]   *Goodman v Gallant* [1986] Fam 106, [1986] 1 FLR 513.
[4]   [2009] EWHC 2954 (Ch).
[5]   [1990] 1 WLR 616.
[6]   (1976) 241 EG 153.
[7]   [1991] 2 FLR 274.
[8]   [1993] 1 FLR 736.
[9]   [2007] UKHL 17.

that the survivor can give a capital receipt. In the absence of an express declaration, the trust principles set out below will be required to justify a different share.

4.10 The TR1 transfer document has space so that the owners may make an express beneficial declaration as to their respective beneficial entitlements and there is really no excuse for not dealing with this. This has been the case since 1 April 1998. However somewhat oddly there is no requirement that this needs to clearly executed before the transfer is registered at the Land Registry, so the TR1 can still be unclear as to the beneficial ownership. Once made, the declaration binds the parties and will be conclusive unless there has been fraud or mistake, or post *Stack v Dowden* possibly a claim under proprietary estoppel. See the judicial comment in *Carlton v Goodman*,[10] stressing that conveyancers should ensure that on purchase there is an express declaration in the transfer as to how the beneficial interest is to be held. See also the helpful summary of the equitable principles relating to co-ownership set out in *Mortgage Corporation v Shaire*,[11] which considers the problems where legal joint tenants have not been advised on the right of survivorship and how this affects their understanding of how the beneficial interest is held.

4.11 A claim may still lie against the conveyancing solicitor in these situations, and this will need to be considered and a claim brought within the limitation period. Specialist advice should be taken if this is considered to be an issue.

4.12 Whilst bankruptcy automatically severs a joint tenancy,[12] it does not determine, or of itself change, the beneficial interests save that the bankrupt's share vests in the trustee.

House in sole name

4.13 The start point if the house is in the bankrupt's sole name is that both the legal and beneficial interest in the property will be held by the bankrupt alone. Following discharge of any outstanding secured debt, the trustee will argue that the entire net proceeds of sale will be available for distribution among the creditors and the wife will have no interest.

4.14 The bankrupt's wife needs to show that she holds a beneficial interest in the property to try to defeat the trustee's application for sale or, more likely, to obtain a share of the sale proceeds.

4.15 To show an interest, the applicant has to rely on the equitable doctrines of implied, resulting or constructive trusts, doctrines which have been the subject of extensive debate since they first came to prominence in the two leading House of Lords cases of *Pettitt v Pettitt*[13] and *Gissing v Gissing*.[14]

---

[10]   [2002] EWCA Civ 545, [2002] 2 FLR 259.
[11]   [2000] 1 FLR 973.
[12]   *Re Gorman* (above).
[13]   [1969] 2 All ER 385.

Lord Bridge updated the position in *Lloyds Bank plc v Rosset and Another*,[15] and more recently the principles have been reconsidered in *Oxley v Hiscock*[16] (where the property was owned in the sole name of one party), and *Stack v Dowden* (where it was owned in joint names).

4.16 The case-law is not, however, always helpful as the judiciary have frequently interchanged the terminology to the extent that the class of trust referred to is not always apparent, nor the application consistent. Quantification of the share is then extremely difficult, and can result in costly and unpredictable litigation.

4.17 It is hard to deduce consistent principles, especially as the facts of each case vary significantly, and *Stack v Dowden* is not the clear statement of the law it should have been. Notwithstanding the principles below there is a large scope for judicial discretion. What is important, however, is not the terminology to be used but the circumstances under which a trust, of whatever description, is considered to have arisen, thereby conferring a beneficial interest upon the wife.

4.18   There are three possible claims.

(1)   **Express trusts.** These claims are the simplest to deal with. There will be clarity that a trust has been created detailing how the beneficial interest is held, and this is conclusive, unless you can show fraud, undue influence, duress or mistake. Care must be taken to consider the wording of the trust, to ensure that it creates a valid trust, and that it has been executed. It remains possible, however, for a wife to make a claim under an implied trust where she has contributed to a property held under an express trust, but where she does not own that property.

(2)   **Implied trusts.** These are not express, but arise from the circumstances of the case. They exist by operation of equity and are either (a) a resulting trust, or (b) a constructive trust. These are dealt with in more detail below. The distinction was considered in detail in *Stack v Dowden*.

(3)   **The doctrine of proprietary estoppel**. There is now a great overlap between this doctrine and that of constructive trusts but the two concepts are different.

Claims arising under resulting trusts, constructive trusts, and proprietary estoppel are dealt with in the following sections of this chapter.

Resulting trusts

4.19   This provides that where the legal estate is conveyed into the name of one person following the payment of some or all of the purchase price by

---

[14]   [1970] 2 All ER 780.
[15]   [1990] 2 FLR 155.
[16]   [2004] EWCA Civ 546.

another, there is a presumption that the payer owns part or all of the beneficial ownership of that property.[17] That presumption is, however, rebuttable. The assumption is that a person will not invest capital in a property without expectation of a return.

4.20 In order to establish the existence of a resulting trust, it is therefore necessary that there should have been a direct financial contribution by the beneficiary to the purchase of a property held by the other. It is also generally considered by most land law textbooks that it does not require a common intention between the parties as to the equitable interest in the property.[18] It is generally the case that the size of the share is in direct proportion to the contribution.[19] Case examples include *Cowcher v Cowcher*,[20] where the wife was held to have a one-third share where she contributed £4,000 towards the purchase price of £12,000. The same principle was applied in *Gordon v Douce*,[21] *Springette v Defoe*[22] and *Evans v Hayward*.[23]

4.21 The contribution can be payment of the deposit, or a proportion of the purchase price.

4.22 It is debatable whether assuming responsibility for any mortgage payment, without making a mortgage payment, creates a resulting trust. Case-law is inconsistent as to how this contribution should be quantified. *Gissing v Gissing*[24] and *Burns v Burns*[25] appear to support the use of mortgage instalments as an extension of the resulting trust theory; the curious case of *Le Foe*[26] appears to extend this principle further but should be treated with caution. In *Carlton v Goodman*,[27] it was noted that, 'in principle, liabilities undertaken by one party in a mortgage, without any direct payment of the purchase price, might be treated as a contribution to the purchase price'. In that case, the mere fact that the claimant had her name on the mortgage (but had not made any of the repayments) meant that her claim for a beneficial interest failed. The matter was also considered by the Court of Appeal in *Ivin v Blake*.[28]

4.23 Contributions that are not financial and directly linked with the purchase will not fall within these categories. This means that resulting trusts have a restricted application.

---

[17]   *Pettitt v Pettitt* [1970] AC 777, following on from *Dyer v Dyer* (1788) 2 Cox Eq 92. See also *Lowson v Coombes* [1999] 1 FLR 799 for an interesting application of the principle.
[18]   *Drake v Whipp* (above).
[19]   *Evans v Hayward* [1995] 2 FLR 511.
[20]   [1972] 1 All ER 943.
[21]   (1983) 4 FLR 508.
[22]   [1992] 2 FLR 388.
[23]   [1995] 2 FLR 511.
[24]   [1970] 2 All ER 780.
[25]   [1984] 1 Ch 317.
[26]   *Le Foe v Le Foe and Woolwich Plc* [2001] 2 FLR 970.
[27]   [2002] EWCA Civ 545, [2002] 2 FLR 259.
[28]   [1995] 1 FLR 70.

4.24 It is possible to rebut the presumption that a beneficial interest was intended by the direct financial contribution. For instance, the contribution may have been made by way of loan or gift.[29] Evidence showing any inconsistency with the intention to acquire a beneficial interest should be sufficient to defeat the claim. Do not forget, however, that the loan can still, if valid, be enforced under an action for debt.

4.25 It is now thought that the presumption of advancement does not apply in such circumstances, although it may still be of use where the husband has transferred the property into his wife's name.

4.26 It may be possible to argue that the level of contribution towards the purchase price does not accurately reflect the parties' intentions as to the extent of the beneficial interest to be acquired under a resulting trust. The court will then consider the parties' actual intentions so far as they can be ascertained. This may result in a beneficial interest less than or greater than the financial contribution towards the purchase price being determined. Any intention to hold the beneficial ownership other than in accordance with the parties' respective contributions to the purchase price must, however, be clearly communicated between them.[30]

4.27 Since *Stack v Dowden* it is clear that the resulting trust is of relatively limited application, and it is entirely justified to plead both a resulting trust and a constructive trust in the same application against the same property, especially if say the direct contribution is small but provable under a resulting trust but the arguments for a constructive trust for a larger sum also exist.

Constructive trusts

4.28 The constructive trust has a much broader application than the resulting trust, and will have a much more common application. The concept is designed to arise where it would be unconscionable for the owner of the legal title in a property to deny that another party holds a beneficial interest in that property. The existence of a constructive trust requires the claimant to prove:

(1)   a common intention that a trust is created;[31] and

(2)   reliance to the claimant's detriment or alteration of the position of the party claiming the interest, which it would be inequitable to ignore.

4.29 It is possible to distinguish two broad categories of constructive trust case:

(1)   those where an express agreement as to the beneficial ownership was communicated between the parties; and

---

[29]   *Richards v Dove* [1974] 1 All ER 888.
[30]   *Springette v Defoe* [1992] 2 FLR 388.
[31]   *Pettit v Pettit* [1969] 2 All ER 385.

(2)   those where, in the absence of such an agreement, the conduct of the parties themselves evidences their common intention.

4.30   In either case, a common intention alone is not sufficient. The party claiming to have a beneficial interest must show as an additional requirement that she acted to her detriment in the reasonable belief that she had or would acquire a beneficial interest in the property. A claim will fail if no detrimental reliance can be proven. Detrimental reliance does not necessarily relate solely to financial expenditure.

The court's approach: *Lloyds Bank v Rosset*

4.31   Prior to *Stack v Dowden* the leading case was *Lloyds Bank plc v Rosset and Another*[32], which was reviewed in *Stack v Dowden*. In *Lloyds Bank* Lord Bridge stated the position as a two-stage process:

(1)   The first fundamental question is: has there at any time prior to acquisition (or exceptionally at some later date) been any agreement, arrangement or understanding reached that the property is to be shared beneficially? This has to be based on evidence of express discussions between the partners, however imperfectly remembered and imprecise.

(2)   Once found, it is only necessary for the party to show that he or she has acted to his or her detriment or significantly altered his or her position in reliance on the agreement.

These points are dealt with in turn below.

(1)   Agreement, arrangement or understanding between the parties

4.32   Whether or not express discussions took place, thereby forming an agreement, arrangement or understanding between the parties is a question of fact for the court to determine.

4.33   In *Lloyds Bank plc v Rosset*, a married couple bought a property in the husband's sole name with the deposit coming from the husband's family trust. The wife argued that they had agreed it was owned jointly when the mortgage company brought possession proceedings, and that she had relied on this when helping to renovate the property.

4.34   The discussions therefore need to be pleaded in great detail and must relate to the beneficial ownership of the property itself so that where, as in *Lloyds Bank plc v Rosset*, the proven common intention was to renovate the property or share it as the family home, such discussions were found to be insufficient to lead to a beneficial interest being found.

---

[32]   [1990] 2 FLR 155.

(2)   Common intention

4.35   Three cases are helpful to the spouse trying to justify her position in such circumstances.

(1)   In *Eves v Eves*,[33] the man sought to justify the absence of the woman's name from the title deeds by reference to the fact that she was under 21 years of age, stating that the house would otherwise have been placed in their joint names. The woman subsequently undertook extensive work on the property. The Court of Appeal accepted that there had been an express understanding between the parties, amounting to a common intention, that the woman was to have a beneficial interest in the house to some extent as the man would not otherwise have needed an excuse as to why her name could not appear on the title deeds. The 'detrimental reliance' required did not necessarily need to be by way of financial contribution and was held to be satisfied by the woman's labours.

(2)   In *Grant v Edwards*,[34] the man had told his cohabitee that her name was to be omitted from the title deeds so that her position in her divorce proceedings would not be prejudiced as might otherwise be the case. This, however, proved to be an excuse. The woman subsequently made substantial contributions to the household finances without which the man would have been unable to discharge the mortgage payments. Nourse J accepted that this amounted to 'conduct on which the woman could not reasonably have been expected to embark unless she was to have an interest in the house'.

(3)   In *H v M (Property: Beneficial Interest)*,[35] Waite J found two particular separate conversations between the parties sufficient to amount to an express understanding that the woman was to have a beneficial interest. In the first, shortly before the purchase, the man explained to the woman that it would be prudent to put the property in his sole name so as to avoid potential tax problems beyond those he was already experiencing. In the second, a short time after the purchase, the man told the woman not to be concerned about her future security as half of the house would be hers once they were married (which they never were).

4.36   All three cases are curious in that the owners did not at any point agree that their partners would have a share; instead, they gave an excuse why they could not. On this basis the common intention to share can either be by express discussion or by drawing inferences from their conduct.

4.37   A couple will not necessarily discuss their intentions so far as the beneficial ownership of their home is concerned in precise terms. In the absence

---

[33]   [1975] 3 All ER 768.
[34]   [1987] 1 FLR 87.
[35]   [1992] 1 FLR 229.

of such discussions, both the common intention and subsequent detrimental reliance previously referred to must be inferred from the parties' conduct.

4.38 Lord Bridge in *Lloyds Bank plc v Rosset and Another* considered that in this situation direct contributions to the purchase price by the partner who is not the legal owner, whether initially or by payment of mortgage instalments, will justify the inference necessary to the creation of a trust but it is extremely doubtful whether 'anything less will do'. This clearly causes a confusing overlap with resulting trust cases, and is not the position as has been taken in *Stack v Dowden*.

4.39 As we have seen, under *Rosset* principles the beneficiary's contribution must be substantial. The reference to 'substantial' seeks to exclude daily repair and maintenance on a small scale. For instance, in *Harnett v Harnett*,[36] the wife's contribution of £100 towards materials, driving a van and some limited labour was not regarded as substantial, whilst in *Re Nicholson*[37] funding the installation of central heating was held to be of a substantial nature.

4.40 It is now felt post *Stack v Dowden* that this is too narrow an interpretation, and this is considered further below.

4.41 Once the common intention to share has been established a detriment for the wife or change of her position must also be established. The detriment must follow the establishment of the common intention.

(3) Detrimental reliance

4.42 This can be either express or inferred, and must be in reasonable expectation of acquiring an interest in the property. This will generally relate to acts involved in the acquisition or improvement of the property. This was considered in depth in *Gillett v Holt*.[38] There needs to be a significant link between the promises relied upon and the conduct which constitutes the detriment.

4.43 Lord Bridge's closing comments as to the nature of contributions are inconsistent with earlier Court of Appeal decisions where both indirect financial and non-financial contributions have been held to be sufficient to establish a beneficial interest. For instance, in *Cooke v Head*,[39] the female cohabitee had made no direct financial contribution towards the property but had undertaken a number of tasks requiring a great deal of her own labour. The Court of Appeal was of the opinion that these efforts warranted the woman receiving a one-third share in the property. In *Hall v Hall*,[40] it was

---

[36] [1973] 2 All ER 593.
[37] [1974] 2 All ER 386.
[38] [2000] 2 FLR 266.
[39] [1972] 1 WLR 518.
[40] (1982) 3 FLR 379.

accepted that the female cohabitee's contribution towards the joint household expenses was sufficient to establish a beneficial interest.

4.44 It is clear that the contributions must be substantial. Lord Bridge considered that had the women in *Eves v Eves*[41] and *Grant v Edwards*[42] not been able to rely upon the express discussions with their respective partners, the work undertaken fell far short of such conduct as would by itself have supported the claim. He considered Mrs Rosset's contributions, which primarily comprised painting, decorating and co-ordinating renovation works, to be insufficient, considering it the most natural thing in the world for any wife to do irrespective of any expectation she might have of enjoying a beneficial interest in the property. In *Burns v Burns*,[43] which involved an unmarried couple, it was held that the mere fact that the parties live together and do 'the ordinary domestic tasks' does not amount to an indication that they intended to alter their property rights.

4.45 The most generous interpretation is in *Gissing v Gissing*[44] where a 'material sacrifice by way of contribution to or economy in the general family expenditure' was deemed sufficient.

4.46 The common intention may be satisfied by the party seeking to claim a beneficial interest having assumed responsibility for the mortgage payments. There is, however, uncertainty as to whether the beneficial interest should be quantified with reference to the whole amount of the mortgage liability or restricted to the level of payments actually made.

4.47 The continued discharge of the mortgage payments following a partner's bankruptcy will not confer upon the paying party any greater beneficial interest, although such payments will be considered during the equitable accounting process.[45] The quantification will be determined according to the corresponding increase, if any, in the value of the property.[46]

4.48 Once the common intention has been established there is need to quantify the beneficial entitlement.

Quantification of beneficial entitlement

4.49 The two different types of trust require different calculations.

---

[41] [1975] 3 All ER 768.

[42] [1987] 1 FLR 87.

[43] [1989] Ch 317.

[44] [1970] 2 All ER 780.

[45] *Re Gorman (A Bankrupt)* [1990] 2 FLR 284; *Re Pavlou (A Bankrupt)* [1993] 2 FLR 751.

[46] *Re Nicholson, deceased; Nicholson v Perks* [1974] 2 All ER 386.

Resulting trust

4.50 Under a resulting trust, the calculation is based on the proportion of the financial contribution made relative to the equity, whether by deposit, outright purchase, or mortgage repayments. See an interesting review of the law in *Parrott v Parkin*[47] which concerned the ownership of a boat.

4.51 The only way to refute a resulting trust is to provide clear evidence that the beneficial interest should be held differently, generally either because the monies were paid as a gift or loan.

4.52 The recent case law including *Oxley v Hiscock* reinforces the position in *Drake v Whipp* and *Midland Bank v Cooke* that a constructive trust can still be argued in such cases and will then override the resulting trust.

Constructive trust

4.53 With the constructive trust, the aim is to quantify the share pursuant to the intentions of the parties as to how they should be held. This is not an easy task especially as in most cases this will be both unclear and contested between the parties.

4.54 In *Springette v Defoe*[48] Dillon LJ was of the view that if two (or more) persons purchase property in their joint names and there has been no declaration of trusts on which they are to hold the property, they will, as a matter of law in the absence of evidence to the contrary, hold the property on trust for the persons who provided the purchase money in the proportions in which they provided it.

4.55 If the court is satisfied that there has been an express agreement, arrangement or understanding between the parties as to the beneficial ownership, their interests will be quantified in accordance with those express terms without further investigation.

4.56 Thus, in *Savill v Goodall*,[49] Mrs Goodall had been a local authority tenant when the property was acquired jointly by the parties under the statutory 'right to buy' scheme. There was no express declaration as to the beneficial ownership. After the discount allowed to Mrs Goodall of 42%, the purchase price amounted to £20,445. A mortgage was obtained to facilitate the purchase for which Mr Savill agreed to be responsible. The Court of Appeal held that the parties' respective interests must be quantified by the terms of their agreement and not by their contributions. The agreement had been that Mr Savill would receive a half share in the property in return for assuming responsibility for the mortgage. Upon sale, he would, therefore, receive a

---

[47] [2007] EWHC 210 (Admlty).
[48] [1992] 2 FLR 388.
[49] [1993] 1 FLR 755.

one-half share from which the amount outstanding under the mortgage would be deducted. Had there been no express agreement, the parties' contributions would have been decisive.

4.57 The real difficulties for the practitioner are the non-financial contributions and those not directly related to the purchase or mortgage. If such contributions are held to warrant a beneficial interest, despite the view adopted by Lord Bridge, how should they then be quantified? In *Eves v Eves*,[50] the cohabitee's interest was quantified by reference to the interest which she had expected to acquire. Alternatively, the court could have attempted to attribute some artificial value to the actual contributions made. This will prove to be a difficult task especially where the relationship is long and the contributions have been many throughout the years.

4.58 Two cases which show the different approaches of the court to the same problem are *Midland Bank plc v Cooke*[51] and *Drake v Whipp*.[52] In *Cooke*, on appeal, the court moved away from quantifying Mrs Cooke's share as 6.57% of the equity (being the gift from her parents she invested in the property) and held that the common intention was that she should receive 50%. Mrs Drake's capital expenditure on a property, however, of some 20% led her to acquire one third of the property.

4.59 The court in each case has to search for the common intention. This is where *Stack v Dowden* has marked the most significant change. The previous case law very much looked at the actual intention, whether or not it was express or inferred from conduct. Under *Stack v Dowden* it is now possible to impute that conduct. This was also the test that *Oxley v Hiscock* required. In that case it was held that each party was entitled to the share which the court considered fair with regard to 'the whole course of dealing between them in relation to the property'. That included meeting outgoings on the property, and possibly improvements (this being endorsed in *Stack v Dowden*).

4.60 In *Stack v Dowden* the parties bought a house in joint names which was funded by a joint mortgage, the proceeds of sale of a property in Ms Dowden's sole name, and savings in Ms Dowden's sole name. There was no express declaration of trust. At first instance it was held that the property was owned as tenants in common as to equal shares. This was overturned in the Court of Appeal and upheld in the House of Lords on the ground that they held the property as to 65% to Ms Dowden, with the balance to Mr Stack.

4.61 The key points from the case are:

(1) The start point is to look at the legal ownership. If the property was held in one party's sole name then they own 100% of the beneficial interest. If it is in joint names they each own 50% of the interest.

---

[50] [1975] 3 All ER 768.
[51] [1995] 4 All ER 562.
[52] [1996] 1 FLR 826.

(2) If one party wished to argue away from this then the onus was on them to do so.

(3) In this, the approach should be the same whether the property was held in joint legal title or in the sole name of one party, albeit that the fact that the parties agreed to put the property into joint names must be a factor to consider when looking at the course of dealing.

(4) That cases where the joint beneficial interest was different from joint legal interest should be different would be 'very unusual'. *Stack* fitted into this as they had deliberately kept their financial affairs rigidly separate despite a very long relationship with children; hence they must have intended to share the property unequally.

(5) That said, Lord Neuberger adopted the strict resulting trust approach which he felt was clearer for the layperson to understand. He did not like the idea of imputing an intention into the way parties own their properties.

(6) Baroness Hale set out a sample list of factors that she thought were relevant to work out the parties' true intentions – which is broadly drawn and includes:
     • how the property was financed both initially and subsequently;
     • how they re-organised their finances;
     • how they met the outgoings and their household expenses.

As such, it is fair to say this covers most cases where a property is jointly owned and more recent case law such as *Fowler v Barron*[53], *Lasker v Lasker*[54], *Abbott v Abbott*[55] and *James v Thomas*[56] has attempted to clarify this.

4.62 *Lasker v Lasker* raises the issue of property where it is acquired in a commercial context, ie it was a property acquired as an investment not a home. In that case there is not the same burden of a presumption of equality, and a stricter test was applied.

The equitable doctrine of exoneration

4.63 Once the beneficial ownership has been determined in accordance with the principles discussed above, an adjustment may be warranted which will affect the parties' eventual shares in the net proceeds. The equitable doctrine of exoneration provides that, where the husband borrows monies with, as is common practice, security being provided by way of a charge against the

---

[53] [2008] 2 FLR 831.
[54] [2008] EWCA 347.
[55] [2008] 1 FLR 1451.
[56] [2008] 1 FLR 1598.

jointly owned family home, and the wife does not derive any direct benefit from those monies, she should, notwithstanding that she signed the legal charge, be exonerated from any liability.

4.64 The doctrine applies strictly between husband and wife and will not affect the level of monies which the lender receives. The lender's concern is the security which the home provides and not the division of the beneficial ownership. In the first instance, the husband's share of the proceeds of sale will be used to discharge the particular debt, with recourse being made to the wife's share only where there is a shortfall. The lender will receive the same amount, albeit in different proportions from the parties.

4.65 For example, the home (held by the parties beneficially in equal shares) is worth £100,000 subject to a mortgage of £50,000 obtained solely to facilitate the purchase. The husband then borrows £20,000 to fund his business interests with security provided by way of a second charge against the home. Upon his bankruptcy, the net proceeds will initially be distributed as follows:

Value of home		£100,000
Mortgage		£50,000
Second charge		£20,000
Net available		£30,000
Division:	Wife	£15,000
	Trustee	£15,000

4.66 If the wife's claim that she should be exonerated from liability for her husband's business debts is successful, the distribution will then be:

Value of home	£100,000
Mortgage	£50,000
Net available	£50,000
Less wife's share	£25,000
Available to trustee	£25,000
Less second charge	£20,000
Trustee's share	£5,000

4.67 The lender is able to recover the entire £20,000 from the husband's share of the proceeds. If the husband's share had, however, been insufficient to discharge the debt in full, the lender would still be able to recover the outstanding balance from the wife's share.

4.68 The wife and her legal advisers should consider the position carefully before putting forward such claims. For example, if the husband's business had not borrowed monies, it may be that there would have been no financial support for the family. In such circumstances, it would be difficult to prove that the wife received no benefit, and the trustee will undoubtedly contend that she did derive some benefit. The same will be true where there is a marked disparity between the parties' income so that some financial dependence upon the husband will have been necessary.

4.69 Whether or not the doctrine is applicable will be apparent from the circumstances of each individual case. There is, however, no automatic presumption in favour of the wife which the husband or trustee must then rebut.[57] A wife will experience difficulty in establishing a case in the following circumstances:

–   where the monies have been used to discharge debts which the husband incurred in maintaining the extravagant lifestyle enjoyed by both himself and his wife;

–   where the monies were used wholly or partly for the wife's benefit, for instance, towards general household and family living expenses;

–   where the wife intended to make a gift to the husband;

–   where the monies were raised to discharge in part the wife's debts and the husband then had the benefit of the surplus.

4.70 The leading modern-day cases are *Re Pittortou (A Bankrupt), ex parte Trustee of the Property of the Bankrupt*,[58] which supports the view that the wife cannot be exonerated from debts incurred for domestic as opposed to business purposes, and *Judd v Brown*[59]. In that case, the husband ran a restaurant business. The family home, which was in the parties' joint names, was used to secure the husband's bank account which he used for the business and general household expenses. In 1981, the husband left the family home and went to live with another woman whom he had been supporting. In 1982, he became bankrupt. The issue before the court related to the manner in which the indebtedness on the husband's bank account should be discharged. Monies from the account had been used to discharge:

(1)   debts arising from the business;

(2)   debts which the husband incurred when he left the family to set up home with the other woman;

(3)   payments for the family's benefit such as the mortgage and the living expenses for himself, his wife and the parties' daughter.

---

[57]   *Paget v Paget* [1898] All ER 1150.
[58]   [1985] 1 All ER 285.
[59]   [1998] 2 FLR 360.

4.71   Scott J held that monies from the bank account used for the first two purposes, not being the wife's debts, should be discharged solely from the husband's share of the proceeds, although the parties remained jointly responsible for the monies used towards the third purpose. For an up-to-date view, see also *Williams v Bateman*.[60]

Equitable accounting

4.72   Although the process of equitable accounting does not affect the beneficial ownership of the home, it may nevertheless alter the division of the net proceeds of sale.

4.73   The principle provides that where the family home is held in the parties' joint names (or the sole name of the other and a beneficial interest is claimed – see *Re Pavlou*) and the husband leaves, he may be entitled to a payment equivalent to rent from the wife if she continues to reside there. This right can be passed to the trustee in bankruptcy.[61] However where she does remain in the house and continues to discharge the mortgage payments in full, she may be entitled to credit for one-half of the capital element of those repayments before the net proceeds of sale are divided.[62] The interest element may, however, be regarded as payment equivalent to rent for her use and occupation of the home and, not having reduced the outstanding mortgage itself, will not necessarily be given any credit.

4.74   The principle was reviewed in depth in *Stack v Dowden*, although this did not relate to bankruptcy in that case. Baroness Hale made it clear that the principle was now governed by TLATA 1996 and in particular s 13(3) which provided that the trustees could impose reasonable conditions on any beneficiary regarding his statutory right to occupy a property. Where one beneficiary had been excluded from the property – in this case most likely the trustee in bankruptcy – financial or other considerations could be imposed. In the context of bankruptcy, see also *French v Barcham*[63] at **4.81** below, and *Williams v Bateman*.

4.75   It was recognised however that often the results would be the same as under the previous principles. A more recent review of those principles was set out in *Murphy v Gooch*[64] in which it was noted that co-owners should be given credit for monies and expenditure paid on a jointly owned property just as a co-owner in sole occupation of a property may be charged with or required to

---

[60]   [2009] EWHC 1760 (Ch), [2009] All ER (D) 317 (Jul), affirming *Bateman v Williams* [2009] BPIR 748.

[61]   *Cooke v Head* [1972] 1 WLR 518; *Bernard v Josephs* 4 FLR 178.

[62]   *Leake (formerly Bruzzi) v Bruzzi* [1974] 2 All ER 1196; *Suttill v Graham* [1977] 3 All ER 1117.

[63]   [2008] EWHC 1505 (Ch).

[64]   [2007] EWCA Civ 603.

give credit to his co-owner for an occupation rent and those credits may be offset against each other. See also *Clarke v Harlowe*[65] for an alternative judicial view on the subject.

4.76 Vinelott J in *Re Gorman (A Bankrupt)*[66] was, however, of the view that such an approach was not a rule of law to be applied in all circumstances, irrespective of, on the one hand, the amount of the mortgage debt and the instalments paid and, on the other hand, the value of the property and the amount of the occupation rent that ought fairly to be charged. It is a rule of convenience and more readily applies between husband and wife, or cohabitants, than between a spouse and the trustee in bankruptcy of the other co-owner.

4.77 In that case, the wife was credited with one-half of all the mortgage payments which she had made and the trustee was held to be entitled to one-half of 'proper occupational rent' from the date of the bankruptcy order (1982) until the eventual sale. Vinelott J expressed the hope that the parties would agree that the adjustments should cancel each other rather than incur the expense of full accounting. This may not always be the case and each case will be specific to its own facts.

4.78 In *Re Pavlou (A Bankrupt)*,[67] the wife remained in the family home following her husband's departure in January 1983. She continued to discharge the mortgage instalments as they fell due and funded repairs and improvements to the property. In March 1987, a bankruptcy order was made against the husband. It was agreed between the wife and the trustee that the property should be sold. The issue before the court related to the equitable accounting to be undertaken. The court held that:

(1)   the wife should be credited with one-half of the increase in the value of the home resulting from her expenditure on repairs and improvements, both before and after her husband's bankruptcy, or one-half of her actual expenditure if less;

(2)   the wife should be credited with one-half of the increase in the equity resulting from the capital element of the mortgage payments which she discharged from January 1983;

(3)   there would have to be an enquiry as to whether an occupational rent (which the wife was prima facie liable to pay) should be set off against the interest element of the mortgage payments, the court having insufficient material before it to make such a decision.

---

[65]   [2007] 1 FLR 1.
[66]   [1990] 2 FLR 284.
[67]   [1993] 2 FLR 751.

4.79   Equitable accounting only applies to the period after separation (save in exceptional circumstances), as that is the point that the common purpose of the trust comes to an end.

4.80   The level of the occupational rent and how it is determined is considered in *Stack v Dowden*. The position appears to be that it is based on the notional rental of the house or the cost of alternative accommodation. Generally the court will take a broad brush approach. The balance will be the liability for the occupation rent against the fact the occupier may well have paid the mortgage.

4.81   The lead bankruptcy case on equitable accounting is *French v Barcham*[68]. The facts here were that Mr and Mrs Barcham purchased a property together in 1992. Mr Barcham was bankrupted in 1994. His share vested in the trustee who did not seek to enforce until 2006. The two issues were what deductions should be made for the costs that the wife had made towards the property and what occupation rent the trustee was entitled to claim. The district judge held that the trustee was not entitled to occupy the property under s 12 of TOLATA 1996 and so could not charge an occupation rent under s 13. This was overturned on appeal – there was no reason why the occupying co-owner should not be charged an occupation rent. This approved the case of *Byford v Butler*[69] which also dealt with occupation rent on a bankruptcy case.

4.82   In most cases it is submitted that the mortgage interest paid offsets the rent and possibly the occupier is entitled to a 50% credit for half the capital part of the mortgage repayments but this is not a hard and fast rule. Where repairs/improvements have been carried out the person who has done so is entitled to a credit for 50% of the increase in the value of the property or if lower 50% of the monies spent.

Proprietary estoppel

4.83   Proprietary estoppel is a broad and loosely defined remedy. As is set out in *Gillett v Holt*,[70] 'in the end the court must look at the matter in the round'. It is an equitable doctrine arising where (i) a party is encouraged to act to his detriment by (ii) the representations or encouragement of another so that (iii) it would be unconscionable for the active party not to have a beneficial interest. The encouragement in this context may be active or passive.

4.84   For instance, a declaration that a beneficial interest exists under a trust does not actually create the interest. It simply confirms a situation which may have been created many years earlier when, for example, a contribution was made to the purchase price. In contrast, a declaration that a beneficial interest exists through proprietary estoppel actually does create the interest. Until that time, no interest can be recognised. There is also no need for a common

---

[68]   [2008] EWHC 1505 (Ch).
[69]   [2004] 1 FLR 56.
[70]   [2001] Ch 210. For earlier cases with this approach, see, for instance, *Habib Bank Ltd v Habib Bank AG Zurich* [1981] 1 WLR 1265.

intention to exist between the parties; conduct by the legal owner alone will suffice. Although a beneficial interest may be granted under the doctrine, the court may alternatively award no more than a personal right to occupy the house, or even the payment of a lump sum – see *Jennings v Rice*[71]. *Holman v Howes*[72] is an example where a claimant was found to be entitled to live in a property bought in the defendant's sole name for as long as she wished. The court will not, however, give the claimant a greater interest than that he or she had expected to receive.

4.85 It is a useful remedy where the contribution by the claimant has not been financial, but *Rosset* blurred the distinction between constructive trusts and proprietary estoppel.

4.86 The distinction between proprietary estoppel and the principles governing trusts has not been assisted by the apparent confusion within the judiciary. Although attempts have been made to clarify the position,[73] the doctrine is perhaps best explained by example. In *Stack v Dowden*, Lord Walker considered the interrelationship and seemed to accept that the two did not always produce the same result.

4.87 In *Pascoe v Turner*,[74] an unmarried couple lived together in the man's house. Following the breakdown of their relationship, the man moved out, informing the woman that the house and its contents were hers. In reliance upon this, the woman remained in the property, carrying out various improvements.

4.88 The Court of Appeal held that the gift of the house to the woman should be perfected, through the doctrine of proprietary estoppel, by ordering a conveyance of the property into her sole name.

4.89 In *Greasley v Cooke*,[75] the woman began a relationship with one of the sons of her employer, in whose house she lived. The family assured her that, if she continued to look after them, she could remain in the home. Following the death of the son and another one of the employer's children whom the woman had looked after during illness, the remaining members of the family sought to remove her. The Court of Appeal held that she had acted to her detriment as a consequence of the family's assurances and, accordingly, had a right to remain at the property during her life.

---

[71] [2002] EWCA Civ 159.
[72] [2007] EWCA Civ 877.
[73] Eg in *Stokes v Anderson* [1991] 1 FLR 391.
[74] [1979] 1 WLR 431.
[75] [1980] 1 WLR 1306.

4.90   Other cases of interest include *Campbell v Griffin*,[76] and *Jennings v Rice*,[77] both involving long-term carers of elderly individuals who died intestate. In each case, the carer was able to demonstrate that she had acted to her detriment.

4.91   The contractual licence may prove to be of assistance where there has been no express agreement, common intention or contribution intended to acquire a beneficial interest. It will, however, be necessary to show the existence of a contract to occupy the property, whether express or implied. There must be actual consideration coupled with an intention to create legal relations.

4.92   In *Tanner v Tanner*,[78] the property was purchased by the man for himself, his girlfriend and their two children. The woman relinquished her rent-controlled flat so as to enable her to join her boyfriend. When he subsequently sought to remove the woman, the court held that a contract could be implied under which the woman and children had been granted a right to occupy the property so long as the children were of school age and the accommodation was reasonably required for them.

4.93   In *Re Sharpe*,[79] the trustee in bankruptcy was held to be bound by an irrevocable licence given by the bankrupt to a relative who had provided £12,000, by way of a loan, to assist in the purchase of the family home where she also lived.

4.94   Most recently the case of *Yeoman's Row Management Limited and another v Cobbe*[80] has reviewed the principles of proprietary estoppel and has been held to be an attempt to tighten up the principle.

4.95   It is probably the case that most wives should be advised of the cost of an application using this remedy as outcomes are uncertain and very expensive to run.

---

[76]   [2001] EWCA Civ 990.
[77]   [2002] EWCA Civ 159.
[78]   [1975] 1 WLR 1346.
[79]   [1980] 1 WLR 219.
[80]   [2008] UKHL 55.

Chapter 5

REALISATION OF THE FAMILY HOME

INTRODUCTION

The Enterprise Act 2002: 'use it or lose it'

5.1   Inserting s 283A into the Insolvency Act 1986, the provisions of the Enterprise Act compel a trustee in bankruptcy to deal with the matrimonial home within a period of 3 years beginning on the date on which a bankruptcy order was made. This applies to all bankruptcy orders made under IA 86; if a bankruptcy order was made prior to 1 April 2004 limitation would have expired on 1 April 2004.

5.2   In the past, wives were left in the unenviable position of the trustee applying to realise the husband's interest 10-20 years later when the property had sufficient equity to make the application worthwhile.

5.3   The 3 year rule applies to a bankrupt's interest in a dwelling house which, as at the commencement of bankruptcy, is a sole or principal residence of:

(a)   the bankrupt;

(b)   the bankrupt's spouse; or

(c)   the former spouse of the bankrupt.

5.4   In the event that the trustee believes that a property he seeks to enforce against falls under these provisions he must file a notice to that effect (Insolvency Rules 1986, r 6.237; such notice must be filed no less than 14 days prior to the expiry of the 3 year period).

5.5   If the 3 years expire without the trustee dealing with the asset it will *automatically re-vest in the bankrupt*.

5.6   There are five ways in which a trustee can prevent re-vesting:

(1)   selling the property;

(2)   applying for an order for sale pursuant to s 335A of the IA 86;

(3)   applying for possession pursuant to s 336 IA 86;

(4) applying for a charge on the property pursuant to s 313 IA 86;

(5) by agreeing with the bankrupt that he shall incur a liability to his estate in consideration of which the interest in the property shall cease to be part of the estate.

5.7 As we have seen in chapter 3, the bankrupt's estate (including the bankrupt's interest in the family home) vests automatically in the trustee in bankruptcy. Of course, the trustee has a duty to realise assets for the benefit of creditors, and the dilemma in a bankruptcy situation is the balance of the interests of the bankrupt and his family facing eviction from their home against those of the bankrupt's creditors seeking prompt payment from the sale of the property. The bankrupt's home, or his interest in it, is likely to represent the last remaining or main capital asset available for realisation and distribution. Any other assets of value are likely to have been disposed of so as to avoid the onset of bankruptcy. The relevant provisions of the IA 1986[1] effectively tip the scales in the direction of the creditors, although the balance has tipped back slightly in favour of the bankrupt and his family in recent years – see the Enterprise Act 2002. It has been suggested that Art 8 of the European Convention on Human Rights will confirm this trend.[2]

5.8 The concept of 'realised' for the purposes of s 283A was recently considered in *Lewis and Anor v Metropolitan Property Realisations Ltd*[3] where the property company had agreed with the trustee in bankruptcy to purchase an assignment of the husband's beneficial interest for the sum of £1 and 25% of the subsequent proceeds of sale. The wife maintained that the property had re-vested under s 238A(2), whilst the property company argued that the trustee had 'realised' their interest by the assignment made to them.

5.9 The Court of Appeal held that a sale of the beneficial interest for a future price, or a partially future price did not fit into the exceptions in s 283A. Such a transaction was not a 'realisation' within s 283A(3)(a).

5.10 Generally, the bankrupt's family will have 12 months from the first appointment of a trustee, either to secure alternative accommodation or to put forward realistic proposals for the acquisition of the bankrupt's interest in the property. Once 12 months have elapsed, it is likely that an order for sale will be made upon the trustee's application. The creditors' interests outweigh all other considerations unless the circumstances of the case are exceptional (IA 1986, s 336(5)) (see below).

---

[1] Sections 336 and 337.

[2] C Gearty and S Davies *QC Insolvency Practice and the Human Rights Act 1998 – A Special Bulletin* (Jordans, 2000).

[3] [2009] EWCA Civ 448, [2009] WLR (D) 189.

Between 1 and 3 years after bankruptcy: *'no man's land'*

5.11 The interplay with the *use it or lose it* provisions of the Enterprise Act and s 336(5) now provides a transitory period between 1 and 3 years from the date of the bankruptcy where they are highly vulnerable to an order for sale application. For the first year the wife and children will be given a reasonable measure of security in the home being able to argue their interests as against those of the creditors; within 1 and 3 years the creditors interests will 'outweigh all other considerations'; and after 3 years the house will automatically vest back in the bankrupt unless the trustee has taken steps to protect his interest.

RIGHTS OF OCCUPATION

5.12 A wife's entitlement to occupy the family home may arise from the existence of her marriage or by virtue of her own interest in the property. A cohabitee is, however, primarily dependent upon being able to prove some beneficial interest in the property. In certain circumstances, the husband may be entitled to continue to occupy the property independently of his wife's rights of occupation.

Wife with no legal or beneficial interest

5.13 'Matrimonial home rights' as provided by s 30 of the Family Law Act 1996 are the rights:

(a) not to be evicted or excluded from the home by the husband if already in occupation, except with permission of the court; and

(b) if not already in occupation, a right to enter and occupy the home with permission of the court.[4]

5.14 The property must have been, or have been intended to be, the matrimonial home.[5] Whether the property constitutes a matrimonial home will depend on the circumstances of the case.[6]

5.15 When determining whether the husband has a right to occupy the home, any right to possession conferred on a mortgagee is disregarded, whether or not the mortgagee is in possession.[7] A wife claiming to have an equitable interest in the home will be treated, for the purpose only of determining whether she has matrimonial home rights, as not being entitled to occupy the home by virtue of that equitable interest.[8] Such a wife will not, therefore, be prejudiced should her

---

[4]   FLA 1996, s 30(2).
[5]   Ibid, s 30(7); *Syed v Syed* (1980) 1 FLR 129.
[6]   See *Collins v Collins* (1973) Fam Law 133, *Kinzler v Kinzler* [1985] Fam Law 26 and *Hall v King* [1988] 1 FLR 376.
[7]   FLA 1996, s 54(1) and (2).
[8]   Ibid, s 30(9).

claim to have an equitable interest subsequently fail. Matrimonial home rights are personal to the wife and cannot be assigned to another party.

5.16 If a wife is able to establish a statutory right of occupation then the chances of success of a trustee's application for an immediate sale are greatly reduced, whether or not that right is registered. Where the husband is entitled to occupy the property by virtue of a legal estate, the wife's matrimonial home rights form a charge on the bankrupt's estate which is capable of registration at the Land Charges Department or at the Land Registry, as appropriate.[9] Where the husband's entitlement to occupation is by virtue of a beneficial estate or interest, the wife's matrimonial home rights form a non-registrable charge. The rights conferred on the wife should be protected by the immediate registration of a class F land charge if the home has an unregistered title or a notice where the title is registered, although in practice the trustee is unlikely to consider the nature of the wife's occupation or to place any importance on the absence of registration if she is in actual occupation. The wife does not have to be in actual occupation at the time of registration, although there must be a genuine intention to occupy.[10]

5.17 Matrimonial home rights do not constitute overriding interests in relation to registered land where the wife is in actual occupation,[11] and do not entitle the wife to lodge a restriction or notice. It is important that a wife without a legal interest in the home registers her statutory right of occupation as a charge prior to the presentation of her husband's bankruptcy petition, although (as indicated above) in practice this may not prove to be critical. If she does so, the charge continues notwithstanding the bankruptcy. It binds the trustee of the husband's estate[12] so that, in the absence of the wife's consent to a sale, the trustee must make an application to the bankruptcy court for an order for terminating the wife's matrimonial home rights pursuant to FLA 1996, s 33. Such applications are discussed in further detail below. Generally, where the wife is in occupation of the property, the trustee will issue his application and serve it on the wife as well as the bankrupt.

5.18 The wife's rights will continue to subsist until one of the following events occurs:

–   the death of either party or the termination of the marriage (otherwise than by death, for example by decree absolute);[13] or

–   the termination of the husband's entitlement to occupy the home, except where the wife's rights are a charge on an estate or interest in the property;[14] or

---

[9]   Ibid, s 31.
[10]   *Barnett v Hassett* [1981] 1 WLR 1385.
[11]   FLA 1996, s 31(10)(b).
[12]   IA 1986, s 336(1) and (2)(a).
[13]   Ibid, s 30(8)(a).
[14]   Ibid, s 30(8)(b).

- the coming into effect of a court order terminating the wife's matrimonial home rights pursuant to FLA 1996, s 33(3); or

- the completion of a release in writing.[15]

5.19 The wife may apply under FLA 1996, s 33(5) for an order that her matrimonial home rights will not be brought to an end by the death of her husband or by the termination of the marriage. However, in practice a pending land action or restriction will be registered if possible to protect the wife's position following decree absolute because the procedure is more cost effective and less complex; alternatively decree absolute is delayed until after determination of the ancillary relief.

5.20 The application to register matrimonial home rights is currently made on Form MH1 to the appropriate District Land Registry. There is no requirement to produce the land or charge certificate in order that the notice may be registered. An application to renew the registration (after the making of an order continuing matrimonial home rights under FLA 1996, s 33(5)) is made on Form MH2, again to the District Land Registry. An official copy of any order must accompany the application. No fee is payable for an application on Form MH1 or Form MH2.

5.21 The timing of an application may prove to be critical. If the application reaches the Land Registry before 9.30 am on a working day, it will be deemed to have been delivered that day. Applications received after 9.30 am will be deemed to have been delivered the following day at 9.30 am.

Wife with a legal or beneficial interest

5.22 If the wife has a legal or beneficial interest in the property, she is entitled to occupy it as of right and does not, therefore, need to rely upon the provisions of the FLA 1996. It would, nevertheless, be prudent for the wife claiming to have a beneficial interest in the property to register a restriction or notice if she is not a registered proprietor. See chapter 4 in relation to the determination of the extent of the parties' beneficial interests.

5.23 In a bankruptcy situation, in the absence of the wife's consent to a sale, the trustee must apply to the bankruptcy court for an order for possession and sale of the property pursuant to Trusts of Land and Appointment of Trustees Act 1996 (TLATA 1996), s 14. Such applications are discussed in further detail below.

---

[15] Ibid, Sch 4, para 5.

APPLICATION FOR SALE

5.24   In the absence of the wife's consent to a sale, the trustee must apply to the court for an order for possession and sale either pursuant to FLA 1996, s 33 (where the wife has matrimonial home rights but no legal or beneficial interest) or TLATA 1996, s 14 (where the wife has a legal or beneficial interest). In reality the distinction is academic. In a bankruptcy situation, an application is to the bankruptcy court[16] where the proceedings are taking place, and the relevant provisions of the IA 1986 apply. The matters set out in TLATA 1996, s 15(1) as relevant to an application under s 14 do not apply on an application by a trustee (s 15(4)). For some useful background to principles applied and the approach of the courts in a non-bankruptcy situation, see *Mortgage Corporation v Shaire and others*[17] and *Re MCA; HM Customs & Excise Commissioners and Long v A and A; A v A (Long Intervening)*.[18]

The relevant factors

5.25   The court must make such order 'as it thinks just and reasonable' having regard to the factors set out in IA 1986, s 335A(2) (which applies to applications under TLATA 1996, s 14) and s 336(4) (which applies to applications under FLA 1996, s 33) rather than those set out in TLATA 1996, s 15(4). The relevant factors are as follows.

(1)   The interests of the bankrupt's creditors

5.25   The degree of weight to be placed on this factor will depend on the financial position of the creditor. A delay in payment may have a serious impact where the creditor is a small business, whereas different considerations may apply where the creditor is a financial institution.

5.27   In *Re Holliday (A Bankrupt), ex parte Trustee of the Property of the Bankrupt v the Bankrupt*[19] the main creditors were a bank and the husband's former solicitors to whom approximately £6,250 was owed. At the date of the appeal hearing in December 1979, the family home was worth in the region of £34,000 subject to an outstanding mortgage of £6,864. Balancing the interests of the husband's creditors against those of the wife (who would have to provide a home for the children of the marriage) the court ordered that the house should not be sold without the wife's consent until July 1985, by which time the two eldest children would be over 17 years of age.

5.28   In *Re Bailey (A Bankrupt)*[20] consideration was given to the monies which the creditors themselves would pay by way of interest on borrowing which proved necessary pending payment from the bankrupt's estate.

---

[16]   IA 1986, ss 335A and 336(2)(b).
[17]   [2001] 4 All ER 364.
[18]   [2002] 2 FLR 274, QBD and FD; [2003] 2 WLR 210, CA.
[19]   [1980] 3 All ER 385.
[20]   [1977] 1 WLR 278.

(2)   The conduct of the spouse or former spouse, so far as contributing to the bankruptcy

5.29   If the wife's conduct has only served to add to the parties' financial difficulties, especially if she was aware of the situation but continued an extravagant lifestyle, she is likely to receive little sympathy from the court. If the wife assisted the husband in his business, it may be argued that the warning signs should have been all that more easily noticeable.

(3)   The needs and financial resources of the spouse or former spouse

5.30   The availability of alternative accommodation, whether purchased or rented, will clearly be a significant consideration. In *Re Densham (A Bankrupt)*,[21] the local authority was actively attempting to find accommodation for the family which Goff J (as he then was) felt was of particular relevance. However, care should be taken to ensure that the family is not seen as making itself intentionally homeless for the purposes of s 191 of the Housing Act 1996, which will then prejudice its chances of local authority accommodation; see also *Re Haghighat (A Bankrupt)*.[22]

(4)   The needs of any children

5.31   The court must have regard to the needs of the children, but their needs are not the paramount consideration. In *Re Bailey (A Bankrupt)*,[23] the wife appealed against an order for sale before her son's full-time education had been completed on the basis that a move would prove to be too disruptive. The court reached the conclusion that there would be, at most, only a slight interference with the son's educational prospects and that it was probable that he would have to move to another school in any event. The younger the children are, the more difficult it is likely to be to establish that the potential disruption will have adverse consequences for them.[24]

(5)   All the circumstances of the case other than the needs of the bankrupt

5.32   The court has a wide discretion to take into account a variety of relevant factors. The presence of third parties such as elderly relatives, who may have even provided some financial assistance to the parties, may persuade the court to defer an immediate sale. In *Re Mott*,[25] the elderly mother of the bankrupt had lived in the house for 40 years and was in poor health. A sale was postponed until after her death.

---

[21]   [1975] 1 WLR 1519.
[22]   [2009] EWHC 649 (Ch), [2009] 1 FLR 1271, [2009] BPIR 268.
[23]   [1977] 1 WLR 278.
[24]   *Re Lowrie* [1981] 3 All ER 353.
[25]   [1987] CLY 212.

5.33   In *Re Ng*,[26] the trustee made an application for sale, even though there
were insufficient assets to meet the debts due to the secured creditor and so
there would be no benefit to unsecured creditors. Lightman J reluctantly made
the order sought, despite regarding the procedure adopted by the trustee as an
abuse of process, since the wife accepted that any subsequent application by the
secured creditor would be successful. It is unclear what motivated the trustee to
take action for the benefit of the secured creditor. Lightman J's comments were
applied by the Court of Appeal in *Trustee in Bankruptcy of Syed Bukhari v
Bukhari and another*.[27]

'Exceptional circumstances' justifying postponement of sale

5.34   The Insolvency Act 1986, ss 335A(3) and 336(5), provide that where the
trustee's application is made 12 months after the bankrupt's estate first vested
in him, the court shall assume that the interests of the bankrupt's creditors
outweigh all other considerations, unless the circumstances of the case are
'exceptional'. In such circumstances, the scales are, therefore, heavily weighted
in favour of the creditors.

5.35   The definition of exceptional is now largely agreed to be that expounded
by Mr Paul Morgan QC (as he then was) in *Hosking v Michaelides*:

> '. . . a circumstance . . . which is out of the ordinary course, or unusual or special,
> or uncommon. To be exceptional, a circumstance need not be unique,
> unprecedented or very rare, but it cannot be one that is regularly or routinely
> encountered.'

5.36   The court is required to undertake a value judgment and needs to look at
all the circumstances of the case in considering exceptionality. In the majority
of cases, it will be simply a matter of time before the creditors' interests prevail.
The onus is on the bankrupt's family to demonstrate that their particular
circumstances are exceptional. This has shown to be a difficult test.

5.37   Even a relatively small outstanding amount will not of itself amount to
an 'exceptional circumstance' on an order for sale application nor will be the
eviction of an 'innocent' wife and small children – see *Dean v Stout (The
Trustee in Bankruptcy of Dean)*.[28]

Art 8 European Convention for the Protection of Human Rights and Fundamental Freedoms

5.38   Article 8 has led to a review of 'exceptional circumstances' (*see Donohoe
v Ingram*[29]); however it appears that the domestic legislation is adequate to take
account of Art 8 considerations. The arguments traversed are to be balanced in

[26]   [1998] 2 FLR 386.
[27]   [1999] BPIR 157.
[28]   [2006] 1 FLR 725.
[29]   [2006] 1 FLR 725, [2006] 2 FLR 1084.

the court's value judgment of 'exceptional' (see *Nicholls v Lan*[30]). It has also been held that the possible shift in considerations does not give rise to a 'significant modification of the approach hitherto adopted'.[31]

5.39 The IA 1986 offers no guidance as to which circumstances are to be regarded as exceptional, and so inevitably the courts have been called on to clarify and interpret the relevant statutory provisions. The following heads of argument have emerged:

(1) needs of the children;

(2) solicitor's negligence;

(3) illness;

(4) lack of equity.

(1) Delay

5.40 As s 283A provides a 3-year window to bring claims, this means that arguments based on delay should fall away. All IA 1986 bankruptcies have a 3-year limitation under s 283A. This limitation period runs for those made bankrupt prior to 1 April 2004, so in reality by 1 April 2007, all transitional cases should be out of time.

5.41 Even arguments about delay in the transitional cases have met with difficulty. His Honour Judge Pelling QC (sitting as a High Court Judge) in *Turner v Avis and Avis*[32] held that a delay of some 19 years did not amount to an 'exceptional circumstances' for the following reasons:

(1) There was no time-limit on the trustee's application (the bankruptcy order was 1989).

(2) Although the effect of the delay was to increase interest and costs this had not materially or disproportionately affected the (wife) because:
    (a) the whole of the bankrupt's one third would have been required at the time of the bankruptcy to pay the debts due;
    (b) the increase in property values had out-performed the interest;
    (c) there was no evidence that showed the expenses of the procedure were greater than they would have been in 1989;
    (d) although the wife argued she had no chance now to obtain a mortgage there was no evidence she could have obtained a mortgage in 1989.

---

[30] [2007] 1 FLR 744.
[31] *Boyle v Turner* [2007] BPIR 43 at 50.
[32] [2007] EWCA Civ 748, [2008] Ch 218.

(2)   Difficulties identifying alternative accommodation and the educational interests of the bankrupt's children

5.42   The judgment of Walton J, pre-1986, in *Re Lowrie*[33] provides a starting point. In 1974, the newly married husband purchased the family home in his own name for £12,000 with the assistance of a mortgage of £11,500. Within one year he became insolvent, and in 1979 was adjudicated bankrupt. The parties had two young children. The husband's only asset was his interest in the family home. At first instance, an order for possession and sale was made but postponed for 30 months primarily due to the presence of the young children and the difficulty which the family would face in securing alternative accommodation. On appeal, Walton J was of the view[34] that:

'It is desirable to step back for a moment and look at the situation which must in these cases inevitably occur, or at any rate must occur so frequently as to be almost inevitable. The first one of course is that the whole family is going to be rendered homeless. That is not an exceptional circumstance. It is a normal circumstance and is the result, the all too obvious result, of a husband having conducted the financial affairs of the family in a way which has led to bankruptcy. The second result almost invariably is that it is going to be incredibly hard and incredibly hard luck on the innocent co-owner, the wife, who is in most cases a totally innocent person who has done nothing to bring about the bankruptcy. Of course, as against that, one has to realise that she has been enjoying, over whatever period it may be, the fruits of the debts which the bankrupt has contracted and which debts are not at the moment being paid.'

5.43   Earlier, the Court of Appeal in *Re Holliday*[35] had made a similar order for possession and sale but suspended enforcement for an exceptionally long period of 5 years. This appeared to be because of the wife's inability to purchase a house for herself and the children from her available resources, the possible disruption to the children's education and the fact that, as the court held, no great hardship would be caused to the creditors (primarily the husband's bank and former solicitors) by the postponement.

5.44   Subsequent cases (post-1986) have cast serious doubt on the *Re Holliday* decision since few situations are likely to arise where creditors will not suffer some form of significant hardship during a lengthy postponement of the sale.

5.45   In *Re Citro (Domenico) (A Bankrupt); Re Citro (Carmine) (A Bankrupt)*,[36] two brothers who operated a business together in partnership became bankrupt in 1985 owing in excess of £60,000 each. Their only assets were their respective interests in their homes, owned jointly with their wives, which could expect to realise in the region of only £27,500 and £38,900. One brother was judicially separated from his wife who had remained in the

---

[33]   [1981] 3 All ER 353.
[34]   At 356.
[35]   [1980] 3 All ER 385.
[36]   [1991] 1 FLR 71.

matrimonial home with their three children, the youngest of whom was 12 years old. The other lived with his wife and their three children, the youngest of whom was 10 years old.

5.46 At first instance, orders for sale were made in respect of each property but enforcement was postponed until the youngest child in each family reached the age of 16. The trustee appealed, seeking removal of the postponement. Nourse LJ considered what might constitute exceptional circumstances and held[37] that:

'As the cases show, it is not uncommon for a wife with young children to be faced with eviction in circumstances where the realisation of her beneficial interest will not produce enough to buy a comparable home in the same neighbourhood, or indeed elsewhere; and, if she has to move elsewhere, there may be problems over schooling and so forth. Such circumstances, while engendering a natural sympathy in all who hear of them, cannot be described as exceptional. They are the melancholy consequences of debt and improvidence with which every civilised society has been familiar.'

5.47 The potential educational difficulties for the children and the inevitable lack of resources to purchase alternative accommodation were still not sufficient to outweigh the interests of the creditors. The trustee's appeal was allowed and the order for sale varied to provide for a period of postponement no longer than 6 months.

5.48 *Re Citro* does, however, need to be considered in the light of *Abbey National plc v Moss and Others*.[38] In this case, there was an agreement that the property would not be sold during the lifetime of one of the joint owners (who were not spouses), and this constituted a collateral purpose beyond joint occupation. However, in most cases which are dealt with by a family lawyer, the property will have been intended for joint occupation and so *Re Citro* will be applicable. It has since been applied in the post-IA 1986 High Court decision in *Harrington v Bennett*.[39]

5.49 In *Barca v Mears*[40] an order for sale was resisted on the basis that the child who spent the majority of the week at the property had special educational needs. This was characterized by absent-mindedness, lack of organisation and poor performance at school. Nicholas Strauss QC confirmed on appeal that this did not amount to 'exceptional circumstances'; see also *Re Haghighat (A Bankrupt)*[41] on the issue of alternative accommodation.

---

[37] At 82.
[38] [1994] 1 FLR 307.
[39] [2000] BPIR 630.
[40] [2005] 2 FLR 1.
[41] [2009] EWHC 649 (Ch), [2009] 1 FLR 1271.

5.50 It has now been clarified that 'needs' of children in this context must be given a very broad interpretation and refer to needs of any kind, and is certainly not confined to needs of a financial nature; see *Everitt v Budhram (A Bankrupt) and Another.*[42]

(3) Solicitors' negligence

5.51 In *Re Gorman (A Bankrupt)*[43] the former matrimonial home was purchased in 1968 in the parties' joint names. The marriage ran into difficulties and a divorce followed in 1978. Mrs Gorman remained in occupation. Mr Gorman was ordered at the ancillary relief hearing to discharge the mortgage repayments. He failed to do so and arrears soon built up. Mrs Gorman was faced with the prospect of possession proceedings and discharged the arrears in full. Mr Gorman was then adjudicated bankrupt owing over £155,000 and the trustee sought an order for possession and sale of the former matrimonial home, then worth over £100,000 with a nominal mortgage. Mrs Gorman's solicitors had failed to apply for a property adjustment order in the ancillary relief proceedings.

5.52 The court at first instance dismissed the trustee's application for an order for sale and the trustee appealed. At the same time, Mrs Gorman commenced negligence proceedings against her former solicitors. The Divisional Court found that the trustee was entitled to an order for sale, but that this should be postponed until the conclusion of the negligence proceedings so as to enable Mrs Gorman to put forward proposals to the trustee for the purchase of Mr Gorman's interest in the property. Costs at both first instance and on the appeal were awarded against Mrs Gorman and provision made for interest at a commercial rate to be paid on the trustee's share of the property until payment was forthcoming. In a market of falling property prices and a potential wait of 2 years until the conclusion of the negligence proceedings, Mrs Gorman may have been left with very little in any event. It is, however, understood that Mrs Gorman subsequently put forward acceptable proposals based on the monies which she received from her negligence claim.

5.53 *Re Gorman* appears to have been an exceptional case primarily as a result of the presence of the negligence proceedings which were likely to enable Mrs Gorman to purchase her former husband's interest in the property. It has since been distinguished in *Jackson v Bell.*[44]

(4) Illness

5.54 Circumstances may be exceptional where the non-bankrupt spouse is suffering from cancer, as in *Judd v Brown, Re Bankrupts (Nos 9589 and 9588 of 1994)*,[45] or even where the bankrupt has a terminal illness and the

---

[42] [2009] WLR (D) 167, (2009) *The Times*, 14 July.
[43] [1990] 2 FLR 284.
[44] [2001] BPIR 613.
[45] [1998] 2 FLR 360.

non-bankrupt spouse needs to be able to care for her dying husband in the family home, as in *Re Bremner (A Bankrupt).*[46]

5.55 In *Judd v Brown*, the non-bankrupt wife had been diagnosed with ovarian cancer 4 months prior to the trustee's application for an order for sale. Harman J said:[47]

'This event must have been sudden, unforeseeable, of very recent occurrence, of gravity and is directly affected by the orders now sought … when recovery from the attack is directly related to the order sought, it is, in my judgment, what is properly to be described as an exceptional reason for refusing the orders.'

5.56 The trustee sought orders for possession and sale either immediately, or suspended for 8 months, to enable the wife's course of chemotherapy to be completed and to allow a short period of recovery thereafter. Harman J refused the trustee's applications. He found the 'occurrence of life-threatening illness' to be an exceptional circumstance and declined to impose an order for possession suspended for 8 months, because to do so would cause increasing stress to the non-bankrupt spouse.

5.57 In *Re Bremner*, the bankrupt spouse had inoperable oesophageal cancer and a life-expectancy of probably no more than 6 months. His wife was his only carer, and although it was accepted that his needs were not relevant, her needs (to be able to care for her husband as effectively as possible) were compelling and justified the suspension of an order for possession until 3 months after his death.

5.58 Sales have also been postponed where the non-bankrupt spouse suffered from paranoid schizophrenia and required time to locate to alternative accommodation,[48] and where the non-bankrupt spouse suffered from renal failure and chronic osteoarthritis causing severely restricted mobility.[49] In the latter case, a sale would not have produced any dividend for creditors because the proceeds of sale would have been consumed in costs. The order for sale was suspended indefinitely.

5.59 In the recent and exceptional case of *Re Haghighat (A Bankrupt)*[50] the court held that exceptional circumstances did exist. The bankrupt and his wife's son was severely disabled, he had congenital quadriplegic cerebral palsy with learning disability and epilepsy, was doubly incontinent, with no speech and little comprehension, used a wheelchair, and had to be carried between his bed, his chair, and the shower. He required continuous care. The result of this case was to delay possession for 3 years to enable the disabled child and the wife to be re-housed in suitable accommodation.

---

[46] [1999] 1 FLR 912.
[47] At 364E.
[48] *Re Raval (A Bankrupt)* [1998] 2 FLR 718, where the order for sale was postponed for one year.
[49] *Claughton v Charalambous* [1999] 1 FLR 740.
[50] [2009] 1 FLR 1271.

(5)   Lack of equity

5.60 In *Trustee of Eric Bowe (A Bankrupt) v Bowe*[51] the wife sought unsuccessfully to postpone the sale of the matrimonial home. The fact that the entirety of the bankrupt's share in the net proceeds of the sale was likely to be applied to pay the expenses of the bankruptcy was not an exceptional circumstance. *Harrington v Bennett,*[52] referred to above, has confirmed this. The Enterprise Act 2002 introduced a statutory *de minimis* amount, which at the date of publication, is £1,000 in relation to the trustee's interest in the property.

5.61 There appears to be no *de minimis* rule to the amount claimed in the bankruptcy; see *Dean v Stout (The Trustee in Bankruptcy of Dean).*[53]

Exceptional circumstances – summary

5.62 The circumstances which will be regarded as exceptional, thereby advancing the interests of the bankrupt's family above those of his creditors, are clearly limited. The inevitable consequences of a sale, comprising disruption, unhappiness and extreme inconvenience to the family, are not exceptional.

5.63 If there is no future date which can be identified as that to which a sale should be postponed (such as the conclusion of other court proceedings or the end of a school term), or there is little prospect of the wife being able to raise sufficient funds to purchase her husband's interest, an order for an immediate sale may be even more likely.

5.64 Whilst the chances of success of the trustee's application for an order for sale are greatly enhanced on the expiration of the 12-month period, there may nevertheless be circumstances which warrant an earlier application, for instance where the equity is rapidly reducing and there is no prospect of realistic proposals being put forward. The trustee may decide to delay an application where, for instance, an improvement is anticipated in the housing market, thereby increasing the eventual sale price and, in turn, the monies available for distribution. In such circumstances, the bankrupt's wife would be well advised to negotiate with the trustee to achieve an early sale to herself wherever she is able to raise the necessary funds. The trustee may otherwise seek a charge against the bankrupt's interest in the home pending the eventual sale. There may be limitation issues around this charge; see *Gotham v Doodes.*[54] In reality a trustee can only have a charge for a fixed figure plus interest so the added value (after costs) goes back to the bankrupt.

---

[51]   [1998] 2 FLR 439.
[52]   [2000] BPIR 630.
[53]   [2006] 1 FLR 725.
[54]   [2006] EWCA Civ 1080, [2007] 1 FLR 373.

5.65 Where extreme circumstances exist (see *Re Haghighat*) a delay may be achievable but even there it was only for 3 years.

BANKRUPT'S RIGHTS OF OCCUPATION

5.66 Under s 337 of the IA 1986, a bankrupt husband is entitled to occupy the family home himself, independently of his wife's rights of occupation, if:

(a) he was entitled to occupy the house by virtue of a beneficial interest prior to the bankruptcy; and

(b) any person under the age of 18, with whom the husband has at some time occupied the property, shares the home both at the time the bankruptcy petition is presented and at the commencement of the bankruptcy.

5.67 It is the interests of the children and not those of the bankrupt which are being balanced against the interests of the creditors. Where matrimonial home rights cannot be conferred upon the bankrupt's partner (where, for instance, the bankrupt's partner is a cohabitant without a beneficial interest), any children for whom the bankrupt is responsible should, nevertheless, be protected. The children do not need to be the natural children of the bankrupt. The only requirement is that they have at some time occupied the home with him and were doing so both at the time the bankruptcy petition was presented and at the time the bankruptcy order was made.

5.68 The husband has similar rights to those conferred upon his wife by virtue of FLA 1996, s 30 (ie the right not to be evicted without a court order and, if not in occupation, the right to apply to the court to regain entry[55]). In the event that the bankrupt is the sole occupant (except for children) and no other person has an equitable interest, the trustee must apply for an order for possession and sale against the bankrupt pursuant to FLA 1996, s 33.

5.69 An application for an order for sale is made to the bankruptcy court, and the court must make such order as it thinks just and reasonable having regard to the factors set out in IA 1986, s 337(5):

(a) the interests of the creditors;

(b) the bankrupt's financial resources;

(c) the needs of the children; and

(d) all the circumstances of the case other than the needs of the bankrupt.

---

[55] IA 1986, s 337(2)(a).

5.70   Where such an application is made 12 months from the date on which the bankrupt's estate vested in his trustee, the court shall assume, unless the circumstances of the case are exceptional, that the interests of the bankrupt's creditors outweigh all other considerations.[56]

ORDERS PENDING SALE

5.71   On the making of an order for possession and sale under FLA 1996, s 33, or at any time thereafter, the trustee may seek one or more of the following additional provisions:

–   that the wife is obliged to repair and maintain the property;[57] or

–   that the wife is obliged to discharge rent, mortgage payments or other outgoings affecting the property;[58] or

–   that the wife should make payments to the trustee in bankruptcy by way of rent in respect of her occupation of the home if the husband would be entitled to occupy it but for the occupation order.[59]

5.72   Whether the court is prepared to make such orders will depend on all the circumstances of the case, including the financial needs and financial resources of the parties, and the financial obligations which they have or are likely to have in the foreseeable future, including obligations to each other and to any relevant child.

5.73   Where the husband continues to occupy the property, whether by virtue of IA 1986, s 337 or otherwise, on condition that he makes payments towards the mortgage or other outgoings, he does not, by virtue of those payments, acquire any interest or greater interest in the property.[60]

NEGOTIATING WITH THE TRUSTEE

5.74   It is difficult to imagine in what circumstances it is not advisable to attempt to negotiate with the trustee in bankruptcy. It is only the husband's share of the property which forms part of his estate and as such the wife should at the earliest available opportunity negotiate in order to attempt to prevent sale.

---

[56]   Ibid, s 337(6).
[57]   FLA 1996, s 40(1)(a)(i).
[58]   Ibid, s 40(1)(a)(ii).
[59]   Ibid, s 40(1)(b).
[60]   IA 1986, s 338.

5.75 A stark word of warning was provided by *Bank of Baroda v Patel*[61] where the wife successfully negotiated the release of a charging order in exchange for the sum of £22,000. The bank later sought to prove their much larger sum in the husband's bankruptcy and as a result an order for the sale of the property was applied for. The wife argued that she had already concluded matters with the bank and the £22,000 was not only for the removal of the charging order but also the husband's underlying debt. The bank appealed successfully and it was held that no reference had been made in correspondence to full and final satisfaction of the underlying debts: 'The clear language used in the relevant letters must be the primary source of the court's construction of the agreement'. Be clear in your negotiations and have the outcome properly documented.

---

[61] [2009] 2 FLR 753.

Chapter 6

ANCILLARY RELIEF AND BANKRUPTCY

INTRODUCTION

6.1   The issue of bankruptcy proceedings against a husband will inevitably cause the wife great concern and make her question how this will affect the financial position of herself and the children in relation to their home, their other assets and their income on divorce.

6.2   Once the bankruptcy petition has been issued, and the bankruptcy order made, there are essentially only two options open to the wife. The first is to challenge the bankruptcy to try to set it aside if it is at an early stage; the second is to review the position in the ancillary relief proceedings where the advice will depend on what stage the proceedings have reached. Both these situations are discussed below.

CHALLENGING THE BANKRUPTCY

6.3   It would be wrong to assume that a wife faced with the issue of bankruptcy proceedings has automatically been presented with a 'fait accompli' and that she must accept the repercussions without question. There will inevitably be cases where a wife considers that bankruptcy proceedings should not have been issued. In particular, where the bankruptcy order follows from the presentation of a petition by the bankrupt husband himself, the wife may suspect that he has followed this route with the intention of defeating her claims for financial provision and that in effect the bankruptcy is a fraudulent device.

6.4   There are four possible options to consider in this case:

(1)   an application under MCA 1973, s 37;

(2)   annulment of the bankruptcy order;

(3)   rescission of the bankruptcy order;

(4)   pleading the bankruptcy as conduct in the ancillary relief proceedings.

These are dealt with below. The first three will be applicable in most cases where divorce proceedings have just begun at the very latest, the fourth is applicable where the divorce case is well underway.

(1)   Matrimonial Causes Act 1973, s 37

6.5   MCA 1973, s 37 provides that a court can protect a party to proceedings for financial relief where the other party to the proceedings has made a reviewable disposition with the intention of defeating the claim for financial relief and if the disposition was set aside, financial relief or different financial relief would be granted to the applicant. In such circumstances, the court may make an order setting aside the disposition. In the context of a wife's suspicions that her husband has presented the bankruptcy petition as a fraudulent device to defeat her claim, the question arises as to whether the action that he has taken is a reviewable disposition under s 37 of the MCA 1973.

6.6   'Disposition' is defined by s 37(6) of the MCA 1973 as:

> 'In this section "disposition" does not include any provision contained in a will or codicil but with that exception includes any conveyance, assurance or gift of property of any description, whether made by an instrument or otherwise.'

6.7   In *Woodley v Woodley*[1] Ewbank J suggested that the route of applying for review of a disposition under s 37 of the MCA 1973 may be open to a wife in this position. This was on the hearing of Mrs Woodley's appeal against a decision to allow her husband's appeal against a committal order made when he failed to pay a lump sum payable under court order, the husband having presented his own bankruptcy petition before the sum due had been paid.

6.8   When Mrs Woodley issued a second judgment summons on which the court refused to make an order, Mrs Woodley again appealed, and Balcombe LJ, before considering the main issue, dealt with two subsidiary matters, one of which was the possibility of the bankruptcy being set aside under s 37 of the MCA 1973.[2] He concluded that this was not a route open to the wife because in bankruptcy, a disposition of the bankrupt's property takes effect by the operation of s 306 of the IA 1986. This provides that the bankrupt's estate vests in the trustee immediately on his appointment taking effect or, in the case of the Official Receiver, on his becoming trustee. The disposition is not, therefore, the act of the bankrupt himself even though the bankruptcy was initiated by his petition, and hence there is no disposition that is capable of review under s 37 of the MCA 1973.

6.9   The usefulness of s 37 was considered further, albeit not in a bankruptcy context, in *Trowbridge v Trowbridge and Trowbridge*.[3] In that case the wife tried to enforce a lump sum due to her under a consent order against her former

[1]   [1992] 2 FLR 417.
[2]   *Woodley v Woodley (No 2)* [1993] 2 FLR 477.
[3]   [2002] All ER (D) 207.

husband. He lived in a property owned in the sole name of his second wife, but towards which he had made significant contributions. The wife successfully showed that the husband's contributions gave him a beneficial interest in the property against which she could enforce her charging order. However, had this beneficial interest not been proved, the judge held that the wife could still have used either s 37 of the MCA 1973, or s 423 of the IA 1986 to set aside the payments made. Note that any recoveries made under s 423 will be for the benefit of all the creditors and not just the wife. There may therefore be circumstances where this route is worth considering, but it comes with a significant concern as to whether it will be effective.

(2) Application for annulment

6.10 This is the most commonly reported approach taken by the wife's solicitors. On occasion it has succeeded, but very careful thought needs to be taken before such an application is made, as when it fails the costs consequences can be very high. The application is made under s 282(1)(a) or 282(1)(b) of the IA 1986. Section 282(1)(a) deals with the situation where the bankruptcy order should not have been made, where the principal respondent to the annulment application is the petitioner. Section 282(1)(b) deals with the situation where all of the creditors and the bankruptcy costs and expenses have been paid or secured. In this application the principal respondent is the trustee. In Balcombe LJ's view in *Woodley v Woodley*, a s 282(1)(a) application was the appropriate route to pursue a husband attempting to defeat the wife's claims. Before such an application is made it is worth considering the case law carefully.

6.11 In the case of *Re Holliday (A Bankrupt)*[4] the wife sought an annulment when, on the day that she gave notice of her intention to proceed with her application for ancillary relief within the divorce proceedings, the husband filed his own petition for bankruptcy and was subsequently adjudicated bankrupt. She sought an order to annul the adjudication of the husband's bankruptcy. On appeal it was held that even if the husband's motive in petitioning for his own bankruptcy was not to protect himself from undue pressure by creditors or to secure a fair distribution of his assets between them, but instead to defeat the claim of his wife for a transfer of property order, that alone could not make the petition an abuse of process. Since the reality was that on the day he filed his petition he was in fact unable to pay his debts, then the judge had been right to refuse to annul the adjudication.

6.12 To succeed on an annulment application under s 282(1)(a), in most cases a wife must show that the bankruptcy order ought not to have been made because at the time it was made the husband was able to pay his debts. This has remained the consistent approach of the court ever since, on some occasions to the wife's benefit and on some occasions to her detriment.

---

4   [1980] 3 All ER 385.

6.13   Such an application by the wife for the annulment of a bankruptcy order under s 282(1) of the IA 1986 succeeded in the case of *F v F (Divorce: Insolvency: Annulment of Bankruptcy Order).*[5] In this case, Thorpe J had no doubt that the bankruptcy order ought not to have been made on the grounds existing at the time the order was made. The husband's petition, on which the bankruptcy order had been made, presented a false picture of the husband's financial position, since he had omitted assets outside the jurisdiction which should have been included. The bankruptcy order was hence an abuse of process and should be set aside.

6.14   This approach has been reinforced in the case of *Roker International Properties Inc and Another v Couvaras v Wolf,*[6] where the bankruptcy court transferred the case to the Family Division, despite the bankrupt husband's strong opposition. The bankruptcy order was then annulled and the petition was dismissed as a sham, as the husband clearly had the resources available. Also of interest is *F v F (S intervening),*[7] where again the annulment was granted.

6.15   The most recent authorities on annulment are two cases, *Whig v Whig*[8] in the High Court and *Paulin v Paulin and Cativo Limited*[9] in the Court of Appeal. The two cases have different outcomes but appear to follow the same principles, and both need to be considered carefully.

6.16   *Whig v Whig* is clear authority for the need to relate any application back to s 282(1)(a) of the IA 1986. As Munby J made clear at para 54:

> 'It is important to appreciate that if in fact the husband was "unable to pay his debts" on [the date he presented his petition], the fact that his motive may have been to spite the wife and frustrate her claim to ancillary relief is neither here nor there. If his motive was corrupt then no doubt the court will scrutinize with some care the self serving assertion that he was insolvent, but if satisfied that he was indeed insolvent then the court cannot annul the bankruptcy order under section 282(1)(a).'

Importantly he went on to make it clear that when considering such applications if they fall in the Family Division:

> 'The Family Division applies precisely the same principles, and in precisely the same way, as the Chancery Division, or for that matter the Queen's Bench Division. A creditor is not to be prejudiced because a wife's application to annul the bankruptcy order on which he depends is heard by a Family Division judge . . .'.

---

[5]   [1994] 1 FLR 359.
[6]   [2000] 2 FLR 976.
[7]   [2002] EWHC 2814 (Fam), [2003] 1 FLR 911.
[8]   [2007] EWHC 1856 (Fam).
[9]   [2009] EWCA Civ 221.

Munby J also gives a very clear analysis of the reasons why the successful annulment cases referred to above can be distinguished, and the case report must be read before any practitioner decides to proceed with such an application.

6.17 In *Paulin v Paulin* in the Court of Appeal however the annulment application was (eventually) successful. The case is curious as the Deputy High Court Judge reversed his initial refusal to annul the decision, but it is more important in that it was held that:

> 'A person who is made bankrupt on his own petition who is shown both to have made a substantially dishonest Statement of Affairs and on the date of presentation to have held assets which substantially exceeded his liabilities will find it hard to resist annulment of the basis that he was nevertheless unable to pay his debts.'

6.18 The two cases are not necessarily inconsistent but it is submitted that the costs of a failed annulment application make it very important that such an application is very carefully thought through before it is made. In particular in *Whig* the costs of the trustee and the other parties' representatives meant that there was nothing left to be divided in the subsequent ancillary relief proceedings.

(3) Rescission

6.19 Rescission under s 375 of the IA 1986, was successfully used in the case of *Fitch v Official Receiver*.[10] Although rarely used in family proceedings, this section confers a general power on the courts to review, rescind or vary orders on bankruptcy matters, in a situation where the circumstances of the case have changed since the order was properly made ie: there is no allegation it was incorrectly made. In *Fitch* the creditors as a group decided they did not want to pursue the bankruptcy. However, the circumstances of this case are very unusual. For a more detailed explanation of rescission, see *Papanicola v Humphreys*.[11] In most if not all cases it would appear better to proceed via annulment.

(4) Pleading the bankruptcy as conduct under s 25(2)(g) of the MCA 1973

6.20 Once the trustee in bankruptcy has been appointed, the assets of the bankrupt will vest in him under s 306 of the IA 1986. Nothing save such assets as are exempt,[12] which are likely to be of limited value, remain against which the divorce court can make a lump sum or property adjustment order. As will be seen, pension sharing may well be an option for recovery. Property

---

[10] [1996] 1 WLR 242.
[11] [2005] EWHC 335 (Ch), [2005] 2 All ER 418.
[12] See **3.2** et seq.

adjustment and lump sum orders against the husband are not possible,[13] except as against the husband's after-acquired property which has not been claimed by the trustee under ss 307 and 309 of the IA 1986, which again will have little value.

6.21   It is likely therefore that there will be little point in the wife pursuing an application for ancillary relief at that stage, and depending on the stage of the case she will either need to refrain from making her application or to seek an adjournment, until such time as the bankrupt has been discharged.[14] It may then be appropriate to argue that a previous bankruptcy should be taken into account in a subsequent financial division.

6.22   How far the court would then take the bankruptcy into account as conduct will very much depend on the facts of the case. Personal bankruptcy is not generally now seen as a particularly blameworthy issue (the liberalisation of the bankruptcy laws was designed specifically to remove the apparent stigma of bankruptcy), and it is likely that the success of any conduct application will depend on the underlying reasons for the bankruptcy, e g gambling. See *Beach v Beach*[15] and *Le Foe v le Foe*[16] for interesting judicial views on this. Simple economic bad luck, in the author's view, would not justify a successful application.

BANKRUPTCY AND ANCILLARY RELIEF

6.23   The impact upon a wife of a bankruptcy order in the following circumstances is now considered:

(i)   where the bankruptcy order is made before the ancillary relief order is made;

(ii)   where she has an enforceable ancillary relief order and the bankruptcy order follows;

(iv)   where the bankruptcy has been discharged.

(1)   Bankruptcy order made and assets vested before ancillary relief order has been made

6.24   Where the bankruptcy order has been made before ancillary relief proceedings have completed then, if the wife fails to have the bankruptcy order annulled or rescinded on one of the grounds above, she is faced with the

---

[13]   *Davy-Chiesman v Davy-Chiesman* [1984] 1 All ER 321, CA.
[14]   For instance, in *Pearce v Pearce* (1980) 1 FLR 261, where a lump sum was made after a delay of 9 years. See also *MT v MT* [1992] 1 FLR 362.
[15]   [1995] 2 FLR 160, [1995] 2 FCR 526.
[16]   [2001] 2 FLR 970.

insurmountable difficulties caused by the vesting provisions under the IA 1986.[17] Any proactive action taken will always be subject to the scrutiny and (likely) attack of the trustee in bankruptcy.

The realistic options for ancillary relief she will have are essentially limited to considering:

(1)   whether a maintenance order for her may be appropriate;

(2)   whether pension sharing is an option.

For the reasons set out below there will be no point in pursuing an application for property adjustment or lump sums. Considering the main possible orders:

Maintenance

6.25   The income of the bankrupt, unlike his capital assets, will not automatically vest in the trustee in bankruptcy. The existence of bankruptcy proceedings will not prevent the wife from applying to the court for a maintenance order for herself. The bankruptcy court can, however, stay such proceedings under s 285(1) of the IA 1986 if it considers it appropriate to do so. The question of a stay is at the discretion of the bankruptcy court. However, there is also jurisdiction under s 285(2) for any court, in which proceedings are pending, to stay those proceedings.

6.26   Since the maintenance arrears are not automatically discharged on the bankrupt's discharge, it may be that the court will refuse such a stay, but there is no helpful case law on the subject. If there is no such stay sought or granted, then the wife can pursue her application.

6.27   In theory, the trustee can seek to recover what might be seen as excessive maintenance paid once the bankruptcy petition has been issued under s 284(1), which covers the period from presentation of the bankruptcy petition to appointment of the first trustee. Although a wife may pursue an application for maintenance after the appointment of the trustee and the vesting of assets in him, any payment made pursuant to an order in the period between presentation of the petition and vesting may be caught by s 284(2) of the IA 1986. This applies the provisions of s 284(1) to a payment, whether in cash or otherwise, and provides that where any such payment is void, the person paid shall hold the sum paid for the bankrupt as part of his estate. This embargo ceases once the vesting has taken place.

6.28   Whilst, therefore, the making of a maintenance order may not be prevented by the terms of s 284, it would appear that during this relevant period payment under any order will in theory be caught by s 284(2) although,

---

[17]   *Hellyer v Hellyer* [1996] 2 FLR 579, CA (where the court held that it was valid to make an order against an undischarged bankrupt where there would be a surplus in the bankruptcy); *Albert v Albert* [1997] 2 FLR 791; *McGladdery v McGladdery* [1999] 2 FLR 1102, CA.

if the money were to be claimed back, the wife could apply for an order ratifying the payment. The reality is that a trustee is unlikely to be interested in recouping modest maintenance, although they would probably wish to consider anything collusive; see *Hill v Haines*[18] below. As most maintenance payments are determined based on reasonable needs, there should not be an issue as to collusion here. However in most cases there is insufficient income to justify a spouse or maintenance order during the term of the bankruptcy.

6.29 When considering maintenance orders it must be remembered that, under s 310(1) of the IA 1986, if the trustee applies to the court, the court may make an order that the bankrupt must pay a specified amount for the benefit of his creditors. This is known as an income payments order. There is also statutory provision under s 310A for an income payments agreement to be entered into between the trustee and the bankrupt. The court also retains the power under s 310(4) of the IA 1986 to discharge or vary any attachment of earnings order already in place. Under s 310(6) of the IA 1986, an income payments order can last beyond the discharge of the bankruptcy. In the case of an automatic discharge, it should not last more than 3 years from the date of the order.

6.30 The court should not, make an income payments order which would reduce the income of the bankrupt below the amount that the court considers he needs to meet the reasonable domestic needs of his family and himself. However, under s 385(1) of the IA 1986, the family is defined as those living with and dependent upon the bankrupt. Hence, no account should be taken, in assessing the appropriate amount to be paid under an income payments order, of the needs of a spouse and children from whom the bankrupt is separated.

6.31 It is important to consider the timing of obtaining a maintenance order. Whilst, in theory, the maintenance order should not be taken into account by the trustee, in practice a maintenance order already made presents a 'fait accompli' to the bankruptcy court. It will be much more difficult for the spouse if the bankruptcy court has already made an income payments order. Note should be taken of *Re Rayatt*[19] where school fees were held to be a 'reasonable domestic need', although this case has very unusual facts. In most cases this will simply not be an issue as there will not be any surplus income for a maintenance order to be made. As was made clear in *Albert v Albert (A Bankrupt)*:[20] '*the size of the cake remaining is liable to be determined by any order made in the Insolvency Court*'. Care must also be taken that if an order is made, the balance of the claims under the MCA 1973 are left open post discharge if at all possible, to enable a subsequent variation application to take place.

6.32 The position in relation to a Child Support Act 1991 calculation differs. The existence of an income payments order will not prevent the making of a

[18]   [2008] 1 FLR 1192.
[19]   [1998] 2 FLR 264.
[20]   [1997] 2 FLR 791.

calculation under the Child Support Act 1991 (as now amended by the Child Support, Pensions and Social Security Act 2000 and the Child Maintenance and Other Payments Act 2008), nor will it affect the amount of the calculation, since there is no provision in the Child Support Act 1991 for an income payments order to be taken into account as a deduction in the calculation of child maintenance payable. A father faced with a maintenance calculation when he is already paying the sum due under an income payments order would have to apply to the bankruptcy court and try to persuade that court that the income payments order should be reduced.

6.33　At the end of the bankruptcy, the bankrupt can apply to the court for an order under IA 1986, s 281(5) releasing him from accrued arrears. It would appear unlikely that the bankruptcy court will wish to interfere in an order made by the family court. At the same time under s 32(1) of the MCA 1973, leave is required to enforce arrears of periodical payments more than one year old in family proceedings, so there is a reasonable chance that the wife will not recover her arrears, unless the bankrupt has improved his finances swiftly on discharge.

6.34　In *Re G*,[21] Singer J held that he would make an order because the mother should not be precluded from the possible remedy of future enforcement, so making a maintenance order to collect the arrears at a later date is in certain circumstances a very real possibility. Do not forget that arrears of maintenance or outstanding lump sums due under a separation agreement or deed are provable and can form part of the basis of a bankruptcy petition.[22] This is dealt with in more detail below but practitioners need to be aware that it is likely that any liability under a separation agreement will not survive the bankruptcy.

Property adjustment and lump sum orders

6.35　It might appear that the wife may proceed with such applications, since, under s 306(1) of the IA 1986, the bankrupt's estate does not vest in the trustee in bankruptcy until his appointment takes effect or, in the case of the Official Receiver, on his becoming trustee. In the usual case, the trustee in bankruptcy is appointed at the creditors' meeting and the Official Receiver has 12 weeks from the date of the bankruptcy order in which to decide whether or not to convene a meeting of creditors to appoint a trustee. The court may appoint a trustee on the making of the bankruptcy order, but this is rare.

6.36　Once the assets have vested in the trustee in bankruptcy then the bankrupt himself will no longer have assets against which a lump sum or property adjustment order in the divorce proceedings can be made. Between the presentation of the petition and the vesting of the bankrupt's assets in the

---

[21]　*Re G (Children Act 1989, Schedule 1)* [1996] 2 FLR 171; *sub nom Re X* [1996] BPIR 494.
[22]　*McQuiban v McQuiban* [1913] P 208.

trustee in bankruptcy, could it be argued that the assets are available to the bankrupt and that there is nothing to prevent the making of financial provision orders within the divorce?

6.37   If the bankrupt were free to deal with his assets simply because they had not vested in the trustee in bankruptcy under s 306, then a bankrupt might be tempted to dispose of his assets following the presentation of a bankruptcy petition, leaving little or nothing for the trustee to realise, and apply to the debts. To avoid this possibility, s 284(1) of the IA 1986 provides:

> 'Where a person is adjudged bankrupt, any disposition of property made by that person in the period to which this section applies is void except to the extent that it is or was made with the consent of the court, or is or was subsequently ratified by the court.'

6.38   By s 284(3), the period to which the section relates is the period between the day of the presentation of the petition for the bankruptcy order and the vesting of the bankrupt's estate in the trustee in bankruptcy, so that any disposition of property by the bankrupt between these dates would be void, unless made with the consent of the court, or subsequently ratified by it.

Property adjustment orders

6.39   Where the assets have vested in the trustee, no transfer will be effective without the trustee's consent and the bankrupt's interest in the property concerned remains with the trustee. Clearly this does not prevent a property adjustment order in circumstances say where the trustee does not consider there is any value in the property concerned for the creditors, provided his consent is obtained first. An approach to the trustee will need to be made to find out if this is an issue, if it is intended that a property is to be retained rather than sold.

Lump sum orders

6.40   No effective lump sum order can be made against the bankrupt's assets without the consent of the trustee. It is unlikely in most cases that there will be any benefit in making an order before the bankrupt is discharged. Care has to be taken if a lump sum order is made, as the lump sum is provable and becomes an unsecured debt automatically in any subsequent bankruptcy. For a full discussion of this, see **6.56** onwards below.

6.41   There may be assets in specific circumstances which are not caught by the bankruptcy, or which the trustee has waived any claim to, against which a lump sum order can be made. Reference is made to *Hellyer v Hellyer*[23] where this was the case. This is likely to be a rare occurrence.

---

[23]   [1996] 2 FLR 579.

6.42 It is likely therefore that the best solution will be either to wait to make the claim on discharge, or adjourn the claim if already made for a period of time. In the case of *Pearce v Pearce*[24] this was 9 years. In very rare family cases there may be a surplus due under a bankruptcy. That was the issue in *Re G*[25] and that was resolved in the wife's favour with a lump sum order against part of the surplus.

Pensions

6.43 The position on pensions on bankruptcy altered significantly post 29 May 2000. Since that point the position is that all HMRC approved personal pensions do not vest in the trustee provided they are not in payment. The position is more complicated for certain final salary schemes (see **3.11**). Specialist advice should always be taken in such cases from an actuary and it is worth checking the scheme rules carefully to see whether there are any specific references to bankruptcy.

6.44 In terms of the benefits payable under the pension then the position is slightly more complex. If the individual is declared bankrupt but has not exercised his right to take a lump sum during the period that he remains un-discharged from bankruptcy then there is no action that the trustee in bankruptcy can take to compel such benefits to be taken for the benefit of the bankrupt's creditors.

6.45 In the event that the bankrupt elected to exercise his entitlement to take a lump sum payment during his bankruptcy, then that lump sum would not automatically vest in his trustee in bankruptcy pursuant to s 306 of the Insolvency Act 1986. However, it would be income for the purposes of s 310 IA 1986, against which the court could make an income payments order.

6.46 Pension lump sums have been held to be income for the purposes of s 310(7) IA 1986 which provides that the definition of income includes:

> 'any payment in respect of the carrying on of any business in respect of any office or employment and (despite anything in section 11 or 12 of the 1999 Act) any payment under a pension scheme,'

but this appears to exclude any payments by way of guaranteed minimum pension or payments giving effect to the bankrupt's protected rights. In the case of *Kilvert v Flackett and another*[26] the court held that the entirety of an individual's lump sum would be caught by the terms of an income payments order in circumstances where the individual's income from other sources was sufficient to meet the reasonable domestic needs of the individual and his family.

---

[24] (1980) 1 FLR 261.
[25] [1996] 2 FLR 171.
[26] [1998] 2 FLR 806.

6.47   It is the case, however, that if the bankrupt has drawn his tax free lump sum prior to bankruptcy, that sum will vest with the trustee as part of the bankrupt's property and will not be treated as income.

Ratification

6.48   As is clear from the terms of s 284 of the IA 1986, any relevant disposition of property or payment is void unless it is made with the consent of the court or subsequently ratified by the court. A decision whether or not to ratify a disposition under s 284 of the IA 1986 is a matter of discretion. See *Treharne and Sands v Forrestor*[27] for some general principles, and see also *Rio Properties Inc v Al-Midani*.[28]

6.49   In *Re Flint (A Bankrupt)*,[29] the judge observed that s 284 was a new provision in personal insolvency with as yet no reported cases offering guidelines for the exercise of the discretionary jurisdiction. However, s 284 is closely modelled on what used to be s 227 of the Companies Act 1948 and is now s 127 of the IA 1986, and he therefore felt it would be legitimate to look for guidelines in cases concerning ss 227 and 127. What is clear from these cases is that the court should consider what is just and fair in all the circumstances, having particular regard to good faith and honest intention.[30]

(2)   Bankruptcy proceedings after ancillary relief order has been made

Maintenance

6.50   Where there is an existing order for maintenance or a Child Support Act 1991 assessment under which the bankrupt husband is ordered to pay maintenance for his former spouse or children, that order or assessment does not cease to have effect on the making of a bankruptcy order. The bankrupt will remain liable for payments due under the order, and arrears, throughout the duration of the bankruptcy order and after discharge from bankruptcy.

6.51   The bankruptcy may provide the bankrupt husband with the grounds to make an application to vary an existing maintenance order, or suspend it, if there has been a change in his financial circumstances resulting from his bankruptcy and particularly if an income payments order is made within the bankruptcy.[31] However, there is no provision to allow the variation of a Child Support Act 1991 assessment to take into account an income payments order.[32]

---

[27]   [2003] EWHC 2784 (Ch), [2004] 1 FLR 1173.
[28]   [2003] BPIR 128, [2002] All ER (D) 135 (Oct).
[29]   [1993] 1 FLR 763.
[30]   *Re Steane's (Bournemouth)* [1950] 1 All ER 21; *AI Levy Ltd* [1964] Ch 19; *Re Clifton Place Garage* [1970] Ch 477.
[31]   See **3.54**.
[32]   Ibid.

6.52 Neither maintenance nor maintenance arrears are provable within the bankruptcy.[33] The wife will have to wait until the bankruptcy is discharged. As noted already, she will need leave if the arrears are over 12 months old.

6.53 The wife must rely on the usual remedies to enforce payment. However, she may find herself in a better position in relation to continuing maintenance than say the wife seeking to enforce a lump sum order against capital because, unlike capital, income does not automatically vest in the trustee in bankruptcy, although the trustee may seek a share for the creditors under an income payments order which will inhibit the bankrupt's ability to meet his maintenance obligations.

6.54 In the case of a pre-existing secured periodical payments order, if the husband is made bankrupt, the bankrupt husband's liability to pay under the order continues and arrears will accrue in the event of non-payment. The advantage of such an order for the wife is that she will become a secured creditor (and as such her claims will prevail over those of unsecured creditors), provided the bankruptcy petition is issued after the secured periodical payments order is made. The transaction may, however, be vulnerable as a transaction at an undervalue,[34] or a preference[35] if made at a relevant time.[36] It is therefore important to consider with an insolvency specialist in a case where solvency may be an issue whether a secured maintenance order is worth making.

6.55 Although the maintenance debt is not provable in the bankruptcy, and although discharge does not automatically release the bankrupt from a bankruptcy debt which arises under any order made in family or domestic proceedings, the bankruptcy court has power to release the bankrupt from the debt.[37] It is, however, difficult to envisage circumstances in which a court would consider the bankrupt's release to be appropriate concerning unpaid maintenance but there are no decided cases which give guidance on this point.

Lump sum orders

6.56 Many court orders, made either by consent or following a contested final hearing, include provision for a lump sum to be paid to the wife. The most frequent problem facing the wife when her husband is made bankrupt following the making of such an order is whether, if the husband fails to pay, she can still enforce the lump sum payment.

6.57 The first relevant question is therefore whether the order for payment of a lump sum by the bankrupt husband is a provable debt within the bankruptcy proceedings. The position has been changed by amendments to r 12.3 of

---

[33] *James v James* [1963] 2 All ER 465.
[34] IA 1986, s 339.
[35] Ibid, s 340.
[36] See **3.52**.
[37] IA 1986, s 281(5).

Insolvency Rules 1986 which have been effective since 1 April 2005. This provides that lump sums and costs orders are provable debts in bankruptcy. Maintenance orders are not, however.

6.58   This has removed what was seen as a long standing unfairness, as before the implementation of the 1986 insolvency legislation, a lump sum order was provable in bankruptcy, and a wife seeking payment of a lump sum due under such an order would thus proceed to enforce payment in the bankruptcy proceedings.[38] Post 1986 although a lump sum order was a bankruptcy debt, it was not provable in the bankruptcy by virtue of r 12.3(2)(a) of the Insolvency Rules 1986.

6.59   Rule 12.3(2)(a) stated that any obligations arising under an order made in Family Proceedings (and also a maintenance order under the Child Support Act 1991) were not provable. This was reviewed in a short paper Debts arising in Family Proceedings in December 2004 which is on the Insolvency Services website at *www.insolvency.gov.uk*, and is well worth a read if you are dealing in detail with this issue. The current position is that a lump sum or costs order is automatically provable (the creditor wife has no choice in the matter) and she will be paid out as an unsecured creditor in any bankruptcy.

6.60   The key issue which follows on from that is will the balance of the unpaid debt survive the discharge? It is clear from the paper referred to above that it was intended that the balance of the debts would remain to be enforced by the wife at a later date if she was able to do so. That is not however clear from the rules which provide at s 281(5) that the bankruptcy court has the discretion as to whether the balance of the sum survives. If you are acting for the wife in that situation you need to consider applying to the court post discharge of the bankruptcy for a declaration that the balance of the lump sum survives the discharge. It might be sensible to write to the bankrupt asking for consent to this before making the application. As discussed at **6.150**, s 281(5) of the IA 1986 provides that:

> 'Discharge does not, except to such extent and on such conditions as the court may direct, release the bankrupt from any bankruptcy debt which ... (b) arises under any order made in family proceedings or under a maintenance calculation made under the Child Support Act 1991.'

6.61   The position on maintenance however is that it is not provable whether via the Child Maintenance and Enforcement Commission or for spousal maintenance. So if a wife wishes to bankrupt her husband for an unpaid lump sum she can do so. She still however needs to approach the matter with caution as this may not be the best way to recover the sum due to her, and to date the point is untested as to whether the balance of the lump sum should survive. It would be thought however that public policy considerations would make sure that a husband could not avoid his obligations to pay a costs order or lump sum to his wife by simply bankrupting himself.

---

[38]   *Curtis v Curtis* [1969] 1 WLR 422.

6.62 What if the lump sum has already been paid? Is the law the same for lump sums as for property adjustment orders? The answer is no, and is dealt with in *Burton v Burton and Another*, where Butler-Sloss J, when referring to orders made under s 23(1)(c) MCA 1973 providing for the payment of a lump sum or sums by one party to another, said:[39]

> 'It is an order to the party to pay, and that is a payment in the future. That cannot, in my judgment, transfer the beneficial interest at the moment of the order. It is an order for money, and the wife is entitled to enforcement of that order, but it does not vest in her at the moment of the order.'

6.63 If that is correct, then a lump sum order is not in itself a disposition, although the payment of monies under the terms of such an order would be a disposition. The position is therefore that if the payment has been paid it will not be recouped unless it falls foul of the undervalue provisions dealt with below.

6.64 The particular circumstances which arose in the case of *Re Mordant; Mordant v Halls*[40] resulted in a finding that allowed a lump sum order (made following the presentation of a bankruptcy petition but before the making of the bankruptcy order) to stand and the wife to receive payment even though the order was made during the period to which s 284 relates. The justification for this, however, was that on the occasion of the ancillary relief hearing, when the judge had reserved full judgment (which was then delivered after the presentation of the bankruptcy petition), the judge had ordered a sum of money standing to the credit of the husband's Dublin bank account with the Allied Irish Bank to be paid by the husband to his solicitors.

6.65 Sir Donald Nicholls, hearing the wife's application to review the district judge's dismissal of her s 284 application, took the view that the payment of monies by the husband to his solicitors in accordance with the order of the court was akin to a payment into court and that when the money reached the husband's solicitors it ceased to be part of the husband's estate. Since the money had been earmarked before the bankruptcy petition was issued as the source for any lump sum payment for the wife, and the purpose of ordering that it should be paid to the husband's solicitors was to protect it for this purpose, it was not the bankrupt's property by the time the bankruptcy petition was presented and it could not fall within s 284.

6.66 Perhaps surprisingly, the same 'earmarking' argument was applied by the court to a further sum also paid by the husband to his solicitors before the bankruptcy petition was presented. This money was not the subject of a court order or undertaking as was the money from the Allied Irish Bank, and hence the position was not so clear cut. However, since the intention of the husband was that this further sum also should be set aside by the solicitor, an officer of the court, and earmarked as available to meet the lump sum payment, the court

---

[39] Ibid at 425.
[40] [1996] 1 FLR 334.

took the view that this money was also no longer part of the bankrupt's estate by the time the bankruptcy petition was issued. Hence, the trustee was not entitled to take the money, and the lump sum to the wife could be paid.

6.67   Thus, whenever the opportunity arises for funds to be earmarked, the wife's interests clearly dictate that it should be taken.

6.68   In contrast to payments due under a court order, capital sums, or arrears of maintenance, etc, due under a deed of separation are provable.[41] Query whether the balance on discharge survives the bankrupt's discharge. It would appear that it does not but there is no case law on this point.

Property adjustment orders

6.69   For the purposes of this section, it is assumed that a property adjustment order involves a transfer of an interest in property by the husband to the wife.

Summary

6.70   The case of *Hill v Haines* now contains the clearest statement of how property adjustment orders work in bankruptcy. In summary it provides that where a property adjustment order has been made before the presentation of the bankruptcy petition, it will defeat any claim by the trustee in bankruptcy if:

(1)   A court order has been made containing the ancillary relief order (whether by consent or final hearing), and

(2)   The decree absolute in the proceedings has been pronounced, and

(3)   The order is not deemed to be collusive as described by Thorpe LJ in *Hill v Haines* in the Court of Appeal.

6.71   In most cases this will mean that the wife will be protected provided she is able to meet these 3 criteria. The law therefore at the moment is very much weighted in the wife's favour.

6.72   The two cases which need to be considered carefully below are *Hill v Haines* in the Court of Appeal and *Ball v Jones*[42], which deals with the issue of collusion. These have substantially simplified the previous case law. It is also worth considering *Burke v Chubb*[43] on the issue of solicitor negligence if the decree absolute has not been pronounced.

6.73   It should also be borne in mind that *Hill v Haines* is seen (as least by most insolvency practitioners) as perhaps too advantageous to the wife, and at

---

[41]   *McQuiban v McQuiban* [1913] P 208 and *Victor v Victor* [1912] 1 KB 247.
[42]   [2008] 2 FLR 1969.
[43]   [2008] 2 FLR 1207, QBD.

some stage in the future it may again be challenged, although many insolvency practitioners see the doors as closed. The grey area remains the issue of consideration, as the old case law and in particular the case of *Re Kumar* remains relevant, and needs to be considered.

When does the transfer take place?

6.74 Dealing with the points above, the first question is why the wife does not need to get the TR1 signed and executed once the order has been made. In addition what is the position if the order itself does not provide for the transfer to take place for a period of time?

6.75 The law that has lead to this position is interesting and is dealt with briefly below. In summary, the equitable principle is that if an order has been made then equity will ensure that it is effected, notwithstanding it is yet to be implemented. This is different from a lump sum order. The key case law is however complex and worth considering.

6.76 In *Re Flint (A Bankrupt)*,[44] the question raised was whether a transfer of property order made in favour of Mrs Flint under s 24 of the MCA 1973 was an order which was void under s 284 of the IA 1986 as a disposition of property made by the bankrupt, unless ratified by the court dealing with Mr Flint's bankruptcy.

6.77 A consent order which, inter alia, ordered Mr Flint within 28 days to transfer all his estate and interest in the former matrimonial home to Mrs Flint, was made in July 1990. A bankruptcy petition had been presented against Mr Flint in May 1990. Only 6 days after the property adjustment order was made, a bankruptcy order was made against Mr Flint before there had been any transfer or other document to implement the property adjustment order. The property adjustment order was thus made in the period covered by s 284.

6.78 The trustee in bankruptcy eventually sought to rely on s 284, arguing that the property adjustment order made in July 1990 was a disposition of property caught by s 284 and was hence void against the trustee in bankruptcy. The judge declared that the property adjustment order and the terms of it were void as against the trustee and that the house be held on trust for the trustee in bankruptcy and Mrs Flint in equal shares. Mrs Flint appealed, seeking an order that the property adjustment order of July 1990 was valid and effective on the basis that the judge had been wrong to hold that the order was a disposition by Mr Flint falling within s 284, that he ought to have held that it was a disposition by the court, or that alternatively, if s 284 was applicable, the judge had failed properly to exercise his discretion whether to ratify the transaction.

---

[44]   [1993] 1 FLR 763.

6.79   Mr Nicholas Stewart QC, sitting as a deputy judge of the High Court, took the view that the property adjustment order of July 1990 had the effect that Mr Flint's equitable interest passed immediately to the wife, equity treating as done that which ought to have been done. It was, hence, a disposition and the fact that the transfer of property was in accordance with a court order and thus had become compulsory, whether that court order had been made by consent or not, did not prevent it being a disposition by the bankrupt himself. Thus, once Mr Flint had been adjudged bankrupt, the disposition of his interest in the house by the property adjustment order became void under s 284 unless, of course, it was subsequently ratified by the court.

6.80   Central to the judge's conclusion was his view that the order had the effect that the husband's equitable interest in the house passed to the wife immediately upon the making of the order. That view was challenged by Sir Donald Nicholls in his judgment in the case of *Re Mordant; Mordant v Halls*,[45] to which further reference is made in relation to the question of lump sum orders below.

6.81   In challenging *Flint*, Sir Donald Nicholls referred to the case of *Burton v Burton and Another*,[46] a case to which no reference had been made during the course of *Flint*. In *Burton*, Butler-Sloss J was asked to consider, inter alia, whether the beneficial interest in the net proceeds of sale of a property vested in a party to the proceedings in whose favour the order had been made on the making of or the perfecting of the order, or only when the property was sold and the proceeds of sale handed over. Butler-Sloss J concluded:[47]

> 'In my judgment, again the beneficial interest in that transfer of property does not pass until the consequential document has taken effect, ... But it is the moment of transfer, in my judgment, pursuant to the comprehensive code of the Law of Property Act, and in accordance with the order properly made under s 24 of the Matrimonial Causes Act 1973 that the beneficial interest in that property or part of that property, whether it be in money or in land, will pass to the wife petitioner and not before.'

6.82   It was not necessary for Sir Donald Nicholls to state any conclusion on the divergence of views, since *Mordant v Halls* did not involve a transfer of property but the payment of a lump sum order.

6.83   If, however, Butler-Sloss J was correct in the view she formed in *Burton v Burton*, then the property adjustment order in *Flint* would not have been a disposition of property, and a disposition would only have occurred if the terms of the order had been implemented and the transfer documentation completed.

---

[45]   [1996] 1 FLR 334.
[46]   [1986] 2 FLR 419.
[47]   At 425.

6.84 As an aside, even if the court in *Flint* had been made aware of *Burton v Burton*, Mrs Flint would have fared no better than she actually did. If the order itself was not a disposition, a transfer of property to her by way of implementation would have been a disposition and hence void under s 284. In the absence of a valid transfer effected by the appropriate documentation, Mr Flint's interest in the property would have vested in the trustee in bankruptcy and, either way, the end result would have been that Mrs Flint retained only her one-half share of the property.

6.85 The decision of the Court of Appeal in *Mountney v Treharne*[48] is an important contribution to the understanding of the position albeit in a scenario where the order preceded the petition and so was not governed by s 284. In that case, the husband was ordered, further to s 24(1)(a) of the MCA 1973, to transfer a property vested in his sole name 'forthwith' to the wife. The decree absolute was pronounced on 13 July 2002 at which point, under s 24(5) of the MCA 1973, the order could take effect. On 14 July 2002 the husband was adjudicated bankrupt on his own petition.

6.86 The Court of Appeal considered three points:

(1) that it was not appropriate to argue that there was a constructive trust in favour of the wife – her right under s 283(5) of the IA 1986 did not require trust law;

(2) that authorities dating back to *Maclurcan v Maclurcan*[49] provided that the property adjustment order conferred an equitable interest to the wife in the property, conditional solely on the making of the decree absolute;

(3) that this equitable interest bound the trustee under s 283(5). On this basis it was held that *Beer v Higham*[50] was wrongly decided, and that the observations of Butler-Sloss J in *Burton v Burton*[51] concerning s 24(1)(a) were also incorrect.

6.87 In the light of the disapproval of *Burton v Burton*, the criticisms of *Re Flint* should be regarded as unfounded so that a property adjustment order made in the period governed by s 284 would be void unless validated under that section. It is vital to have regard to the date of the decree absolute as this implements the terms of the property adjustment order.

6.88 If the transfer has not been completed before the presentation of the bankruptcy petition, but is completed before the vesting of the assets in the trustee, the transfer may be caught by the provisions of s 284 of the IA 1986.[52]

---

[48] [2002] EWCA Civ 1174, [2002] 3 WLR 1760.
[49] 1897 77 LT 474.
[50] [1997] BPIR 349.
[51] [1986] 2 FLR 419.
[52] *Burton v Burton and Another* [1986] 2 FLR 419.

However, if the beneficial interest in the property has passed to the wife, it is the case that a transfer will be permitted.

6.89   In *Harper v O'Reilly and Harper*[53] the consent order provided for a deferred sale in respect of the jointly owned home from which the wife was entitled to the net sale proceeds. The consent order did not state under which section of the MCA 1973 the order for sale had been made. Before the property had been sold, or transferred to the wife, the husband was made bankrupt. The wife argued that the beneficial interest vested in her from the date of the order, and hence the husband's share did not form part of the bankrupt's estate. The trustee submitted that the husband's interest was not extinguished until sale, and hence formed part of the bankrupt's estate. The judge held the order on its true construction to have been made further to s 24(1)(c) or, possibly, (d) of the MCA 1973. On this basis, it was held that it was a variation of settlement and hence passed the beneficial interest on the order being made, not on the transfer being executed. On that basis, if an order is made under s 24(1)(c) or (d) of the MCA 1973 that constitutes a variation of a post-nuptial settlement for the benefit of one of the parties or an extinguishing of the interest of one party thereby benefiting the other, the beneficial interest vests or passes immediately upon the making of the order.

6.90   It will be appreciated from the above that, until the intervention of the Court of Appeal in *Mountney v Treharne*, there appeared to be a distinction drawn between orders made under s 24(1)(a) and (b) compared to orders made under s 24(1)(c) and (d). Such a distinction could be regarded as unfortunate when considering how s 24(1) was intended to operate in the context of a bankrupt's spouse. It is therefore fortunate that the Court of Appeal in *Mountney v Treharne* overturned *Beer v Higham* when allowing the appeal before them. The basis of the reasoning of the Court of Appeal was that a line of authority starting with *MacLurcan v MacLurcan*[54] indicated that an order made under s 24(1)(a) conferred on Mrs Mountney an equitable interest in the property at the moment when the order took effect, ie on the making of the decree absolute. The beneficial interest in the property had therefore passed to Mrs Mountney, and the trustee in bankruptcy took subject to the same. For the sake of completeness, it should be borne in mind that the decision in *MacLurcan* was made pursuant to the predecessor of s 23(1)(b) and would therefore govern an order made under the same. The distinctions envisaged above have therefore been eradicated by virtue of *Mountney v Treharne*. Whilst the result is obviously desirable, it should be mentioned that all is not completely clear given that Laws LJ considered that the *MacLurcan* line of authority was open to question as a matter of principle. Nevertheless, as the Court of Appeal was bound by the same, he also allowed the appeal. For the moment, however, the position is as described above.

---

[53]   [1997] 2 FLR 816.
[54]   1897 77 LT 474.

6.91 It is vital that there is a decree absolute as well as a court order. The case of *McMinn v McMinn*[55] makes it clear, as does *Hill v Haines* that the order has to be effective, as is made clear by s 23 of MCA 1973 where ancillary relief orders only can be enforced on decree absolute. The case of *Burke v Chubb* is a good warning of the problems if it is not applied for and the advising solicitor needs to be very clear and careful on this point. If a delay takes place in applying for the decree and there is an intervening bankruptcy, then the solicitor may have an action for negligence to deal with.

How does the trustee attack the order?

6.92 Where a property adjustment order provides for the transfer of property to a wife and the transfer has subsequently been completed, the wife, on learning that her former husband has been made bankrupt, will no doubt seek to be reassured that she will be able to keep the property.

6.93 Unfortunately, the property, or at least what would have been the husband's interest in it, will not necessarily be safe from attack by the trustee in bankruptcy even though the transfer into the wife's name has been completed. The trustee will wish to maximise the bankrupt's estate for the benefit of the creditors and has wide powers to take back into the bankrupt's estate assets which belonged to the bankrupt but which he has since disposed of in particular circumstances. Even if the husband has transferred assets because the court ordered him to do so, this will not prevent the transfer being open to attack by the trustee in bankruptcy as a transaction at an undervalue.[56]

The pre-1986 position

6.94 Before the implementation of the IA 1986, the trustee in bankruptcy's powers to attack a property adjustment order arose under s 42 of the Bankruptcy Act 1914. Section 42 of the 1914 Act rendered transfers of property which were not for valuable consideration to a purchaser in good faith void as against the trustee in bankruptcy if the transferor was made bankrupt within 2 years from the date of the transfer.

6.95 The leading pre-1986 case is *Re Abbott (A Bankrupt), ex parte Trustee of the Property of the Bankrupt v Abbott (PM)*.[57] In this case, an ancillary relief order was obtained by consent within divorce proceedings in December 1978. It provided that the former matrimonial home should be sold, the wife should receive £18,000 from the net proceeds of sale plus one-half of the balance remaining, as a result of which the wife gave up her right to pursue her claims under s 24 of the MCA 1973. The husband was adjudged bankrupt on his own petition in May 1980 and the trustee subsequently made an application to the bankruptcy court for a declaration that the ancillary relief order was void

---

[55] [2003] 2 FLR 839.
[56] MCA 1973, s 39.
[57] [1983] 1 Ch 45.

under s 42 of the Bankruptcy Act 1914. The court accepted that the wife had been unaware of the husband's insolvency and had acted in good faith, but had she given valuable consideration?

6.96   The court at first instance dismissed the trustee's application, holding that the wife was a purchaser for valuable consideration within s 42 of the Bankruptcy Act 1914 because she had given up a legal right to pursue her capital claims under s 24 of the MCA 1973. The court considered this to be valuable consideration.

6.97   The trustee appealed but the appeal was dismissed, the court holding that the words 'purchaser for valuable consideration' as used for the purpose of s 42(1) were wide enough to cover a spouse whose claim for a property adjustment order under s 24 of the MCA 1973 had been compromised.

Post 1986

6.98   Since the decision in *Re Abbott*, the IA 1986 has been enacted and transactions taking place after December 1986 will be governed by s 339 and 340 of this Act which are complex. Under these provisions, the trustee in bankruptcy can attack transactions effected at an undervalue or preferences given by the bankrupt if effected or given at a relevant time.

Section 339 – transactions at an undervalue

6.99   If a trustee wishes to attack a transfer of property made in pursuance of a court order, he can apply to the court under s 339 of the IA 1986 for an order that the transfer be set aside as a transaction at an undervalue. An individual enters into a transaction at an undervalue with a person if:

(1)   he makes a gift to that person or he otherwise enters into a transaction with that person on terms that provide for him to receive no consideration;

(2)   he enters into a transaction with that person in consideration of marriage; or

(3)   he enters into a transaction with that person for a consideration the value of which, in money or money's worth, is, significantly less than the value in money or money's worth, of the consideration provided by the individual.[58]

6.100   However, in order for the transaction at an undervalue to be open to attack, it must have been entered into at the relevant time. If this is the case, then the court can set aside the transfer and restore the position to what it would have been if the individual had not entered into the transaction.

---

[58]   Ibid, s 339.

'Relevant time' (s 339)

6.101   The relevant time in the case of a transaction at an undervalue is within the period of 5 years preceding the presentation of the bankruptcy petition on which the individual is adjudged bankrupt. However, if the transaction takes place within the 5-year period but more than 2 years before the date on which the petition is presented, then that will not be a relevant time unless the bankrupt was insolvent at the time or became insolvent as a result of the transaction.[59] It is assumed that the husband was insolvent or became insolvent as the result of the transaction, unless the contrary can be shown, where the transaction is with an associate.

6.102   A transaction entered into within a 2-year period ending with the day on which the petition is presented will always be at a relevant time and hence open to attack.

'Associate' (s 339)

6.103   An 'associate' is defined by s 435 of the IA 1986 as, inter alia, the husband or wife, former spouse of the bankrupt or reputed spouse. The Act does not define 'reputed'.

A comparison between s 42 and s 339

6.104   The *Abbott* case was decided under s 42 of the Bankruptcy Act 1914, under which the test, if the transaction was to be safe against the trustee, was whether the person to whom the property had been transferred was a purchaser in good faith for valuable consideration.

6.105   The test under s 339 of the IA 1986 differs in that the transaction will be vulnerable to attack by the trustee if it was a gift, if it was for no consideration, if it was in consideration of marriage, or if it was for a consideration the value of which, in money or money's worth, was significantly less than the value in money or money's worth of what was given in exchange.

6.106   Thus, s 339 (unlike s 42) involves placing a value on the consideration given so that it can be judged whether it is worth significantly less than what the wife receives in exchange. How, in reality, would this affect a wife who, as in *Abbott*, has given up financial claims against a husband in exchange for a transfer of the matrimonial home into her sole name?

The case-law

Re Kumar

6.107   Until 1993, there had been no reported cases on the application of s 339 of the IA 1986. Then, in 1993, the case of *Re Kumar (A Bankrupt), ex parte*

---

[59]   Ibid, s 341.

Lewis v Kumar[60] was decided. The wife petitioned for divorce in July 1990. The husband agreed to transfer all his interest in the matrimonial home to the wife subject to the existing mortgage. The transfer was executed in June 1990. It was not until 19 April 1991 that a consent order was obtained which provided, inter alia, that the wife's claims under ss 23 and 24 of the MCA 1973 and the Married Women's Property Act 1882 and any other relevant statutory provision be dismissed in consideration of the husband having transferred his interest in the jointly owned property to the wife with the wife assuming sole liability for the mortgage. There was also a provision for periodical payments for the wife.

6.108   In July 1991, a bankruptcy order was made against the husband and the trustee in bankruptcy sought to set aside the transfer of the matrimonial home under s 339 as being a transaction at an undervalue. The transfer had clearly taken place within the 'relevant time' but was it a transaction at an undervalue? The court approved *Abbott* to the extent that it accepted that a compromise of a claim to provision in matrimonial proceedings was capable of being consideration in money or money's worth, but under s 339 there would still then remain the question of the value of that consideration.

6.109   It was held that the transfer was at an undervalue for the purpose of s 339 of the IA 1986. The only consideration given by the wife for the transfer was the assumption of sole liability under the mortgage secured on a property with considerable equity and the value of that was significantly less than the value of consideration provided by the husband.

6.110   At the time of the transfer, the husband had sought nothing from the wife and in return had received nothing. Although an order dismissing her capital claims had later been made, she had in reality given up little of value since she could not have made further claims in any event, the matrimonial home being the husband's only remaining significant asset. The wife also had a superior earning capacity. Even if she had compromised her claims for financial relief at the time of the transfer (which she did not), the value of that consideration (ie the giving up of her claims), in the circumstances, would have been significantly less than the value of the husband's interest in the house which she received in exchange.

6.111   The *Kumar* case therefore provided that accepting the compromise of a claim for financial provision within matrimonial proceedings can be for consideration in money or money's worth but that the consideration must be given at the time of the transaction. Where it does not assist the family lawyer is in relation to the valuation of the consideration given, such as the wife giving up her claim for maintenance.

---

[60]   [1993] 2 FLR 382.

6.112 A further example of the problem is given in *Claughton v Charalamabous*,[61] where a gift by the husband to the wife 7 months before the bankruptcy was set aside.

6.113 The issue was to be considered by the Court of Appeal in *Jackson v Bell and Another*.[62] However, the case did not proceed, although the Court of Appeal gave leave for three issues to be considered:

(1) whether a property adjustment order could be a preference under s 340; or

(2) whether it could be a transaction at an undervalue under s 339; and

(3) whether s 335A of the IA 1986 is Human Rights Act 1998-compliant? This is dealt with in chapter 5.

Hill v Haines

6.114 The background of the case of *Hill v Haines* was that after a contested ancillary relief hearing the wife was ordered to have the former matrimonial home transferred to her from their joint names, and had her lump sum and maintenance claims adjourned on the basis that the husband was at the time of the order (possibly) insolvent, in a case where the disclosure and valuations of the assets was far from clear. The district judge at first instance commented that the case could well be looked at by a trustee if the husband subsequently bankrupted himself, which he duly did (but not before the decree absolute has been pronounced).

6.115 At first instance it was held that sufficient consideration had passed for the transfer not to be at undervalue under s 339 IA 1986. Before His Honour Judge Pelling QC in the Chancery Division this was overturned and the order set aside on the basis that no consideration passed in ancillary relief settlements.

6.116 This was overturned by the Court of Appeal who held that consideration did pass in ancillary relief settlements, and constituted consideration for the purpose for s 339 of IA 1986. The only exception would be where the case was exceptional and it could be demonstrated that the property transfer order was obtained by fraud, or some broadly similar exceptional circumstance. It did not matter whether the order was by compromise or contested hearing, only fraud, misrepresentation or mistake would get around this. The one uncertainty the case introduced was that if the case was the subject of collusion (which remains undefined) designed to affect the creditors adversely, or there was some other vitiating factor, then the transfer could be set aside. It was also made clear that *Kumar* remained good

---

[61] [1999] 1 FLR 740.
[62] [2001] EWCA Civ 387, [2001] Fam Law 879.

case law and that in certain circumstances there could be insufficient consideration in a matrimonial case involving a property adjustment order.

6.117   *Hill v Haines* did leave certain issues unresolved, the key two being what constituted collusion and whether s 340 was now the way to attack such orders.

Ball v Jones

6.118   These issues were however dealt with swiftly in the case of *Ball v Jones*. In that case the husband and wife had agreed after protracted negotiations that the husband would receive the vast majority of the assets to let him stay in the matrimonial home and look after the 3 children. The wife subsequently was bankrupted, and it became clear that she had entered into the deal against the advice of her lawyer, and had allegedly misstated her position to make it far better than it was on her statement of information. The trustee argued that this was collusion, and was preferring the husband and children to the other creditors.

6.119   It was held by Chief Registrar Baister that collusion did not mean an order that as a collateral effect of what was commonplace in matrimonial proceedings, put assets out of reach of a creditor. It is fair to say that if this is not collusion, then collusion has to be at the level of fraud, and it is hard to see many matrimonial orders, provided they are negotiated at arms length, that can be attacked.

6.120   The case also looked at preferences.

Section 340 – preferences

6.121   The trustee may, alternatively, seek to set aside a transfer of property as being a preference under s 340 of the IA 1986. A preference is given if the bankrupt did anything the effect of which was to put one creditor, surety or guarantor in a better position than he would have been in had he not been given the preference. If a bankrupt has given a preference to any person, the court may make such order as it thinks fit for restoring the position to what it would have been if the bankrupt had not given that preference. A trustee has to show that the bankrupt was influenced by a desire to place the creditor in a better position than the other creditors. Hence, a wife who is also a creditor and to whom property has been transferred in satisfaction of her debt, and in preference to other creditors, will be vulnerable under this section.

'Associate' (s 340)

6.122   Section 340(5) provides that where a preference is given to an associate, which would include a spouse or former spouse,[63] then the desire to prefer is presumed unless the contrary is shown.

---

[63]   IA 1986, s 435.

'Relevant time' (s 340)

6.123 The wife's status also affects the relevant time within which the trustee can attack a transaction. A trustee can attack a transaction as being a preference if the transaction is not a transaction at an undervalue and is given to an associate at a time in the period of 2 years ending with the day on which the bankruptcy petition was presented. In any case which does not involve a preference to an associate, merely to another creditor, the relevant time is the period of 6 months ending with the day on which the petition was presented. Again, if the wife can show that the husband was not insolvent at the time of the transaction and did not become insolvent as a result of the transaction then the preference will not have been given at a relevant time.

6.124 *Ball v Jones* found that the husband was not a creditor of the wife within the meaning of the 1986 Act and so there could not be a preference.

Section 423 – transactions to defraud creditors

6.125 The court may set aside a transaction, even if the husband was solvent at the time of transfer, as being a transaction at an undervalue beyond the 5-year limit, if it can be shown that the husband intended to put assets beyond the reach of creditors or potential creditors or otherwise prejudice the interests of potential claimants.[64] See *Trowbridge v Trowbridge and Trowbridge*,[65] where the provision was made available to the wife of a bankrupt, where she was seeking to enforce a lump sum order against him. He argued that his financial contribution to his second wife's property (in her sole name) did not give him a beneficial interest against which she could enforce. He failed, the court indicating that under s 423 his financial contributions could be set aside. A trustee can look back as far as he wishes under s 423 but any claim must be made within the limitation period; see *Hill (Trustee in Bankruptcy of Nurkowski) v Spread Trustee Co Ltd*[66] and *Giles v Rhind*.[67] The case of *Commissioners of Inland Revenue v Hashmi*[68] made it clear that it was not necessary for the 'dominant' purpose of any transference of property to be to put the asset beyond the creditors; it was purely based on the interpretation of the statute. The non-matrimonial case of *The Law Society v Southall*,[69] however, makes it clear that the courts are reluctant to reopen transactions going back many years.

6.126 It is hard to see, following the *Hill v Haines* and *Ball v Jones* decisions, that such an application can be made against a property adjustment order.

---

[64] Ibid, s 423.
[65] [2002] All ER (D) 207. See also *Kubiangha and Another v Ekpenyang and Another* [2002] EWHC 1567, (unreported) 10 July 2002, ChD.
[66] [2006] EWCA Civ 542, [2007] 1 All ER 1106.
[67] [2008] EWCA Civ 118, [2009] Ch 191, [2008] BPIR 342.
[68] [2002] BPIR 271.
[69] [2001] EWCA Civ 2001, [2001] BPIR 303.

6.127 Section 342 of the IA 1986 provides that a third party will be vulnerable only if he can be shown to have had knowledge of the bankruptcy or pending bankruptcy, or if he was either an associate of the bankrupt or an associate of the person benefiting by the preference or transaction at an undervalue. A wife is unlikely to be affected by the provisions of s 342 in any event since she is unlikely to be on the receiving end of a transfer of property from someone who has received property from the bankrupt. However, if she is, this Act will not assist her since it does not offer protection to associates.

6.128 Do not forget that arrears of maintenance or outstanding lump sums due under a separation agreement or deed are provable and can form part of the basis of a bankruptcy petition.[70]

Financial undertakings

6.129 Financial undertakings are required to deal with aspects of an agreement which cannot be incorporated into the main terms of a court order because there is no power under the MCA 1973 to make an order in such terms. Such an undertaking might be by the husband to pay the mortgage instalments due on the former matrimonial home.

6.130 Subject to the ongoing issue as to whether undertakings are enforceable as orders, an undertaking is not rendered unenforceable by a bankruptcy order, and, despite the bankruptcy, there is nothing to prevent the wife from using whatever remedies would have been available to her had the husband not been made bankrupt, in an attempt to secure the promised payment. *Mubarak v Mubarak*[71] has made it extremely hard to use committal proceedings to enforce such an undertaking; see also *L v L*[72] where Munby J stated that such undertakings are just as enforceable as court orders.

6.131 The bankrupt husband may apply for a stay of any committal proceedings, based upon *In re Smith*,[73] although that case is distinguishable as the House of Lords considered that s 285 was concerned with a situation where an unsecured creditor was seeking to obtain an advantage. It can be argued in the case of the undertaking here that the debt is not provable and the wife is not in that sense seeking to obtain an advantage.

6.132 Whether, however, the husband will have the means to pay will depend on whether the undertaking is to make payment or payments that would usually be made from: (1) income; or (2) capital.

---

[70] *McQuiban v McQuiban* [1913] P 208.
[71] [2002] EWHC 2171 (Fam), [2003] 2 FLR 553.
[72] [2006] EWHC 956 (Fam), [2008] 1 FLR 26.
[73] [1990] 2 AC 215.

(1) Income

6.133 If the undertaking is one to pay sums which would usually be paid out of income, such as to pay the mortgage instalments, assuming the bankrupt continues in remunerative employment, whether or not he has the means to pay will depend on whether an income payments order has been made under which a part of his income has been taken by the trustee in bankruptcy for the benefit of creditors. When making the income payments order, the court must leave the bankrupt sufficient income to meet the reasonable domestic needs of himself and his family,[74] but since 'family' is defined by s 385(1) of the IA 1986 as those living with and dependent upon the bankrupt, the wife and family from whom the bankrupt is separated may not have been taken into account. Reference should be made to **6.25** et seq.

(2) Capital

6.134 If the undertaking is to pay a sum that would usually be paid out of capital (for example to meet a capital gains tax liability as in *M v M*[75]), then, if the undertaking has not been complied with by the time the bankrupt's assets vest in the trustee in bankruptcy, he will not be able to pay the sum due (unless the *Mordant v Halls*[76] earmarking argument applies), although he could still in appropriate circumstances (now hard to envisage) be punished for failing to pay, by committal to prison.[77]

6.135 If, prior to vesting, but after issue of the bankruptcy petition, the husband pays the sum due, this is likely to be caught by s 284 of the IA 1986, and hence be void, unless validated by the bankruptcy court.

6.136 In either case, the undertaking, if in any event enforceable, would remain enforceable. It would be open to the wife, if payment had not been made, to enforce the undertaking if the bankrupt's position improved either during the bankruptcy or, more likely, upon discharge.

Non-financial undertakings

6.137 The issue of bankruptcy proceedings will not affect undertakings which are not financial undertakings unless the end result of compliance with such an undertaking has financial repercussions (for example, an undertaking to execute all documents necessary to assign an interest in a joint insurance policy to a wife). If an order contains such an undertaking, then, if the bankrupt husband complied with the undertaking before the vesting of his assets in the trustee in bankruptcy but after presentation of the petition, he would be caught by s 284 of the IA 1986.[78]

---

[74]   IA 1986, s 310(2).
[75]   [1993] Fam Law 469.
[76]   [1996] 1 FLR 334.
[77]   See *Woodley v Woodley* [1992] 2 FLR 417 and *Woodley v Woodley (No 2)* [1993] 2 FLR 477.
[78]   See **6.36** et seq and **6.61** et seq.

6.138 Unless the 'earmarking' argument used in *Mordant v Halls*[79] applies, the assets of the bankrupt will in due course vest in the trustee, thus the husband's interest in the policy will have vested in the trustee and the husband cannot, therefore, comply with the undertaking and assign his interest to the wife.

Possible steps which the family practitioner needs to consider to reduce the effects of s 339 and 340

6.139 It is fair to say that the case law has made it much harder for the trustee to set orders aside. However, what is set out below gives some pointers that may assist to ensure that there is not an unhappy outcome.

(1)   Full disclosure of the husband's position

6.140 The client wife must be warned, if her husband's financial position appears to be precarious, that if a bankruptcy petition is presented and a bankruptcy order is made within the relevant time, the trustee can seek to attack a property adjustment order. Great care must be taken at the time the ancillary relief settlement is reached to preserve all financial information obtained by disclosure, to enable the wife to try to establish the husband's solvency at the relevant time if the trustee later makes an application under s 339 or s 340.

(2)   Documentary evidence of wife's consideration

6.141 The cases of *Re Abbott*[80] and *Re Kumar (A Bankrupt)*[81] confirm the importance of establishing that full consideration had been given by the wife at the time of the transaction or the transfer. That said, *Hill v Haines* and *Ball v Jones* have probably reduced the need to document consideration at the time of the transaction.

(3)   Declaration of solvency

6.142 Under IA 1986, s 341(3), an individual is insolvent if he is unable to pay his debts when they fall due, or if his liabilities, taking into account both his contingent and prospective liabilities, exceed the value of his assets.

6.143 A declaration of solvency includes a statement that the husband is solvent and able to pay his debts and that his assets exceed his liabilities, both contingent and prospective. It is useful to a wife to be able to show that her husband was (or at least considered he was) solvent at the time he entered into a transaction with her. It may assist the wife in a subsequent contest over a property with the trustee if the husband has signed a declaration of solvency,

[79]   [1996] 1 FLR 334.
[80]   [1983] 1 Ch 45.
[81]   [1993] 2 FLR 382.

although different practitioners have different views on this, and because many practitioners do not include them as of right in all orders they could be seen as indicating that there is a concern.

6.144 The contents of the declaration are important and, ideally, the declaration should be separate from the main body of the order (although referred to in it) and with a schedule annexed setting out the husband's assets and liabilities so that his financial position can be seen to support his declaration. A precedent can be found in Appendix 2.

6.145 Some mortgagees insist that where a property is transferred into the wife's sole name the husband provides a declaration of solvency. They may also require indemnity assurance of an amount equal to the mortgage advance, where the transfer is open to attack by a trustee under ss 339 and 340.

(4)   Apply for the decree absolute and get a move on with clear advice

6.146 The need to have applied for decree absolute to make the order enforceable must be considered, further to the remarks in *Mountney v Treharne*, and *Hill v Haines*. The possibility of getting an order by consent and decree absolute to defeat the trustee's possible future claims must always be considered and acted upon quickly. It may not be possible to do but clear advice needs to be given to the client to clarify the options available and the likely timescales.

(3)   Discharge from bankruptcy order

Effect of discharge upon existing orders for ancillary relief

6.147   If a wife has the benefit of an ancillary relief order (the terms of which have not been implemented effectively, as a result of the issue of a bankruptcy petition or the making of a bankruptcy order), she will wish to consider whether the bankrupt husband's discharge from bankruptcy will enable her to pursue the implementation of the ancillary relief order.

6.148   Unfortunately for her, discharge does not have the effect of revesting the bankrupt's property in the bankrupt. There will, hence, be no immediate improvement in the bankrupt's position resulting from the discharge, although assets acquired after discharge will remain the bankrupt's property and it is against such assets that the wife must seek to enforce the terms of the order that she holds.

6.149   The effect of discharge is, inter alia, to release the bankrupt from bankruptcy debts, which are widely defined by s 382(1) of the IA 1986 and include any debts or liability to which the bankrupt is subject at the commencement of his bankruptcy. The unpaid extent of lump sum and costs orders has been dealt with above.

6.150   IA 1986, s 281(5) specifically provides that discharge does not, except to such extent and on such conditions as the court may direct, release the bankrupt from any bankruptcy debt which arises under any order made in family proceedings as defined in s 281(8) or under a maintenance calculation made under the Child Support Act 1991. Whilst, therefore, a bankrupt would not automatically be released from an order for ancillary relief made within divorce proceedings, it would be open to him to apply to the bankruptcy court to obtain a release from orders made in those proceedings.

6.151   It would, however, seem manifestly unjust if the wife, prevented from proving in the bankruptcy her debt as a result of r 12.3(2) of the Insolvency Rules 1986, then found herself unable to enforce the order against her husband because he had applied for and successfully obtained release from the debt from the bankruptcy court.

The commencement of proceedings following discharge

6.152   A wife who has refrained from the issue of ancillary relief proceedings during her husband's bankruptcy will wish to consider the timing of such an application following his discharge. Since the discharge from bankruptcy does not re-vest assets in the bankrupt, she will have to bide her time until his situation improves as a result of his post-bankruptcy efforts. She may then, of course, find herself faced with the argument that, after a lapse of time, it would be unjust to award a lump sum out of assets in the accrual or acquisition of which she has played no part; whether or not this argument will be successful will depend on the particular circumstances of the case.[82]

---

[82]   *Pearce v Pearce* (1980) 1 FLR 261; *Hardy v Hardy* (1981) 2 FLR 321.

Chapter 7

DEBTS

THE NATURE OF DEBTS

7.1   This chapter analyses the relationship between the creditor and debtor prior to bankruptcy.

7.2   Debts are contractual, essentially the creditor provides a sum of money on terms and a contract to that effect is entered into. The creditor is therefore a party to the credit contract rather than the actual recipient of the funds.

7.3   The Matrimonial Causes Act 1973 does not confer power on the court to re-order debts. To do so would be to ride roughshod over the contractual arrangements which exist between the creditor and debtor. However, certain practices have become common to make arrangements in respect of debts by way of undertakings and indemnities and these will be discussed below.

7.4   It is essential that the financial position of the family upon breakdown of the marriage is confronted at a very early stage. It is vital for the wife to ascertain the extent of the family's liabilities as soon as possible. She needs to identify the nature of each unsecured debt, liability for the debt, whether the debt is in joint names or in one party's sole name, and if the latter, whether she is responsible to repay the debt.

Who is liable to pay the debt?

7.5   The wife or the husband or both may be liable to repay debt(s) owed to one or more creditors. The basic rule is that if documentation appears in your name you are liable to pay the debt.[1]

Joint and several liability: bank accounts, credit cards and other credit agreements.

7.6   The wife may believe that she is jointly liable with the husband for a debt because she holds and can use a card in her name, for example, a credit card account. It is worth checking at the outset in whose name the actual account is held: if it is in the husband's name, he is solely liable for the debt, whether or not the wife is a cardholder. She does not assume his liability. It is likely, however, that the husband will ask for an immediate return of the card.

---

[1]   Due to the likelihood that the credit contract was taken out in your name.

7.7   There may be credit cards, store cards or loan accounts in the husband's and wife's joint names, although this is becoming less common. The wife may have had little to do with these accounts and may even have no recollection of having opened these accounts. However, if the wife is named as a joint account holder with the husband, she is jointly and severally liable with him for the whole of the debt owed. The terms and conditions of the credit will have been made clear when the credit was obtained, and the wife will have had to consent to these terms.

7.8   Joint and several liability arises where one debtor is collectively liable with another debtor or other debtors for the whole of a debt. It is governed by the common law on contract. Joint and several liability must be express and is not easily implied, although the contract does not need to include the exact words, provided they can be interpreted as imparting severality to the obligation. In such a case, the creditor may sue either or both of the account holders to the extent of the whole of the debt. It must be distinguished from joint liability where the chasing creditor must pursue all debtor parties, rather than simply the most obvious debtor.

7.9   If the creditor elects to sue both the husband and the wife, a right of contribution *usually* exists between them. The same will apply if the creditor sues only one spouse; he or she will have a right to a contribution from the other.[2]

7.10   If the husband fails to acknowledge service of the creditor's claim or to enter a defence to the claim, judgment in default may be entered against him without prejudicing the creditor's claim against the wife.

7.11   Upon the death of one of the joint debtors, liability for payment of the debt does not pass to his/her personal representatives, provided that at least one of the other joint debtors survives. If jointly and severally liable, however, the death of one party does not release that party's estate from that liability.

TREATMENT OF DEBTS UNDER THE MATRIMONIAL CAUSES ACT 1973

7.12   The court's powers under the Matrimonial Causes Act 1973 do not extend to the ability to re-order debts. Often the assets are adjusted in a manner which allows one party or the other to pay their debts, either by way of lump sum or property adjustment order.

7.13   Another common practice is the 'Undertaking and Indemnity', the usual form of which is as follows:

---

[2]   The right of contribution is dealt with in *Deering v Earl of Winchelsea* (1787) and s 48 of the County Courts Act 1984.

'And upon the Petitioner undertaking to use her best endeavours to procure the Respondent's release from his covenants under the mortgage in favour of [company] [roll number] and to indemnify him in any event against any payments due under the said mortgage.'

7.14 This is essentially an agreement between the parties as to who will be responsible for the mortgage – the wife (typically) agrees, and undertakes that she will attempt to have the mortgage transferred into her sole name (or that she will obtain a fresh mortgage in her sole name to redeem the original) and that even if she is unable so to do she will be responsible for any of the payments due.

7.15 This does not, of course, have the effect of re-writing the contractual obligations between the husband and the mortgage company who are just as likely to enforce the covenants under the mortgage against him as they are against the wife, but it does mean that in the event the mortgage company were to pursue the husband he could rely on the indemnity to counterclaim against the wife for 100% of these payments.

7.16 The approach of mortgage companies to this arrangement has been mixed, some are happy to ignore the husband's liability under the original mortgage on the basis that he is not responsible for the payments, others are more cautious.

METHODS OF ENFORCEMENT

7.17 Assuming that the debt remains unpaid, the creditor's recourse to seek recovery of the monies owed will be to issue court proceedings, obtain judgment and, if the judgment debt is still unpaid, issue proceedings for enforcement of the judgment debt.

7.18 There are available to a judgment creditor three main methods of enforcement of a judgment debt. They are:

(1) seizure of goods;

(2) charging order;

(3) appointment of an equitable receiver.

7.19 Civil Procedure Rules 1998 (CPR) Parts 70–73 contains general rules about enforcement to which this section in the chapter relates.

Seizure of goods

7.20 The principle of this type of enforcement is that the judgment debtor's goods are seized and sold to repay the judgment debt. A county court bailiff or a High Court sheriff's officer is empowered to seize and take possession of the judgment debtor's goods, which are sold at public auction and the proceeds utilised to pay off the judgment debt in full as well as meeting the expenses of obtaining the order. Any surplus is repayable to the debtor.

7.21 A creditor may obtain an order if the judgment debt has not been repaid or repayment instalments are in arrears. Execution is the responsibility of the sheriff in the High Court, and the bailiff in the county court, in whose area the debtor's goods are to be found. The county court will usually send the judgment debtor a notice stating that the warrant has been issued and that payment in respect of the judgment debt must be made within 7 days. If payment is not received within the required time, the sheriff's or bailiff's officers will call at the judgment debtor's address within 15 working days of the warrant being issued. The first contact from the sheriff's officer will be a visit. The sheriff/bailiff is not entitled to enter the premises unless the owner consents. The sheriff/bailiff will try to collect payment there and then to satisfy the judgment debt or take sufficient goods to be sold at auction to repay the debt. It is possible to have a 'walking possession agreement' by which the debtor agrees not to part with identified goods for a short period; if the debtor does not raise the cash to pay the debt and the cost of execution, then the goods will be seized and sold at public auction.

7.22 Certain goods are protected from seizure. Essentially the sheriff/bailiff cannot take items which the judgment debtor may need for his or her job or business, such as tools, books, vehicles and other items of equipment needed for work, or basic items which are needed for the family such as clothes, furniture and bedding. The fact that goods are owned jointly by the judgment debtor and another (for example, his wife) does not take them outside the scope of the enforcement provisions. Such goods may be seized and sold as goods of the judgment debtor but the proceeds must be divided between the co-owners according to their shares. Execution against the goods of a private person is not always an effective remedy. No items that are leased, rented or on hire-purchase agreement can be taken as they belong to third parties.

7.23 A wife confronted by a warrant of execution issued against her husband, herself or both of them should be aware that she can take steps to stop the execution order and apply to court for the warrant to be 'suspended' on terms that the debt is paid in instalments. Further, at any time up to the sale of the goods seized, a wife may apply for a stay of execution if there are special circumstances that render it inexpedient to enforce the judgment or order or she is simply unable to pay.[3]

---

[3]   County Courts Act 1984, s 88.

Charging orders

(1)   The nature of a charging order

7.24 The Charging Orders Act 1979 (COA 1979) empowers the court to impose a charge on a beneficial interest in certain types of asset as security for payment of any money due or to become due under the terms of the judgment or order. The property which may be made subject to a charging order is set out in s 2 of the COA 1979 and is defined as:

> 'any interest held by the debtor beneficially ... in any asset of a kind mentioned in sub-section (2) [which includes land] or ... under any trust.'

7.25 The obvious disadvantage of a charging order is that it does not facilitate immediate repayment of the debt. In order to achieve that, the judgment creditor must apply for an order that the property be sold and the proceeds of sale be applied in settlement of the debt. The obvious advantage is that the creditor obtains security quickly and is protected in the event of the debtor's ultimate bankruptcy.

7.26 The remedy is discretionary, but the burden is very much on the debtor to show why a charging order should not be made. Special considerations will apply where the property in question is the former matrimonial home and divorce proceedings are already under way. This is discussed in more detail below. In practice the circumstances where a charging order are not made are virtually non-existent and it is extremely rare for a court not to order the Final Charging Order.

7.27 Where, however a charging order is made in respect of land a debtor owns jointly, the order ranks as a charge on the debtor's beneficial interest rather than upon the land itself (see *National Westminster Bank Ltd v Stockman*).[4]

(2)   Procedure (CPR Pt 73)

7.28 An application for a charging order is made in the county court save in rare circumstances where the property to be charged is a fund lodged in the High Court. The jurisdiction of the county court is unlimited (r 73.3(2)).

7.29 Charging order applications are a two stage process[5], interim order and final order.

7.30 No rule specifically requires the service of the charging order application on a spouse. It is highly likely, however, that the spouse will be served as a result of:

---

[4]   [1981] 1 WLR 67.
[5]   Formerly known as *order nisi* and *order absolute*.

(a)   being a 'creditor' under r 73.5(1)(b) if there are pending proceedings under the Matrimonial Causes Act;

(b)   as a trustee (r 73.5(1)(c));

(c)   as a person 'in possession' (para 4.3(6) of Practice Direction to Part 72);

(d)   as a person who has registered a Class F land charge or notice under s 31(10) of the Family Law Act 1996;

(e)   as a person directed to be served by the court.

7.31   The creditor will initiate proceedings for an interim charging order over land by filing Form N379 (for land) setting out all the details required by the form verified by a Statement of Truth. The application may be made without notice. The application is initially considered without a hearing, usually by a district judge or master. If the judge is satisfied and there is sufficient evidence, he will make an interim charging order in Form N86 and will fix a hearing to consider the application for the final charging order. The interim charging order must be served on the debtor, together with a copy of the application and documents filed in support, at least 21 days before the hearing. The court may direct that other creditors must also be served. The judgment creditor must file a certificate of service not less than 2 days before the hearing.

7.32   The court may direct that any other 'interested persons' are joined as respondents to the application. This is discussed in more detail below. Even though the wife may not be named as an owner of the property in the title deeds, she may have a beneficial interest in the former matrimonial home; if she is living there she should always be served. Where the wife is a joint owner, she should be named in the application, and the court will order that copies of the interim order be served on her (CPR, r 73.5). Where the former matrimonial home is the property to be charged, the spouse should be identified if possible.

7.33   At the final hearing, the court may make the final order or discharge the interim order and dismiss the application.

7.34   The effect of the final charging order is to confirm the continuance of the charge imposed by the interim order.

7.35   Once an interim order has been granted, the judgment creditor should register a restriction against the relevant title at the Land Registry or a land charge upon the property at the Land Charges Department (if unregistered).

7.36   If the judgment debtor or any other person wishes to oppose the application for the final charging order, he must serve on the applicant at least 7 days before the hearing written evidence of his grounds and must file the same at the court.

7.37 If the application for the final charging order is opposed by the judgment debtor or any other person (for example, his wife), the judge may give directions as to the issues and adjourn the hearing. Usually the interim order will continue in force until a final order is made.

7.38 In the event of the debtor's bankruptcy, the charging order claimant will be protected in the event that the order was made final before the presentation of the bankruptcy petition. If the order was only interim at that stage, the question of whether the creditor will obtain a final charging order remains at the discretion of the court.

(3) Who is an 'interested person'?

7.39 It is now established that, regardless of whether the wife is a co-owner of the property, she is an 'interested person' by virtue of her right of occupancy.[6] Competing claims between the judgment creditor and the wife who is occupying the former matrimonial home will usually be resolved in favour of the creditor, in that a final charging order will usually be granted but may not necessarily be enforced by sale.[7]

7.40 Where the wife has not yet applied for ancillary relief, her right of occupation in the home is taken into account by the court hearing the application for a charging order only as 'one of the circumstances of the case' under s 1(5) of the COA 1979. The wife would therefore be well advised to issue divorce and ancillary relief proceedings without delay if it seems likely that the husband's creditors might seek a charging order against the home. However, in cases where the enforcement of the charging order would produce hardship, the court might be persuaded to attach conditions as to the enforceability of the order under s 3(1) of the COA 1979.

(4) The court's duty

7.41 Whether a final order is made is a matter for the court's discretion. Section 1(5) of the COA 1979 states:

> 'In deciding whether to make a charging order, the court shall consider all the circumstances of the case and, in particular, any evidence before it as to –
>
> (a) the personal circumstances of the debtor, and
> (b) whether any other creditor of the debtor would be likely to be unduly prejudiced by the making of the order.'

7.42 Therefore, the court is under a duty to consider 'all the circumstances', but has discretion as to what weight to give to each. The position of the judgment debtor's spouse requires special consideration. If divorce proceedings have been commenced, her interest must be balanced against the creditor's and

---

[6] See *Harman v Glencross* [1986] Fam 81, [1986] 1 All ER 545, CA, [1986] 2 FLR 241.
[7] See **7.45** et seq below.

it may be appropriate to consolidate the application for a final charging order with the wife's application for ancillary relief.[8]

7.43 The charging order may be conditional. In deciding whether or not to make a charging order absolute, the court also has wide discretion under s 3(1) of the COA 1979 to impose certain conditions and terms on the order. For example, the court can attach '*Mesher*'-type terms on any charging order which would have the effect of preventing the judgment creditor from enforcing the charging order by applying for an order for sale of the property until, for example, the youngest child attains the age of 17 or ceases full-time education.

7.44 The exercise of judicial discretion, in determining the competing claims between the judgment creditor seeking a charging order and the wife, has achieved rather disparate results. A basic presumption has emerged in case-law that the judgment creditor is justified in expecting that a charging order will be made in his favour except in exceptional circumstances. The fact that the debtor's wife and children may be rendered homeless as a result of the enforcement of the charging order has been held not to constitute an 'exceptional circumstance'.

(5) Enforcing the charging order

7.45 A charge imposed by a charging order is equivalent to an equitable charge and is enforceable as such.[9] The judgment creditor may be content simply to register the charging order and retain it as security. It is not therefore a foregone conclusion, once the charging order has been obtained, that the property in question will have to be sold.

7.46 If the judgment creditor wishes to enforce his security, a separate set of proceedings must be commenced for an order for sale under CPR, r 73.10. The county court has jurisdiction to deal with an application under Part 73 to enforce the charging order by sale if the amount owed under the charge does not exceed the capital limit (£30,000, pursuant to s 23 of the County Courts Act 1984 and the High Court and County Courts Jurisdiction Order 1991). The court may order the sale of property to enforce a charging order to which it is subject. Before the application is made under CPR, r 73.10, the judgment creditor must consider whether there is sufficient equity in the property to realise the debt if the sale is ordered.

7.47 The application to enforce a charging order by sale should be made in the court that made the original order, provided that court has jurisdiction. If the application has to be made in the High Court, it must be made in the Chancery Division. The application is made using Form N208 under the CPR Part 8 Procedure, and a copy of the charging order must be filed with the claim form. The creditor must file written evidence with the claim identifying:

---

8   *Harman v Glencross* [1986] 2 FLR 241.
9   COA 1979, s 3(4).

- the charging order and the property to be sold;

- the amount in respect of which the charge was imposed;

- the amount due at the date of the issue of the claim, verifying, so far as is known, the debtor's title to the property charged;

- so far as is known, the names and addresses of any other creditors who have a prior charge or other security of the property and the amount owed to each such creditor;

- an estimate of the price which would be obtained on the sale of the property.

7.48 Proceedings to enforce a charging order by sale of property can be taken only where the judgment debtor alone owns the beneficial interest in the property charged. If a charging order has been obtained over the beneficial interest of one or more but not all of the beneficial owners of land, the judgment creditor must apply to the court for an order for sale under s 14 of the Trusts of Land and Appointment of Trustees Act 1996 (TLATA 1996) for sale of the land.

7.49 Section 14 of the TLATA 1996 states:

'(1) Any person who is a trustee of land or has an interest in property subject to a trust of land may make an application to the court for an order under this section.

(2) On an application for an order under this section the court may make any such order –

(a) relating to the exercise by the trustees of any of their functions ...
(b) declaring the nature or extent of a person's interest in property subject to the trust,

as the court thinks fit.'

7.50 Section 15 states that the matters to which the court is to have regard in determining an application for an order under s 14 include:

- the intentions of the person or persons (if any) who created the trust,

- the purposes for which the property subject to the trust is held,

- the welfare of any minor who occupies or might reasonably be expected to occupy any land subject to the trust as his home, and

- the interests of any secured creditor of any beneficiary.

7.51 The case-law noted below gives a flavour of recent decisions in this matter. The earlier case-law, however, is still relevant; for instance, *First*

National Securities Limited v Hegarty and Another,[10] *Harman v Glencross and Another,*[11] *Austin-Fell v Austin-Fell and Midland Bank,*[12] *F v F (S Intervening),*[13] *Barclays Bank v Hendricks,*[14] *Mortgage Corporation v Shaire,*[15] *Bank of Ireland Home Mortgages Limited v Bell.*[16]

Close Invoice Finance Ltd v Pile[17]

7.52 It was held that the creditor was entitled to apply under CPR, r 73.10, irrespective of TLATA 1996. The court held that on considering the application under r 73.10, the court had to take into account the provisions of the European Convention for the Protection of Human Rights and Fundamental Freedoms 1950, namely the rights to respect for private and family life and home and the enjoyment of possessions, in respect of all occupants. As a result, the same considerations as under TLATA 1996, s 15 were likely to apply. Accordingly, possession was postponed for over a year.

7.52 It was held that the creditor was entitled to apply under CPR, r 73.10 irrespective of TLATA 1996. The court held that on considering the application under r 73.10, the court had to take into account the provisions of the European Convention for the Protection of Human Rights and Fundamental Freedoms 1950, and the European Convention rights to respect for private and family life and home and the enjoyment of possessions in respect of all occupants, as a result the same considerations as under TLATA 1996, s 15 were likely to apply. Possession postponed for over a year.

Bank of Baroda v Patel[18]

7.54 This case is a stark warning to those who engage in negotiations with the creditors for removal of their security. In this case the wife had done just that and had written to the bank seeking 'to redeem the bank's charge' (relating to an outstanding balance of £180,000) over the husband's interest in the matrimonial home and informing them that in her view his interest was limited to 10% in any event. Eventually it was agreed with the creditors that they would remove their charging order in exchange for the sum of £22,000. This was paid and the charging order duly removed.

7.55 The bank then approached the husband's trustee in bankruptcy requesting proof of the husband's debt minus the £22,000 paid by the wife. The trustee agreed and brought proceedings for an order for sale of the property within the bankruptcy. The wife applied under s 303 IA 86 (Trustee acting in

---

[10]   [1984] 1 All ER 139, QBD, [1985] 1 QB 850, CA.
[11]   [1986] 2 FLR 241.
[12]   [1989] 2 FLR 497.
[13]   [2002] EWHC 2814 (Fam), [2003] 1 FLR 911.
[14]   [1996] 1 FLR 258.
[15]   [2000] 1 FLR 973.
[16]   [2001] 2 FLR 809.
[17]   [2009] 1 FLR 873.
[18]   [2009] 2 FLR 753.

bad faith) arguing that it must have been understood that the £22,000 was not merely for removal of security but payment of the husband's underlying debt in addition. The wife was successful at first instance, the bank appealed.

7.56 The bank succeeded on appeal. It was held that no reference had been made in the correspondence to full and final discharge of the underlying debt and the agreement did not extend to that obligation at all. The clear language used in the relevant letters must be the primary source for the court's construction of the agreement. In legal and commercial terms there was a clear distinction between the security interest achieved by the charging order and the underlying unsecured debt. Much clearer language than was, in fact, used by the wife would have been needed to make an offer directed to the husband's underlying debt (or by extension his interest in the property).

7.57 See also *C&W Berry Limited and Armstrong-Moakes*;[19] *Putnam & Sons v Taylor*;[20] and *Wright v Nationwide Building Society*.[21]

Appointment of a receiver by way of equitable execution

7.58 An order for equitable execution authorises a receiver to receive rents, profits and monies in respect of the judgment debtor's interest in specified property. Such an order is granted by the court in circumstances where it may be impossible to enforce the judgment debt by any other means or when the debtor has interests in certain property which cannot be realised by any other method of enforcement. Generally, however, a charging order will be a cheaper and more efficient method of enforcement. It is clear that a receiver should be appointed only where there are these impediments to legal execution. The scope for this method of enforcement is now limited but it may be appropriate if, for example, the court refuses to make a charging order. In practice, this method of enforcement is rarely invoked as it is regarded as cumbersome.

INTEREST ON JUDGMENT DEBTS

7.59 Every judgment debt in the High Court carries interest at the statutory rate from the time that judgment is entered.[22] The statutory rate of interest is varied from time to time and is currently 8%.

7.60 Interest arises on county court judgments made on or after 1 July 1999 provided the judgment debt exceeds £5,000,[23] with certain exceptions – in particular, debts under agreements regulated by the Consumer Credit Act 1974. County court judgments being enforced in the High Court, by the sheriff's officer, carry interest in the same way as High Court judgments.

---

[19] [2007] EWHC 2101 (QB).
[20] [2009] EWHC 317 (Ch), [2009] BPIR 769.
[21] [2009] EWCA Civ 811, [2009] 2 BCLC 695.
[22] Judgments Act 1838, s 17.
[23] County Courts (Interest on Judgment Debts) Order 1991, SI 1991/1184.

7.61 In certain circumstances, the amount of interest recoverable on a judgment debt is not limited in time.[24] In *Ezekiel v Orakpo*,[25] more than 6 years of interest was recoverable on a charging order despite no reference having been made in the charging order to interest. However, note the distinction arising from *Lowsley v Forbes*,[26] when the court, in considering the making of a charging order, limited the interest to 6 years. This decision applies to other forms of execution.

SECURED DEBTS

7.62 Secured debts are, far too often, simply entered into the parties' respective asset schedules for the purposes of ancillary relief proceedings without further regard. There are important circumstances which allow argument by the wife against a secured creditor and provide a defence to a claim brought by them – wives are not always bound by these secured debts.

7.63 The relationship between the wife and a secured creditor has been the subject of considerable judicial scrutiny in the last decade or so, such scrutiny having identified the need to protect the wife's interest in certain circumstances, as weighed against the rights of the bank to security for their credit. The courts have also been conscious the wife may wish to enter into certain arrangements, regardless of the risks involved and that if lenders are burdened with highly onerous duties which involve a real danger that the security will be challenged and subsequently found to be unenforceable, they will be extremely unlikely to lend. It will be seen that this policy consideration has played a greater role in the courts' decisions following the landmark case of *Barclays Bank v O'Brien*[27] and the House of Lords' decision in *Royal Bank of Scotland plc v Etridge (No 2)* (hereinafter called *Etridge*).[28]

7.64 These policy considerations have been balanced by requiring the wife to receive independent advice concerning the transaction. The House of Lords in *Barclays Bank plc v O'Brien*, and more recently in *Etridge*, provide a comprehensive review of these issues.

7.65 The relevant circumstances where a wife could argue that she was not bound by a secured charge, or that her occupation rights had priority, on the former matrimonial home are these:

(a)   Where the charge is not valid.

---

[24]   Limitation Act 1980, s 24(2).
[25]   [1997] 1 WLR 340.
[26]   [1999] 1 AC 329.
[27]   [1994] 1 FLR 1.
[28]   [2001] 2 FLR 1364.

(b) Where the borrowing was secured against the former matrimonial home as a result of the undue influence of the husband (implied or otherwise), or by fraud, or by misrepresentation (*Etridge*).

(c) Where the borrowing is secured against the property without proper enquiries being made of the wife's beneficial interest as an occupier (overriding interests); see LRA 2002, s 29.[29]

(d) In the case of a bankrupt, the wife may argue she is entitled to prevail as against her husband ('equity of exoneration') but this would not affect the entitlement of the bank to enforce its security.

VALIDITY OF THE CHARGE

Forgery, Fraud and *Factum*

7.66 Before turning to the defence of undue influence, the family law practitioner should be aware of the obvious effect of forgery, as well as the very narrow doctrine of *non est factum*, which was argued unsuccessfully in *Saunders (Executrix of the Estate of Rose Maud Gallie) v Anglia Building Society (formerly Northampton Town and Country Building Society)*.[30] Per Lord Reid, the doctrine was initially applied in circumstances where the person alleged to be bound did not in fact sign the document. It was then extended to assist those who were unable to read due to blindness or illiteracy. However, Lord Reid stressed that the defence would very rarely be available to a person with ordinary mental capacity, and would not provide an excuse for declining to scrutinise the document, nor for failing to do so sufficiently. In summary, it was held by the House of Lords that, for the defence to be successful, a radical or fundamental distinction must be shown between the document as it is and the document as it was believed to be.[31]

7.67 If a charge was fraudulently entered into by the husband it will not bind the wife, although the creditors would be able to pursue a claim against his equitable interest in the property.

Undue influence

7.68 Where one party has placed unacceptable pressure on a second party which caused the second party to enter into a specific transaction *actual undue influence is proved*. According to the case of *Earl of Aylesford v Morris*,[32] undue influence is 'the unconscientious use by one person of power possessed by him

---

[29] Replacing s 70(1)(g) of the Land Registration Act 1925.
[30] [1970] 3 All ER 961.
[31] See also the case of *Lloyds Bank plc v Waterhouse* [1993] 2 FLR 97 for further judicial consideration of this issue.
[32] (1873) 8 Ch App 484.

over another in order to induce the other to enter into a contract'. Whether or not the issue arises will depend on the particular facts of the case.

7.69 The husband's actions need not go so far as *actual undue influence,* the court *may presume undue influence.* In the words of Baron J in *NA v MA*[33] (a post-nuptial agreement case):

> 'in a case involving a husband and wife where it is clear that the interdependence and mutual influence are the basis of the relationship, I consider that the court has to take special care in assessing the manner in which each party's conduct affected the other. For example, if a wife has been accustomed to placing reliance upon her husband's decisions she might be much more easily influenced than an individual in a commercial transaction.'

Barclays Bank plc v O'Brien: the notice principle

7.70 Mrs O'Brien executed a charge over the matrimonial home, the purpose of which was to secure her husband's liabilities as guarantor of his company's overdraft to the bank. She was induced to sign the charge by her husband's misrepresentations regarding the extent of the indebtedness involved. The bank did not explain the transaction to her nor did it advise her to take independent advice before executing the charge. The bank commenced possession proceedings and Mrs O'Brien resisted the same on the ground that the bank had notice of her husband's wrongdoing. The trial judge held that the bank could enforce its security, but the Court of Appeal allowed the wife's appeal. The bank then appealed to the House of Lords, which affirmed the decision of the Court of Appeal, albeit on different grounds. The House of Lords confirmed that the charge was not enforceable to its full purported extent, due to the husband's misrepresentation and the bank's failure to take reasonable steps to ensure that the wife fully understood the effect of the charge. However, the charge was enforceable to the amount that the wife had understood to be secured, ie £60,000. This is discussed further below.

7.71 The House of Lords held that the true basis for the law in this area is the proper application of the doctrine of notice (per Lord Browne-Wilkinson: 'the key to the problem is to identify the circumstances in which the creditor will be taken to have had notice of the wife's equity to set aside the transaction'). In particular, Lord Browne-Wilkinson held that when a wife offers to stand as surety for her husband's debts, the presence of two factors should put the creditor on enquiry:

- the transaction is on its face to the financial disadvantage of the wife;

- there is a substantial risk in transactions of this kind that in procuring the wife to act as surety the husband has committed a legal or equitable wrong that entitles the wife to set aside the transaction.

---

[33]   [2007] 1 FLR 1760.

7.72 Therefore, under *O'Brien*, unless the creditor who was put on enquiry took reasonable steps to satisfy himself that the wife's agreement to stand as surety had been properly obtained, the creditor had constructive notice of the wife's rights.

7.73 In the cases following *O'Brien*, banks attempted to defeat wives' 'undue influence' defences by obtaining summary judgment. In response, wives' claims were increasingly pleaded on the *O'Brien* test for presumed undue influence. Wives were seeking to challenge the validity of the charge purely on the basis that they could satisfy both requirements of the *O'Brien* presumed undue influence test:

(1)   that the wife placed trust and confidence in her husband;

(2)   that the transaction was to her manifest disadvantage.

7.74 The argument continued that, as the bank had been on notice of the undue influence, it should not be allowed to enforce the charge against the wife (or between cohabitants where there is an emotional relationship).

7.75 The apparent flaw in the argument is that presumed undue influence was being treated by wives as a type of undue influence per se, of which the bank should have been put on notice. Presumed undue influence was clearly easier for wives to establish than actual undue influence; since there was no burden of proof, they did not need to provide evidence of the exertion of undue influence within actual incidents. However, the wives' reliance upon presumed undue influence did not increase their chances of success in defending against banks' claims for possession. As can be seen from what follows, courts often held that the banks' standard practices were sufficient to take them off notice of any presumed undue influence.

7.76 In *O'Brien*, when Lord Browne-Wilkinson considered the reasonable steps a creditor should take to come off notice of undue influence, he indicated that for the future, a creditor would satisfy the requirements if it insisted that the wife attend a private meeting, in the absence of the husband, with a representative of the creditor. She would be told the extent of her liability as surety, warned of the risk she would be running and urged to take independent legal advice. Lord Browne-Wilkinson's system of face-to-face meetings between the bank manager and the wife did not, however, become standard practice.

7.77 In many cases, banks successfully relied on the fact that a solicitor instructed by the wife would give her the necessary advice, thus making her consent free from any undue influence by her husband. Therefore following *O'Brien*, the presence of a solicitor in the background was often held to be enough to take the bank off notice of the husband's legal or equitable wrong, thus defeating the wife's claim of entitlement to set aside the transaction. Banks were found to have taken reasonable steps to come off notice simply by ascertaining that a solicitor was acting for the wife.

7.78 The problem encountered by wives was the ease with which banks were able to defeat their undue influence defences. The banks could simply plead that if indeed they were put on notice by the existence of the actual or presumed undue influence, they had automatically come off notice by ensuring that a solicitor had been instructed by the wife.

Royal Bank of Scotland v Etridge (No 2)

Re-defining meaning of undue influence

7.79 After *O'Brien* wives were held to be subject to presumed undue influence in all cases where they appeared to be at a financial disadvantage as a result of the transaction. In *Etridge* Lord Nicholls opines:

> 'I return to husband and wife cases. I do not think that, *in the ordinary course*, a guarantee of the character I have mentioned is to be regarded as a transaction which, failing proof to the contrary, is explicable only on the basis that it has been procured by the exercise of undue influence of the husband ... [Wives] may be less optimistic than their husbands about the prospects of the husbands' businesses. They may be anxious, perhaps exceedingly so. But this is a far cry from saying that such transactions as a class are to be regarded as prima facie evidence of the exercise of undue influence by husbands.'

7.80 Lord Scott expressed a similar view at paras [159]–[160] of the judgment:

> 'The proposition that if a wife, who generally reposes trust and confidence in her husband, agrees to become surety to support his debts or his business enterprises, a presumption of undue influence arises is one that I am unable to accept. ... More is needed before the stage is reached at which, in the absence of any other evidence, an inference of undue influence can properly be drawn or a presumption of the existence of undue influence can be said to arise.'

7.81 *Etridge* therefore defines presumed undue influence using two criteria:

(1)   a wife who has placed trust and confidence in her husband; and

(2)   a transaction which was not readily explicable by the relationship between the parties.

7.82 If the wife can establish both of these criteria, the bank will have the burden of disproving undue influence.

7.83 See also *Marion Mary Thompson v Julie Ann Foy: Mortgage Business v (1) Julie Ann Foy (2) Marion Thompson*.[34] Mrs Thompson had spent her married life in 'Valley View', a property in her husband's sole name. Mr and Mrs Foy (Mrs Foy was Mrs Thompson's daughter) also lived at the property with their children in an extension they had built with their own expense. The family regarded them as owners of that part of the property although the title

---

[34]   [2009] EWHC 1076 (Ch).

did not reflect this. Mr Thompson died and Mrs Thompson inherited under the terms of his will. She was now overhoused and wished to move out.

7.84 After a great deal of discussion with family members and solicitors Mrs Thompson executed two deeds:

(i) 'Deed of family arrangement' – varying the terms of Mr Thompson's will in order to entitle Mrs Foy to receive under the will a sum of money, equivalent to half the value of the property.

(ii) 'Deed of Gift' – transferring title of the property to Mrs Foy.

These transactions were an attempt to avoid IHT and to enable Mrs Foy to mortgage the property

7.85 Mrs Foy remortgaged and did not pay the money to Mrs Thompson. Mrs Thompson claimed that her daughter had exercised undue influence over her in persuading her to execute the deeds which varied the will and transferred the property to her and that an equity arose protected by her actual occupation of the property as an overriding interest under LRA 2002, Sch 3, para 2.

7.86 An issue arose as to whether Mrs Thompson was in 'actual occupation' at the relevant time, and the judge held:

• If actual occupation must exist at one date only, then the date of disposition (ie the grant) is the relevant date (he left open the question of whether there must be actual occupation at the date of registration as well).

• Unacceptable conduct amounting to undue influence might arise out of a relationship between two persons where one had acquired over the other a measure of influence or ascendancy, of which the ascendant person took unfair advantage. Whether a transaction had been brought about by undue influence was a question of fact, *Royal Bank of Scotland Plc v Etridge (No 2)*[35] applied. On the evidence, there had not been a complete relationship of trust and confidence between Mrs Thompson and Mrs Foy, as Mrs Thompson had appreciated that she was taking a risk, although Mrs Foy had promised to pay Mrs Thompson the £200,000. The kind of trust in play was no more than a trust that a daughter would keep her promise to her mother. No presumption of undue influence arose, therefore, and the burden was on Mrs Thompson to prove that Mrs Foy had actually used undue influence to procure that the transaction went ahead. The fact that Mrs Foy's promise had been repeatedly and sincerely given did not amount to undue influence. Accordingly, the claim to set aside the deed of family arrangement and the gift of the legal title had to fail.

---

[35] [2001] UKHL 44, [2002] 2 AC 773.

Causation

7.87   Despite a wife being able to establish a presumption of undue influence by satisfying the two criteria above, her claim might still fail as a result of *BCCI v Aboody*[36] if the bank could show, on the balance of probabilities, that a wife would have entered into the transaction in any event. The decision of *UCB Corporate Services Limited v Williams*,[37] however, confirmed that the *Aboody* decision could not be sensibly reconciled with Lord Browne-Wilkinson's statement of principle in *CIBC Mortgages v Pitt*[38] that a victim of undue influence is entitled to have the transaction set aside 'as of right', ie regardless of other considerations.

Reasonable steps to avoid notice of undue influence – the *Etridge* review

How can banks avoid being fixed with constructive notice?

7.88

(1)   The bank should make contact with the wife as close to the outset of the proposed transaction as possible. The bank should ask the wife for the name of the solicitor whom she would like to act for her. In that first letter, the bank should explain that it will require written confirmation from the solicitor that he 'has fully explained to her the nature of the documents and the practical implications they will have for her'. Lord Nicholls states that the reason for imposing a duty on banks to receive certification from a solicitor is to prevent the wife being able to dispute, at some later stage, that she is legally bound by the documents which she has signed. The bank should confirm in its initial letter to the wife that the purpose of requiring her to take legal advice is to prevent her from disputing that she is legally bound by the documents at any time after she has signed them.

(2)   The wife's nominated solicitor need not necessarily be a different solicitor from the one already acting for the husband in the transaction. The wife should state to the lender whether she would prefer a different solicitor to advise her where there is already a solicitor acting for the husband.

(3)   The bank should wait to receive an appropriate response from the wife before proceeding with the transaction.

(4)   The bank should disclose to the wife's solicitor the financial information about the transaction which he will need in order to advise her in accordance with his professional duties. Lord Nicholls states that, as a

---

[36]   [1990] 1 QB 923.
[37]   [2002] 3 FCR 448.
[38]   [1994] 1 AC 200.

minimum, the bank must disclose to the wife's solicitor information which enables him to advise properly about the transaction. This will need to cover the following areas:

- the purpose for which the wife is being asked to stand as surety;
- the amount of any existing indebtedness that will be covered by the surety;
- the amount of the current overdraft facility;
- the amount and terms of the new facility;
- any written application received from the husband.

7.89 Lord Hobhouse pointed out that some of the relevant information may be confidential and that banks may need to obtain the husband's consent to give the information to the solicitor and the wife. A refusal to give consent should further alert the bank and the solicitor to the risk that undue influence is being exerted.

7.90 The bank also has a duty to consider whether any further financial disclosure should be provided, including any suspicion that the husband has misled the wife or that she is not entering the transaction of her own free will.

7.91 In addition to the requirements set out above, individual cases call for individual considerations. In *National Westminster Bank Plc v Amin and Another*,[39] where a secured loan had been sought by the parties' son, the parents and legal owners were Ugandan Urdu speakers. A solicitor appointed on behalf of the bank convened a meeting, in English. It was held that the solicitor had not been acting for the parents and as such they had no independent legal advice – further it was held that even with independent legal advice it was not inevitable that the bank would succeed as if the bank knew that the couple did not speak English, they would therefore know that the they were especially vulnerable to exploitation; whilst understanding of the terms described to them might be inferred in ordinary cases that was not necessarily the case if the bank was aware of particular communication problems (per Lord Scott).

7.92 The decision in *Etridge* has largely resolved the confusion amongst bankers as to what steps would, or would not, protect their investment as against the wife.

Misrepresentation

7.93 A defence of misrepresentation is often raised in tandem with one of undue influence, where it is alleged that the husband has misrepresented some material fact relating to the security which has induced the wife to enter into that security. This is referred to in many of the cases discussed above concerning undue influence. The characterisation of the responsibility of the lender for the husband's undue influence is equally applicable to the husband's

---

[39] [2002] 1 FLR 735.

misrepresentation. *O'Brien and Etridge* provide both the definitive legal analysis and the practical guidelines to which a lender should have regard. Evidence of misrepresentation will also be evidence of undue influence.

THE RELIEF AVAILABLE

7.94   While the wife will obviously want a tainted joint security to be set aside as against her, it is necessary to consider whether conditions are capable of being imposed by the courts.

7.95   It is submitted that, as rescission is an equitable remedy, conditions can indeed be imposed by the court. However, there are limitations, and in particular where there has been a misrepresentation as to the limit of security. In *Barclays Bank plc v O'Brien*[40] the wife thought that the security was limited to £60,000 and it was accepted that the creditor could rely upon its security to this extent. In fact, Mr and Mrs O'Brien had already taken out a further loan to repay this sum and Barclays Bank plc had agreed to postpone the balance of its security for that further charge in favour of another lender. The enforceability of the original loan to the extent of £60,000 was confirmed by the Court of Appeal and the House of Lords did not consider the point expressly. A different conclusion was reached in *TSB Bank plc v Camfield*[41] where the Court of Appeal refused to set aside the charge in part or impose conditions.

7.96   In *Barclays Bank plc v Caplan*[42] the court considered the issue of severance and the possibility of setting aside a transaction in part. The facts of the case are relatively detailed and involved company borrowing secured by a guarantee, a charge against the family and a side letter waiving a limitation so that the charge would extend to the guarantee. The court considered that, on the facts, there were two distinct guarantees which were indeed capable of being severed.

7.97   It is well established that a condition of equitable relief is that the party obtaining rescission should make restitution in integrum (counter-restitution) to the other party in respect of all that he or she had obtained from the transaction, ie to the extent of enrichment. In the case of *Dunbar Bank plc v Nadeem*,[43] the condition of rescission was that the beneficial interest in the lease acquired by the wife was to be restored.

---

[40]   [1994] 1 FLR 1.
[41]   [1995] 1 FLR 751.
[42]   [1998] 1 FLR 532.
[43]   [1998] 3 All ER 876.

OVERRIDING INTERESTS

7.98   As a general principle, property rights bind third parties and, therefore, a husband who purports to sell or charge the matrimonial home cannot give a purchaser a greater interest than he in fact owns. However, where the wife's interest is only equitable, a lender may seek to assert that it was unaware of the wife's beneficial interest and, therefore, is not bound by it.

7.99   If the wife was in 'actual occupation' at the time of the charge (or sale) the creditor will take subject to her beneficial interest. Reference must now be made to s 29 of, and to Sch 3, para 2 to, the Land Registration Act 2002.

> '**29**—(1)   If a registrable disposition of a registered estate is made for valuable consideration, completion of the disposition by registration has the effect of postponing to the interest under the disposition any interest affecting the estate immediately before the disposition whose priority is not protected at the time of registration.
>
> (2)   For the purposes of subsection (1), the priority of an interest is protected—
>
> (a)   in any case if the interest . . .
>
> (ii)   falls within any of the paragraphs of Schedule 3.
>
> **Schedule 3**
>
> '2   An interest belonging at the time of the disposition to a person in actual occupation, so far as relating to land of which he is in actual occupation, except for—
>
> (a)   an interest under a settlement under the Settled Land Act 1925 (c 18);
>
> (b)   an interest of a person of whom inquiry was made before the disposition and who failed to disclose the right when he could reasonably have been expected to do so;
>
> (c)   an interest—
>
>   (i)   which belongs to a person whose occupation would not have been obvious on a reasonably careful inspection of the land at the time of the disposition, and
>
>   (ii)   of which the person to whom the disposition is made does not have actual knowledge at that time;
>
> (d)   a leasehold estate in land granted to take effect in possession after the end of the period of three months beginning with the date of the grant and which has not taken effect in possession at the time of the disposition.'

7.100   This replaces the old provisions under s 70(1)(g) of the Land Registration Act 1925:

> '(1)   All registered land shall … be deemed to be subject to such of the following overriding interests as may be for the time being subsisting in reference thereto …
>
> (g)   the rights of every person in actual occupation of the land or in receipt of the rents and profits thereof, save where enquiry is made of such person and the rights are not disclosed …'.

7.101   The case of *Williams & Glyn's Bank Ltd v Boland and Another*[44] brought lenders to an abrupt awareness of their responsibilities in relation to wives who had a beneficial interest in the matrimonial home and who were in actual occupation of that property at the material time. First, where a lender is seeking a possession order, as in *Boland*, the charge may prove to be unenforceable if the lender does not make enquiry of the wife as to her interest in the property. Lord Wilberforce stated that it was not acceptable for lenders solely to deal with the husband.

7.102   This has led to the common practice by lenders of requiring the wife to sign documentation to the effect that the security has priority over her own interest in the property and her right of occupation. Lenders will generally ask any person in occupation over the age of 17 to sign a Consent to Mortgage form, which will effectively give the lender priority over any equitable rights that the person may have in relation to the property. It is also usual to suggest that the person should obtain separate legal advice and, therefore, the practitioner should enquire as to whether this was stressed to the occupants. Indeed, the practitioner will wish to check whether the guidance in *O'Brien* and *Etridge* has been applied to the full.

7.103   If such enquiry has not been carried out, and the creditor was not made aware of other occupiers, the questions of what is the material time for occupation and what amounts to actual occupation must be considered.

7.104   In the case of *Lloyds Bank plc v Rosset and Another*,[45] it was held by the Court of Appeal that the material time for determining whether the wife had been in actual occupation, and, therefore, could claim priority over the lender, was the date upon which the legal estate was transferred or created and not the date of registration. This position was confirmed by the House of Lords in *Abbey National Building Society v Cann and Another*.[46]

7.105   In relation to actual occupation, Lord Denning stated in the Court of Appeal in *Williams & Glyn's Bank Ltd v Boland*[47] that 'actual occupation is a matter of fact, not law'. In the House of Lords in *Boland*, Lord Scarman explained that the legislative provision for an overriding interest in this scenario meant that 'statute has substituted a plain factual situation for the uncertainties of notice, actual or constructive, as the determinant of an overriding interest'.

7.106   The decision went on to confirm that the words 'actual occupation' are ordinary words of plain English and should be read as such, the word 'actual' emphasises that physical presence is required.

[44]   [1981] AC 487.
[45]   [1990] 2 FLR 155.
[46]   [1990] 2 FLR 122.
[47]   See footnote 44 above.

7.107   In *Abbey National BS v Cann*[48] it was confirmed that the occupation can be vicarious – a caretaker or the representative of a company can occupy on behalf of his employer.

7.108   The mere presence of some personal belongings will not usually count as actual occupation – see Russell J in *Strand Securities Ltd v Caswell*.[49]

7.109   If the person said to be in actual occupation at any particular time is not physically present on the land at that time, it will usually be necessary to show that his occupation was manifested and accompanied by a continuing intention to occupy see *Hoggett v Hoggett*[50] and the recent case of *Link Lending v Hussain*.[51] Physical presence is required, not just an entitlement to possession at law. The person in question had been cared for in residential care homes since the sale of the property but her intention had always been to return to her house. Her furniture and personal effects were still in the property. She visited periodically and it was not occupied by anyone else. Regular outgoings relating to the property were paid by her. The court held that the evidence and intention to occupy satisfied the requirement of actual occupation even though she was residing elsewhere. She therefore had an overriding interest which took priority to the charge. The lender was not entitled to possession of the property.

7.110   See also *Marion Mary Thompson v Julie Ann Foy: Mortgage Business v (1) Julie Ann Foy (2) Marion Thompson*[52] (referred to above at **7.83**) for the definition of 'actual occupation'.

7.51   The wife's equitable interest will only bind the lender and defeat the enforceability of the charge if the lender can be said to have had actual or constructive notice of that interest. The question will be whether or not the lender made such inspections as it reasonably ought to have arranged.

7.112   In *Kingsnorth Finance Co Ltd v Tizard and Another*,[53] Judge John Finlay QC stated that, although *Boland* related to regisered land, the decision provided an illustration as to the manner in which the presence of the wife at the property was to be regarded.

7.113   In that case, the matrimonial home was in the sole name of the husband. The couple experienced matrimonial difficulties and it was agreed that their house should be sold and the net proceeds divided equally as between the husband and the wife. The wife ceased to stay at the property, except when the husband was away, but would come to the property during the day to look after the children. The husband at some later stage negotiated a loan, informing

---

[48]   [1991] 1 AC 56, [1990] 2 WLR 833, [1990] 2 FLR 122.
[49]   [1965] Ch 958.
[50]   (1980) 39 P&CR 121.
[51]   [2010] 1 P & CR D16.
[52]   [2009] EWHC 1076 (Ch).
[53]   [1986] 1 WLR 783.

the lender that he was single. Although the lender's agent went through the property, he saw no signs of the wife's occupation.

7.114 The court held that the lender had not satisfied its duty of enquiry, despite the visit to the property. Further inspection or enquiries should have been undertaken. The wife was, therefore, successful in asserting that the lender had constructive notice of her interest in the property and, therefore, the charge was subject to that prior interest.

7.115 However, it may still be possible for the devious husband to charge the property successfully and defeat the wife's claim for occupation, by the application of the decision in *City of London Building Society v Flegg*.[54] In that case, the legal interest in the property was in the joint names of a husband and wife, although the wife's parents also had a beneficial interest in, and occupied, the property. Whilst the parents were aware of the original charge, although they believed it to be for a lesser sum, the husband and wife secured a further two charges against the property without the parents' knowledge. These three charges were discharged by an advance from the City of London Building Society, which was secured by another charge against the property, again without the parents' knowledge. However, the House of Lords found that the building society was entitled to possession, because the legal charge was entered into by two trustees for sale, hence overreaching the parents' right of occupation.

7.116 *Boland* was distinguished on the basis that only one trustee had entered into the charge. *Flegg* obviously gives rise to an unsatisfactory loophole, which the husband owning a property in his sole name may be able to exploit by appointing an additional trustee for sale. The lender would, therefore, on the basis of *Flegg*, be able to claim successfully that the wife's interest of occupation had been overreached and the charge should be enforceable.

7.117 The situation where a wife's rights of occupation may be overreached by a purchaser for value without notice from two trustees of sale has been eroded further in the case of *State Bank of India v Sood*,[55] when the Court of Appeal decided that it was not necessary for capital money to arise on and contemporaneously with the conveyance.

7.118 The case of *Le Foe v Le Foe*[56] concerned judicial separation proceedings involving deceit by the husband who procured a second charge against the former matrimonial home without the wife's knowledge or consent. As the wife was in actual occupation at the time the mortgage was created, her interest overrode that of the lender pursuant to s 70(1)(g) of the Land Registration Act 1925[57] (*Boland* being applied). However, in *Equity and Law Homes Limited*

---

[54]   [1988] 1 AC 54, [1988] 1 FLR 98, HL.
[55]   [1997] Ch 276.
[56]   [2001] 2 FLR 970 (Nicholas Mostyn QC).
[57]   Now replaced by LRA 2002, s 29.

v Prestidge,[58] the Court of Appeal held that the charge of the mortgagee ranked ahead of the beneficial interest of the female partner up to the amount of a previous mortgage to which she had consented and that principle was applied in *Le Foe*. In effect, the mortgagee was subrogated to the rights of the previous mortgagee who had been discharged, which previous mortgage was binding on the female partner.

7.119 Nicholas Mostyn QC (sitting as a deputy High Court judge) did however hold that the husband's behaviour amounted to 'conduct' for the purposes of Matrimonial Causes Act 1973, s 25(2)(g) as it would be conduct which it would be inequitable for the court to disregard (ordering that the amount required to redeem the second mortgage be taken from the husband's share). This approach was also taken in *Re Haghighat (A Bankrupt)*.[59]

7.120 The problem faced by wives in establishing an equitable interest which takes priority over a mortgagee's rights was exemplified in the Court of Appeal's decision in the case of *Bristol and West Building Society v Henning and Another*.[60] In this case, a husband had left his cohabitee in the property but had ceased to pay the mortgage instalments, resulting in a claim for possession by the society. The wife asserted that the society knew or ought to have known of her occupation and therefore had constructive notice of her equitable interest, which took priority over the society's charge. This was rejected by the Court of Appeal who held that the imputed intention of the parties must have been that Mrs Henning's interest was subject to the society's charge, as she knew of and supported the proposal to raise the purchase price on mortgage – this follows the principle of subrogation. The wife cannot claim that her beneficial interest overrides that of the lender where she knew of the borrowing. Furthermore where a second mortgage is taken out (unbeknownst to the wife) which clears an earlier mortgage which she did know about, the second mortgagees are entitled to rely on the subrogated rights of the first mortgagees and can enforce against the wife to the extent of those rights.

---

[58]   [1992] 1 FLR 485.
[59]   [2009] 1 FLR 1271.
[60]   [1985] 1 WLR 778.

Appendix 1

FLOWCHARTS

Figure 1 – Creditor's Petition

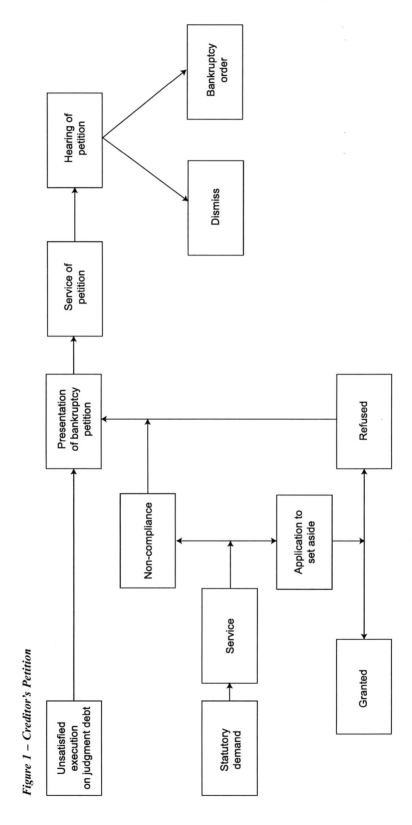

Figure 2 – Debtor's Petition

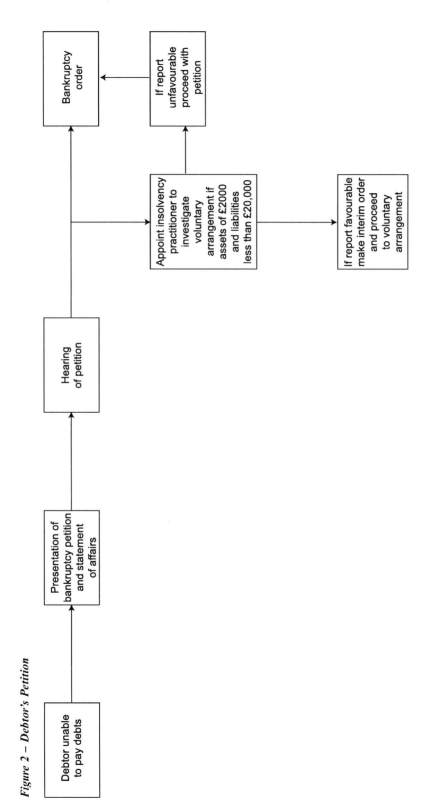

Figure 3 – Individual Voluntary Arrangement – Interim Order Route

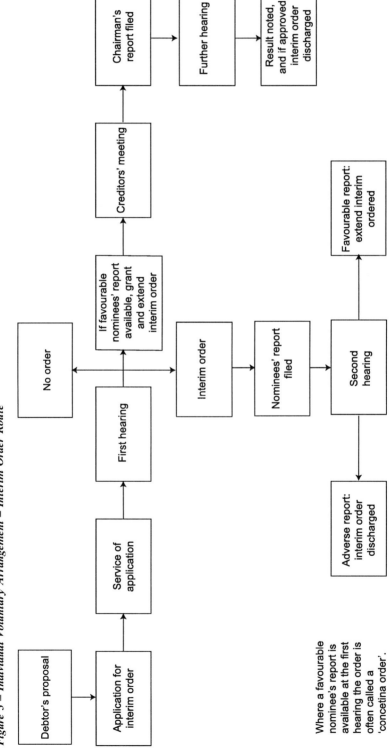

Appendix 2

DECLARATION OF SOLVENCY

To whom it may concern

I, AB of CD, hereby solemnly declare that:

(a)   I have never been adjudicated bankrupt, or entered into an IVA.

(b)   I am not aware of any proceedings which have been commenced with the intention of obtaining a bankruptcy order against me.

(c)   I am solvent at the present time in that:
    (i)   I am able to pay my debts as they fall due; and
    (ii) the value of my assets exceed the amount of my liabilities, both contingent and prospective, in accordance with the schedule below.

Signed ....

Dated ....

Schedule of Assets and Liabilities

Assets		*Liabilities*	
Interest in 1 South Parade – estimated gross value:	£100,000	Outstanding mortgage	£25,000
Building society:	£15,000	Bank overdraft:	£1,000
Shareholding:	£3,000	Credit cards:	£1,000
		Income tax assessment due December 2010 – estimated:	£3,000

Note: consider whether appropriate to attach Form E and other financial disclosure to this declaration or at least to refer to them in this document. Also consider **6.142–6.145** for views on the effectiveness of this declaration.

Appendix 3

QUESTIONNAIRE PURSUANT TO FAMILY PROCEEDINGS RULES 1991, R 2.61B(7)(C)

Please provide the following information.

[Before knowledge of bankruptcy proceedings]

Has the petitioner/respondent ever been bankrupt or subject to an individual voluntary arrangement or any other composition or arrangement with creditors?

[In the event that an individual voluntary arrangement has been made]

Please provide a copy of the following documents:

(a) the proposal;

(b) any amendments;

(c) any interim order or orders;

(d) any order discharging any interim orders;

(e) a copy of the nominee's report;

(f) a copy of the chairman's report.

[In the event of bankruptcy proceedings]

1. Please confirm whether the bankruptcy order was made on a debtor's or creditor's petition and, in either case, provide a copy of the statement of affairs.

2. In the event that the order was made on a debtor's petition, please provide:
    (a) a copy of the petition;
    (b) a copy of the bankruptcy order;
    (c) any other orders or agreements made including an income payments order or agreement.

3. In the event that the order was made on a creditor's petition, please provide:

    (a)   an explanation of the debt upon which the petition is based;

    (b)   a copy of any judgment obtained against the debtor by the petitioning creditor;

    (c)   a copy of the statutory demand;

    (d)   any application to set aside statutory demand;

    (e)   a copy of any evidence sworn;

    (f)   a copy of the petition;

    (g)   a copy of any order made on the petition; and

    (h)   any other orders made including an income payments order.

4.   Please provide the name and address of the trustee in bankruptcy.

Appendix 4

INSOLVENCY ACT 1986

ARRANGEMENT OF SECTIONS

PART IX
BANKRUPTCY

Chapter I
Bankruptcy Petitions; Bankruptcy Orders

Preliminary

Creditor's petition

Debtor's petition

Chapter V
Effect of Bankruptcy on Certain Rights, Transactions, Etc

Rights under trusts of land

Rights of occupation

PART XVI
PROVISIONS AGAINST DEBT AVOIDANCE (ENGLAND AND WALES ONLY)

****

252 Interim order of court

(1) In the circumstances specified below, the court may in the case of a debtor (being an individual) make an interim order under this section.

(2) An interim order has the effect that, during the period for which it is in force –

    (a)   no bankruptcy petition relating to the debtor may be presented or proceeded with,

    (aa)   no landlord or other person to whom rent is payable may exercise any right of forfeiture by peaceable re-entry in relation to premises let to the debtor in respect of a failure by the debtor to comply with any term or condition of his tenancy of such premises, except with the leave of the court and

    (b)   no other proceedings, and no execution or other legal process, may be commenced or continued and no distress may be levied against the debtor or his property except with the leave of the court.

Amendments—Insolvency Act 2000, s 3, Sch 3, paras 1, 2(a), 2(b).

253 Application for interim order

(1) Application to the court for an interim order may be made where the debtor intends to make a proposal under this Part, that is, a proposal to his creditors for a composition in satisfaction of his debts or a scheme of arrangement of his affairs (from here on referred to, in either case, as a 'voluntary arrangement').

(2) The proposal must provide for some person ('the nominee') to act in relation to the voluntary arrangement either as trustee or otherwise for the purpose of supervising its implementation and the nominee must be a person who is qualified to act as an insolvency practitioner, or authorised to act as nominee, in relation to the voluntary arrangement.

(3) Subject as follows, the application may be made –

    (a)   if the debtor is an undischarged bankrupt, by the debtor, the trustee of his estate, or the official receiver, and

    (b)   in any other case, by the debtor.

(4) An application shall not be made under subsection (3)(a) unless the debtor has given notice of the proposal to the official receiver and, if there is one, the trustee of his estate.

(5) An application shall not be made while a bankruptcy petition presented by the debtor is pending, if the court has, under section 273 below, appointed an insolvency practitioner to inquire into the debtor's affairs and report.

Amendments—Insolvency Act 2000, s 3, Sch 3, paras 1, 3(a), (b), (c).

254 Effect of application

(1) At any time when an application under section 253 for an interim order is pending,

    (a)   no landlord or other person to whom rent is payable may exercise any right of forfeiture by peaceable re-entry in relation to premises let to the debtor in respect of a failure by the debtor to comply with any term or condition of his tenancy of such premises, except with the leave of the court, and

    (b)   the court may forbid the levying of any distress on the debtor's property or its subsequent sale, or both, and stay any action, execution or other legal process against the property or person of the debtor.

(2) Any court in which proceedings are pending against an individual may, on proof that an application under that section has been made in respect of that individual, either stay the proceedings or allow them to continue on such terms as it thinks fit.

Amendments—Insolvency Act 2000, s 3, Sch 3, paras 1, 4(a), (b).

255 Cases in which interim order can be made

(1) The court shall not make an interim order on an application under section 253 unless it is satisfied –

    (a)   that the debtor intends to make a proposal under this Part;

    (b)   that on the day of the making of the application the debtor was an undischarged bankrupt or was able to petition for his own bankruptcy;

    (c)   that no previous application has been made by the debtor for an interim order in the period of 12 months ending with that day; and

    (d)   that the nominee under the debtor's proposal is willing to act in relation to the proposal.

(2) The court may make an order if it thinks that it would be appropriate to do so for the purpose of facilitating the consideration and implementation of the debtor's proposal.

(3) Where the debtor is an undischarged bankrupt, the interim order may contain provision as to the conduct of the bankruptcy, and the administration of the bankrupt's estate, during the period for which the order is in force.

(4) Subject as follows, the provision contained in an interim order by virtue of subsection (3) may include provision staying proceedings in the bankruptcy or modifying any provision in this Group of Parts, and any provision of the rules in their application to the debtor's bankruptcy.

(5) An interim order shall not, in relation to a bankrupt, make provision relaxing or removing any of the requirements of provisions in this Group of

Parts, or of the rules, unless the court is satisfied that that provision is unlikely to result in any significant diminution in, or in the value of, the debtor's estate for the purposes of the bankruptcy.

(6) Subject to the following provisions of this Part, and interim order made on an application under section 253 ceases to have effect at the end of the period of 14 days beginning with the day after the making of the order.

Amendments—Insolvency Act 2000, ss 3, 15(1), Sch 3, paras 1, 5(a), (b), Sch 5.

256 Nominee's report on debtor's proposal

(1) Where an interim order has been made on an application under section 253, the nominee shall, before the order ceases to have effect, submit a report to the court stating –

(a)   whether, in his opinion, the voluntary arrangement which the debtor is proposing has a reasonable prospect of being approved and implemented,

(aa)   whether, in his opinion, a meeting of the debtor's creditors should be summoned to consider the debtor's proposal, and

(b)   if in his opinion such a meeting should be summoned, the date on which, and time and place at which, he proposes the meeting should be held.

(2) For the purpose of enabling the nominee to prepare his report the debtor shall submit to the nominee –

(a)   a document setting out the terms of the voluntary arrangement which the debtor is proposing, and

(b)   a statement of his affairs containing –

(i)   such particulars of his creditors and of his debts and other liabilities and of his assets as may be prescribed, and

(ii)   such other information as may be prescribed.

(3) The court may –

(a)   on an application made by the debtor in a case where the nominee has failed to submit the report required by this section or has died, or

(b)   on an application made by the debtor or the nominee in a case where it is impracticable or inappropriate for the nominee to continue to act as such,

direct that the nominee shall be replaced as such by another person qualified to act as an insolvency practitioner, or authorised to act as nominee, in relation to the voluntary arrangement.

(3A) The court may, on an application made by the debtor in a case where the nominee has failed to submit the report required by this section, direct that the interim order shall continue, or (if it has ceased to have effect) be renewed, for such further period as the court may specify in the direction.

(4) The court may, on the application of the nominee, extend the period for which the interim order has effect so as to enable the nominee to have more time to prepare his report.

(5) If the court is satisfied on receiving the nominee's report that a meeting of the debtor's creditors should be summoned to consider the debtor's proposal, the court shall direct that the period for which the interim order has effect shall be extended, for such further period as it may specify in the direction, for the purpose of enabling the debtor's proposal to be considered by his creditors in accordance with the following provisions of this Part.

(6) The court may discharge the interim order if it is satisfied, on the application of the nominee –

(a)   that the debtor has failed to comply with his obligations under subsection (2), or

(b)   that for any other reason it would be inappropriate for a meeting of the debtor's creditors to be summoned to consider the debtor's proposal.

Amendments—Insolvency Act 2000, s 3, Sch 3, paras 1, 6(a), (b), 7.

256A Debtor's proposal and nominee's report

(1) This section applies where a debtor (being an individual) –

(a)   intends to make a proposal under this Part (but an interim order has not been made in relation to the proposal and no application for such an order is pending), and

(b)   if he is an undischarged bankrupt, has given notice of the proposal to the official receiver and, if there is one, the trustee of his estate,

unless a bankruptcy petition presented by the debtor is pending and the court has, under section 273, appointed an insolvency practitioner to inquire into the debtor's affairs and report.

(2) For the purpose of enabling the nominee to prepare a report to the court, the debtor shall submit to the nominee –

(a)   a document setting out the terms of the voluntary arrangement which the debtor is proposing, and

(b)   a statement of his affairs containing –

(i)   such particulars of his creditors and of his debts and other liabilities and of his assets as may be prescribed, and

(ii)   such other information as may be prescribed.

(3) If the nominee is of the opinion that the debtor is an undischarged bankrupt, or is able to petition for his own bankruptcy, the nominee shall, within 14 days (or such longer period as the court may allow) after receiving the document and statement mentioned in subsection (2), submit a report to the court stating –

(a)   whether, in his opinion, the voluntary arrangement which the debtor is proposing has a reasonable prospect of being approved and implemented,

(b)   whether, in his opinion, a meeting of the debtor's creditors should be summoned to consider the debtor's proposal, and

(c)   if in his opinion such a meeting should be summoned, the date on which, and time and place at which, he proposes the meeting should be held.

(4) The court may –

(a)   on an application made by the debtor in a case where the nominee has failed to submit the report required by this section or has died, or

(b)   on an application made by the debtor or the nominee in a case where it is impracticable or inappropriate for the nominee to continue to act as such,

direct that the nominee shall be replaced as such by another person qualified to act as an insolvency practitioner, or authorised to act as nominee, in relation to the voluntary arrangement.

(5) The court may, on an application made by the nominee, extend the period within which the nominee is to submit his report.

Amendments—Inserted by the Insolvency Act 2000, s 3, Sch 3, paras 1, 7.

257 Summoning of creditors' meeting

(1) Where it has been reported to the court under section 256 or 256A that a meeting of the debtor's creditors should be summoned, the nominee (or his replacement under section 256(3) or 256A(4)) shall, unless the court otherwise directs, summon that meeting for the time, date and place proposed in his report.

(2) The persons to be summoned to the meeting are every creditor of the debtor of whose claim and address the person summoning the meeting is aware.

(3) For this purpose the creditors of a debtor who is an undischarged bankrupt include –

(a)   every person who is a creditor of the bankrupt in respect of a bankruptcy debt, and

(b)   every person who would be such a creditor if the bankruptcy had commenced on the day on which notice of the meeting is given.

Amendments—Insolvency Act 2000, s 3, Sch 3, paras 1, 8(a), (b).

258 Decisions of creditors' meeting

(1) A creditors' meeting summoned under section 257 shall decide whether to approve the proposed voluntary arrangement.

(2) The meeting may approve the proposed voluntary arrangement with modifications, but shall not do so unless the debtor consents to each modification.

(3) The modifications subject to which the proposed voluntary arrangement may be approved may include one conferring the functions proposed to be conferred on the nominee on another person qualified to act as an insolvency practitioner or authorised to act as nominee, in relation to the voluntary arrangement.

But they shall not include any modification by virtue of which the proposal ceases to be a proposal under this Part.

(4) The meeting shall not approve any proposal or modification which affects the right of a secured creditor of the debtor to enforce his security, except with the concurrence of the creditor concerned.

(5) Subject as follows, the meeting shall not approve any proposal or modification under which –

   (a)   any preferential debt of the debtor is to be paid otherwise than in priority to such of his debts as are not preferential debts, or
   (b)   a preferential creditor of the debtor is to be paid an amount in respect of a preferential debt that bears to that debt a smaller proportion than is borne to another preferential debt by the amount that is to be paid in respect of that other debt.

However, the meeting may approve such a proposal or modification with the concurrence of the preferential creditor concerned.

(6) Subject as above, the meeting shall be conducted in accordance with the rules.

(7) In this section 'preferential debt' has the meaning given by section 386 in Part XII; and 'preferential creditor' is to be construed accordingly.

Amendments—Insolvency Act 2000, s 3, Sch 3, paras 1, 9.

259 Report of decisions to court

(1) After the conclusion in accordance with the rules of the meeting summoned under section 257, the chairman of the meeting shall report the result of it to the court and, immediately after so reporting, shall give notice of the result of the meeting to such persons as may be prescribed.

(2) If the report is that the meeting has declined (with or without modifications) to approve the debtor's proposal, the court may discharge any interim order which is in force in relation to the debtor.

260 Effect of approval

(1) This section has effect where the meeting summoned under section 257 approves the proposed voluntary arrangement (with or without modifications).

(2) The approved arrangement –

(a)   takes effect as if made by the debtor at the meeting, and

(b)   binds every person who in accordance with the rules –

(i)   was entitled to vote at the meeting (whether or not he was present or represented at it), or

(ii)   would have been so entitled if he had had notice of it,

as if he were a party to the arrangement.

(2A) If –

(a)   when the arrangement ceases to have effect any amount payable under the arrangement to a person bound by virtue of subsection (2)(b)(ii) has not been paid, and

(b)   the arrangement did not come to an end prematurely,

the debtor shall at that time become liable to pay to that person the amount payable under the arrangement.

(3) The Deeds of Arrangement Act 1914 does not apply to the approved voluntary arrangement.

(4) Any interim order in force in relation to the debtor immediately before the end of the period of 28 days beginning with the day on which the report with respect to the creditors' meeting was made to the court under section 259 ceases to have effect at the end of that period.

This subsection applies except to such extent as the court may direct for the purposes of any application under section 262 below.

(5) Where proceedings on a bankruptcy petition have been stayed by an interim order which ceases to have effect under subsection (4), the petition is deemed, unless the court otherwise orders, to have been dismissed.

Amendments—Insolvency Act 2000, s 3, Sch 3, paras 1, 10.

261 Additional effect on undischarged bankrupt

(1) This section applies where –

(a)   the creditors' meeting summoned under section 257 approves the proposed voluntary arrangement (with or without modifications), and

(b)   the debtor is an undischarged bankrupt.

(2) Where this section applies the court shall annul the bankruptcy order on an application made –

(a)   by the bankrupt, or

(b)   where the bankrupt has not made an application within the prescribed period, by the official receiver.

(3) An application under subsection (2) may not be made –

(a)   during the period specified in section 262(3)(a) during which the decision of the creditors' meeting can be challenged by application under section 262,

(b)   while an application under that section is pending, or

(c)   while an appeal in respect of an application under that section is pending or may be brought.

(4) Where this section applies the court may give such directions about the conduct of the bankruptcy and the administration of the bankrupt's estate as it thinks appropriate for facilitating the implementation of the approved voluntary arrangement.

Amendments—Enterprise Act 2002, s 264(1), Sch 22, para 1.

262 Challenge of meeting's decision

(1) Subject to this section, an application to the court may be made, by any of the persons specified below, on one or both of the following grounds, namely –

(a)   that a voluntary arrangement approved by a creditors' meeting summoned under section 257 unfairly prejudices the interests of a creditor of the debtor;

(b)   that there has been some material irregularity at or in relation to such a meeting.

(2) The persons who may apply under this section are –

(a)   the debtor;

(b)   a person who –
    (i)   was entitled, in accordance with the rules, to vote at the creditors' meeting, or
    (ii)   would have been so entitled if he had had notice of it;

(c)   the nominee (or his replacement under section 256(3), 256A(4) or 258(3)); and

(d)   if the debtor is an undischarged bankrupt, the trustee of his estate or the official receiver.

(3) An application under this section shall not be made –

(a)   after the end of the period of 28 days beginning with the day on which the report of the creditors' meeting was made to the court under section 259, or

(b)   in the case of a person who was not given notice of the creditors' meeting, after the end of the period of 28 days beginning with the day on which he became aware that the meeting had taken place,

but (subject to that) an application made by a person within subsection (2)(b)(ii) on the ground that the arrangement prejudices his interests may be made after the arrangement has ceased to have effect, unless it has come to an end prematurely.

(4) Where on an application under this section the court is satisfied as to either of the grounds mentioned in subsection (1), it may do one or both of the following, namely –

(a)   revoke or suspend any approval given by the meeting;

(b)   give a direction to any person for the summoning of a further meeting of the debtor's creditors to consider any revised proposal he may make or, in a case falling within subsection (1)(b), to reconsider his original proposal.

(5) Where at any time after giving a direction under subsection (4)(b) for the summoning of a meeting to consider a revised proposal the court is satisfied that the debtor does not intend to submit such a proposal, the court shall revoke the direction and revoke or suspend any approval given at the previous meeting.

(6) Where the court gives a direction under subsection (4)(b), it may also give a direction continuing or, as the case may require, renewing, for such period as may be specified in the direction, the effect in relation to the debtor of any interim order.

(7) In any case where the court, on an application made under this section with respect to a creditors' meeting, gives a direction under subsection (4)(b) or revokes or suspends an approval under subsection (4)(a) or (5), the court may give such supplemental directions as it thinks fit and, in particular, directions with respect to –

(a)   things done since the meeting under any voluntary arrangement approved by the meeting, and
(b)   such things done since the meeting as could not have been done if an interim order had been in force in relation to the debtor when they were done.

(8) Except in pursuance of the preceding provisions of this section, an approval given at a creditors' meeting summoned under section 257 is not invalidated by any irregularity at or in relation to the meeting.

Amendments—Insolvency Act 2000, s 3, Sch 3, paras 1, 11(1)(a), (b), (2)(a), (b).

262A False representations etc

(1) If for the purpose of obtaining the approval of his creditors to a proposal for a voluntary arrangement, the debtor –

(a)   makes any false representation, or
(b)   fraudulently does, or omits to do, anything,

he commits an offence.

(2) Subsection (1) applies even if the proposal is not approved.

(3) A person guilty of an offence under this section is liable to imprisonment or a fine, or both.

Amendments—Inserted by Insolvency Act 2000, s 3, Sch 3, paras 1, 12.

262B Prosecution of delinquent debtors

(1) This section applies where a voluntary arrangement approved by a creditors' meeting summoned under section 257 has taken effect.

(2) If it appears to the nominee or supervisor that the debtor has been guilty of any offence in connection with the arrangement for which he is criminally liable, he shall forthwith –

(a) report the matter to the Secretary of State, and

(b) provide the Secretary of State with such information and give the Secretary of State such access to and facilities for inspecting and taking copies of documents (being information or documents in his possession or under his control and relating to the matter in question) as the Secretary of State requires.

(3) Where a prosecuting authority institutes criminal proceedings following any report under subsection (2), the nominee or, as the case may be, supervisor shall give the authority all assistance in connection with the prosecution which he is reasonably able to give.

For this purpose, 'prosecuting authority' means the Director of Public Prosecutions or the Secretary of State.

(4) The court may, on the application of the prosecuting authority, direct a nominee or supervisor to comply with subsection (3) if he has failed to do so.

Amendments—Inserted by Insolvency Act 2000, s 3, Sch 3, paras 1, 12.

262C Arrangements coming to an end prematurely

For the purposes of this Part, a voluntary arrangement approved by a creditors' meeting summoned under section 257 comes to an end prematurely if, when it ceases to have effect, it has not been fully implemented in respect of all persons bound by the arrangement by virtue of section 260(2)(b)(i).

Amendments—Inserted by Insolvency Act 2000, s 3, Sch 3, paras 1, 12.

263 Implementation and supervision of approved voluntary arrangement

(1) This section applies where a voluntary arrangement approved by a creditors' meeting summoned under section 257 has taken effect.

(2) The person who is for the time being carrying out, in relation to the voluntary arrangement, the functions conferred by virtue of the approval on the nominee (or his replacement under section 256(3), 256A(4) or 258(3)) shall be known as the supervisor of the voluntary arrangement.

(3) If the debtor, any of his creditors or any other person is dissatisfied by any act, omission or decision of the supervisor, he may apply to the court; and on such an application the court may –

(a) confirm, reverse or modify any act or decision of the supervisor,

(b) give him directions, or

(c) make such other order as it thinks fit.

(4) The supervisor may apply to the court for directions in relation to any particular matter arising under the voluntary arrangement.

(5) The court may, whenever –

(a)   it is expedient to appoint a person to carry out the functions of the supervisor, and

(b)   it is inexpedient, difficult or impracticable for an appointment to be made without the assistance of the court,

make an order appointing a person who is qualified to act as an insolvency practitioner or authorised to act as supervisor, in relation to the voluntary arrangement, either in substitution for the existing supervisor or to fill a vacancy.

This is without prejudice to section 41(2) of the Trustee Act 1925 (power of court to appoint trustees of deeds of arrangement).

(6) The power conferred by subsection (5) is exercisable so as to increase the number of persons exercising the functions of the supervisor or, where there is more than one person exercising those functions, so as to replace one or more of those persons.

Amendments—Insolvency Act 2000, s 3, Sch 3, paras 1, 13(a), (b).

263A Availability

Section 263B applies where an individual debtor intends to make a proposal to his creditors for a voluntary arrangement and –

(a)   the debtor is an undischarged bankrupt,

(b)   the official receiver is specified in the proposal as the nominee in relation to the voluntary arrangement, and

(c)   no interim order is applied for under section 253.

Amendments—Inserted by Enterprise Act 2002, s 264(1), Sch 22, para 2.

263B Decision

(1) The debtor may submit to the official receiver –

(a)   a document setting out the terms of the voluntary arrangement which the debtor is proposing, and

(b)   a statement of his affairs containing such particulars as may be prescribed of his creditors, debts, other liabilities and assets and such other information as may be prescribed.

(2) If the official receiver thinks that the voluntary arrangement proposed has a reasonable prospect of being approved and implemented, he may make arrangements for inviting creditors to decide whether to approve it.

(3) For the purposes of subsection (2) a person is a 'creditor' only if –

(a)   he is a creditor of the debtor in respect of a bankruptcy debt, and

(b)   the official receiver is aware of his claim and his address.

(4) Arrangements made under subsection (2) –

(a)   must include the provision to each creditor of a copy of the proposed voluntary arrangement,

(b)   must include the provision to each creditor of information about the criteria by reference to which the official receiver will determine whether the creditors approve or reject the proposed voluntary arrangement, and

(c)   may not include an opportunity for modifications to the proposed voluntary arrangement to be suggested or made.

(5) Where a debtor submits documents to the official receiver under subsection (1) no application under section 253 for an interim order may be made in respect of the debtor until the official receiver has –

(a)   made arrangements as described in subsection (2), or

(b)   informed the debtor that he does not intend to make arrangements (whether because he does not think the voluntary arrangement has a reasonable prospect of being approved and implemented or because he declines to act).

Amendments—Inserted by Enterprise Act 2002, s 264(1), Sch 22, para 2.

263C   Result

As soon as is reasonably practicable after the implementation of arrangements under section 263B(2) the official receiver shall report to the court whether the proposed voluntary arrangement has been approved or rejected.

Amendments—Inserted by Enterprise Act 2002, s 264(1), Sch 22, para 2.

263D   Approval of voluntary arrangement

(1) This section applies where the official receiver reports to the court under section 263C that a proposed voluntary arrangement has been approved.

(2) The voluntary arrangement –

(a)   takes effect,

(b)   binds the debtor, and

(c)   binds every person who was entitled to participate in the arrangements made under section 263B(2).

(3) The court shall annul the bankruptcy order in respect of the debtor on an application made by the official receiver.

(4) An application under subsection (3) may not be made –

(a)   during the period specified in section 263F(3) during which the voluntary arrangement can be challenged by application under section 263F(2),

(b)   while an application under that section is pending, or

(c)   while an appeal in respect of an application under that section is pending or may be brought.

(5) The court may give such directions about the conduct of the bankruptcy and the administration of the bankrupt's estate as it thinks appropriate for facilitating the implementation of the approved voluntary arrangement.

(6) The Deeds of Arrangement Act 1914 (c 47) does not apply to the voluntary arrangement.

(7) A reference in this Act or another enactment to a voluntary arrangement approved under this Part includes a reference to a voluntary arrangement which has effect by virtue of this section.

Amendments—Inserted by Enterprise Act 2002, s 264(1), Sch 22, para 2.

263E Implementation

Section 263 shall apply to a voluntary arrangement which has effect by virtue of section 263D(2) as it applies to a voluntary arrangement approved by a creditors' meeting.

Amendments—Inserted by Enterprise Act 2002, s 264(1), Sch 22, para 2.

263F Revocation

(1) The court may make an order revoking a voluntary arrangement which has effect by virtue of section 263D(2) on the ground –

(a)   that it unfairly prejudices the interests of a creditor of the debtor, or
(b)   that a material irregularity occurred in relation to the arrangements made under section 263B(2).

(2) An order under subsection (1) may be made only on the application of –

(a)   the debtor,
(b)   a person who was entitled to participate in the arrangements made under section 263B(2),
(c)   the trustee of the bankrupt's estate, or
(d)   the official receiver.

(3) An application under subsection (2) may not be made after the end of the period of 28 days beginning with the date on which the official receiver makes his report to the court under section 263C.

(4) But a creditor who was not made aware of the arrangements under section 263B(2) at the time when they were made may make an application under subsection (2) during the period of 28 days beginning with the date on which he becomes aware of the voluntary arrangement.

Amendments—Inserted by Enterprise Act 2002, s 264(1), Sch 22, para 2.

263G Offences

(1) Section 262A shall have effect in relation to obtaining approval to a proposal for a voluntary arrangement under section 263D.

(2) Section 262B shall have effect in relation to a voluntary arrangement which has effect by virtue of section 263D(2) (for which purposes the words 'by a creditors' meeting summoned under section 257' shall be disregarded).

Amendments—Inserted by Enterprise Act 2002, s 264(1), Sch 22, para 2.

PART IX
BANKRUPTCY

Chapter I
Bankruptcy Petitions; Bankruptcy Orders

Preliminary

264 Who may present a bankruptcy petition

(1) A petition for a bankruptcy order to be made against an individual may be presented to the court in accordance with the following provisions of this Part –

  (a) by one of the individual's creditors or jointly by more than one of them,
  (b) by the individual himself,
  (ba) by a temporary administrator (within the meaning of Article 38 of the EC Regulation),
  (bb) by a liquidator (within the meaning of Article 2(b) of the EC Regulation) appointed in proceedings by virtue of Article 3(1) of the EC Regulation,
  (c) by the supervisor of, or any person (other than the individual) who is for the time being bound by, a voluntary arrangement proposed by the individual and approved under Part VIII, or
  (d) where a criminal bankruptcy order has been made against the individual, by the Official Petitioner or by any person specified in the order in pursuance of section 39(3)(b) of the Powers of Criminal Courts Act 1973.

(2) Subject to those provisions, the court may make a bankruptcy order on any such petition.

Amendments—SI 2002/1240.

265 Conditions to be satisfied in respect of debtor

(1) A bankruptcy petition shall not be presented to the court under section 264(1)(a) or (b) unless the debtor –

  (a) is domiciled in England and Wales,
  (b) is personally present in England and Wales on the day on which the petition is presented, or
  (c) at any time in the period of 3 years ending with that day –
    (i) has been ordinarily resident, or has had a place of residence, in England and Wales, or
    (ii) has carried on business in England and Wales.

(2) The reference in subsection (1)(c) to an individual carrying on business includes –

  (a) the carrying on of business by a firm or partnership of which the individual is a member, and

(b)   the carrying on of business by an agent or manager for the individual or for such a firm or partnership.

(3) This section is subject to Article 3 of the EC Regulation.

Amendments—SI 2002/1240.

266 Other preliminary conditions

(1) Where a bankruptcy petition relating to an individual is presented by a person who is entitled to present a petition under two or more paragraphs of section 264(1), the petition is to be treated for the purposes of this Part as a petition under such one of those paragraphs as may be specified in the petition.

(2) A bankruptcy petition shall not be withdrawn without the leave of the court.

(3) The court has a general power, if it appears to it appropriate to do so on the grounds that there has been a contravention of the rules or for any other reason, to dismiss a bankruptcy petition or to stay proceedings on such a petition; and, where it stays proceedings on a petition, it may do so on such terms and conditions as it thinks fit.

(4) Without prejudice to subsection (3), where a petition under section 264(1)(a), (b) or (c) in respect of an individual is pending at a time when a criminal bankruptcy order is made against him, or is presented after such an order has been so made, the court may on the application of the Official Petitioner dismiss the petition if it appears to it appropriate to do so.

Creditor's petition

267 Grounds of creditor's petition

(1) A creditor's petition must be in respect of one or more debts owed by the debtor, and the petitioning creditor or each of the petitioning creditors must be a person to whom the debt or (as the case may be) at least one of the debts is owed.

(2) Subject to the next three sections, a creditor's petition may be presented to the court in respect of a debt or debts only if, at the time the petition is presented –

(a)   the amount of the debt, or the aggregate amount of the debts, is equal to or exceeds the bankruptcy level,

(b)   the debt, or each of the debts, is for a liquidated sum payable to the petitioning creditor, or one or more of the petitioning creditors, either immediately or at some certain, future time, and is unsecured,

(c)   the debt, or each of the debts, is a debt which the debtor appears either to be unable to pay or to have no reasonable prospect of being able to pay, and

(d)   there is no outstanding application to set aside a statutory demand served (under section 268 below) in respect of the debt or any of the debts.

(3) A debt is not to be regarded for the purposes of subsection (2) as a debt for a liquidated sum by reason only that the amount of the debt is specified in a criminal bankruptcy order.

(4) ' The bankruptcy level' is £750; but the Secretary of State may by order in a statutory instrument substitute any amount specified in the order for that amount or (as the case may be) for the amount which by virtue of such an order is for the time being the amount of the bankruptcy level.

(5) An order shall not be made under subsection (4) unless a draft of it has been laid before, and approved by a resolution of, each House of Parliament.

268 Definition of 'inability to pay', etc; the statutory demand

(1) For the purposes of section 267(2)(c), the debtor appears to be unable to pay a debt if, but only if, the debt is payable immediately and either –

(a) the petitioning creditor to whom the debt is owed has served on the debtor a demand (known as 'the statutory demand') in the prescribed form requiring him to pay the debt or to secure or compound for it to the satisfaction of the creditor, at least 3 weeks have elapsed since the demand was served and the demand has been neither complied with nor set aside in accordance with the rules, or

(b) execution or other process issued in respect of the debt on a judgment or order of any court in favour of the petitioning creditor, or one or more of the petitioning creditors to whom the debt is owed, has been returned unsatisfied in whole or in part.

(2) For the purposes of section 267(2)(c) the debtor appears to have no reasonable prospect of being able to pay a debt if, but only if, the debt is not immediately payable and –

(a) the petitioning creditor to whom it is owed has served on the debtor a demand (also known as 'the statutory demand') in the prescribed form requiring him to establish to the satisfaction of the creditor that there is a reasonable prospect that the debtor will be able to pay the debt when it falls due,

(b) at least 3 weeks have elapsed since the demand was served, and

(c) the demand has been neither complied with nor set aside in accordance with the rules.

269 Creditor with security

(1) A debt which is the debt, or one of the debts, in respect of which a creditor's petition is presented need not be unsecured if either –

(a) the petition contains a statement by the person having the right to enforce the security that he is willing, in the event of a bankruptcy order being made, to give up his security for the benefit of all the bankrupt's creditors, or

(b)   the petition is expressed not to be made in respect of the secured part of the debt and contains a statement by that person of the estimated value at the date of the petition of the security for the secured part of the debt.

(2) In a case falling within subsection (1)(b) the secured and unsecured parts of the debt are to be treated for the purposes of sections 267 and 270 as separate debts.

270 Expedited petition

In the case of a creditor's petition presented wholly or partly in respect of a debt which is the subject of a statutory demand under section 268, the petition may be presented before the end of the 3-week period there mentioned if there is a serious possibility that the debtor's property or the value of any of his property will be significantly diminished during that period and the petition contains a statement to that effect.

271 Proceedings on creditor's petition

(1) The court shall not make a bankruptcy order on a creditor's petition unless it is satisfied that the debt, or one of the debts, in respect of which the petition was presented is either –

(a)   a debt which, having been payable at the date of the petition or having since become payable, has been neither paid nor secured or compounded for, or

(b)   a debt which the debtor has no reasonable prospect of being able to pay when it falls due.

(2) In a case in which the petition contains such a statement as is required by section 270, the court shall not make a bankruptcy order until at least 3 weeks have elapsed since the service of any statutory demand under section 268.

(3) The court may dismiss the petition if it is satisfied that the debtor is able to pay all his debts or is satisfied –

(a)   that the debtor has made an offer to secure or compound for a debt in respect of which the petition is presented,

(b)   that the acceptance of that offer would have required the dismissal of the petition, and

(c)   that the offer has been unreasonably refused;

and, in determining for the purposes of this subsection whether the debtor is able to pay all his debts, the court shall take into account his contingent and prospective liabilities.

(4) In determining for the purposes of this section what constitutes a reasonable prospect that a debtor will be able to pay a debt when it falls due, it is to be assumed that the prospect given by the facts and other matters known to the creditor at the time he entered into the transaction resulting in the debt was a reasonable prospect.

(5) Nothing in sections 267 to 271 prejudices the power of the court, in accordance with the rules, to authorise a creditor's petition to be amended by the omission of any creditor or debt and to be proceeded with as if things done for the purposes of those sections had been done only by or in relation to the remaining creditors or debts.

Debtor's petition

272 Grounds of debtor's petition

(1) A debtor's petition may be presented to the court only on the grounds that the debtor is unable to pay his debts.

(2) The petition shall be accompanied by a statement of the debtor's affairs containing –

(a) such particulars of the debtor's creditors and of his debts and other liabilities and of his assets as may be prescribed, and
(b) such other information as may be prescribed.

273 Appointment of insolvency practitioner by the court

(1) Subject to the next section, on the hearing of a debtor's petition the court shall not make a bankruptcy order if it appears to the court –

(a) that if a bankruptcy order were made the aggregate amount of the bankruptcy debts, so far as unsecured, would be less than the small bankruptcies level,
(b) that if a bankruptcy order were made, the value of the bankrupt's estate would be equal to or more than the minimum amount,
(c) that within the period of 5 years ending with the presentation of the petition the debtor has neither been adjudged bankrupt nor made a composition with his creditors in satisfaction of his debts or a scheme of arrangement of his affairs, and
(d) that it would be appropriate to appoint a person to prepare a report under section 274.

'The minimum amount' and 'the small bankruptcies level' mean such amounts as may for the time being be prescribed for the purposes of this section.

(2) Where on the hearing of the petition, it appears to the court as mentioned in subsection (1), the court shall appoint a person who is qualified to act as an insolvency practitioner in relation to the debtor –

(a) to prepare a report under the next section, and
(b) subject to section 258(3) in Part VIII, to act in relation to any voluntary arrangement to which the report relates either as trustee or otherwise for the purpose of supervising its implementation.

274 Action on report of insolvency practitioner

(1) A person appointed under section 273 shall inquire into the debtor's affairs and, within such period as the court may direct, shall submit a report to the

court stating whether the debtor is willing, for the purposes of Part VIII, to make a proposal for a voluntary arrangement.

(2) A report which states that the debtor is willing as above mentioned shall also state –

(a) whether, in the opinion of the person making the report, a meeting of the debtor's creditors should be summoned to consider the proposal, and

(b) if in that person's opinion such a meeting should be summoned, the date on which, and time and place at which, he proposes the meeting should be held.

(3) On considering a report under this section the court may –

(a) without any application, make an interim order under section 252, if it thinks that it is appropriate to do so for the purpose of facilitating the consideration and implementation of the debtor's proposal, or

(b) if it thinks it would be inappropriate to make such an order, make a bankruptcy order.

(4) An interim order made by virtue of this section ceases to have effect at the end of such period as the court may specify for the purpose of enabling the debtor's proposal to be considered by his creditors in accordance with the applicable provisions of Part VIII.

(5) Where it has been reported to the court under this section that a meeting of the debtor's creditors should be summoned, the person making the report shall, unless the court otherwise directs, summon that meeting for the time, date and place proposed in his report.

The meeting is then deemed to have been summoned under section 257 in Part VIII, and subsections (2) and (3) of that section, and sections 258 to 263 apply accordingly.

274A Debtor who meets conditions for a debt relief order

(1) This section applies where, on the hearing of a debtor's petition –

(a) it appears to the court that a debt relief order would be made in relation to the debtor if, instead of presenting the petition, he had made an application under Part 7A; and

(b) the court does not appoint an insolvency practitioner under section 273.

(2) If the court thinks it would be in the debtor's interests to apply for a debt relief order instead of proceeding on the petition, the court may refer the debtor to an approved intermediary (within the meaning of Part 7A) for the purposes of making an application for a debt relief order.

(3) Where a reference is made under subsection (2) the court shall stay proceedings on the petition on such terms and conditions as it thinks fit; but if following the reference a debt relief order is made in relation to the debtor the court shall dismiss the petition.

Amendment—Inserted by Tribunals, Courts and Enforcement Act 2007, s 108(1), Sch 20, Pt 1, paras 1, 3.

****

276 Default in connection with voluntary arrangement

(1) The court shall not make a bankruptcy order on a petition under section 264(1)(c) (supervisor of, or person bound by, voluntary arrangement proposed and approved) unless it is satisfied –

   (a)   that the debtor has failed to comply with his obligations under the voluntary arrangement, or

   (b)   that information which was false or misleading in any material particular or which contained material omissions –

      (i)   was contained in any statement of affairs or other document supplied by the debtor under Part VIII to any person, or

      (ii)   was otherwise made available by the debtor to his creditors at or in connection with a meeting summoned under that Part, or

   (c)   that the debtor has failed to do all such things as may for the purposes of the voluntary arrangement have been reasonably required of him by the supervisor of the arrangement.

(2) Where a bankruptcy order is made on a petition under section 264(1)(c), any expenses properly incurred as expenses of the administration of the voluntary arrangement in question shall be a first charge on the bankrupt's estate.

277 Petition based on criminal bankruptcy order

(1) Subject to section 266(3), the court shall make a bankruptcy order on a petition under section 264(1)(d) on production of a copy of the criminal bankruptcy order on which the petition is based.

This does not apply if it appears to the court that the criminal bankruptcy order has been rescinded on appeal.

(2) Subject to the provisions of this Part, the fact that an appeal is pending against any conviction by virtue of which a criminal bankruptcy order was made does not affect any proceedings on a petition under section 264(1)(d) based on that order.

(3) For the purposes of this section, an appeal against a conviction is pending –

   (a)   in any case, until the expiration of the period of 28 days beginning with the date of conviction;

   (b)   if notice of appeal to the Court of Appeal is given during that period and during that period the appellant notifies the official receiver of it, until the determination of the appeal and thereafter for so long as an appeal to the Supreme Court is pending within the meaning of subsection (4).

(4) For the purposes of subsection (3)(b) an appeal to the Supreme Court shall be treated as pending until any application for leave to appeal is disposed of and, if leave to appeal is granted, until the appeal is disposed of; and for the purposes of this subsection an application for leave to appeal shall be treated as disposed of at the expiration of the time within which it may be made, if it is not made within that time..

Amendments—Constitutional Reform Act 2005, s 40(4), Sch 9, Pt 1, para 44.

Commencement and duration of bankruptcy; discharge

278 Commencement and continuance

The bankruptcy of an individual against whom a bankruptcy order has been made –

(a)   commences with the day on which the order is made, and
(b)   continues until the individual is discharged under the following provisions of this Chapter.

279 Duration

(1) A bankrupt is discharged from bankruptcy at the end of the period of one year beginning with the date on which the bankruptcy commences.

(2) If before the end of that period the official receiver files with the court a notice stating that investigation of the conduct and affairs of the bankrupt under section 289 is unnecessary or concluded, the bankrupt is discharged when the notice is filed.

(3) On the application of the official receiver or the trustee of a bankrupt's estate, the court may order that the period specified in subsection (1) shall cease to run until –

(a)   the end of a specified period, or
(b)   the fulfilment of a specified condition.

(4) The court may make an order under subsection (3) only if satisfied that the bankrupt has failed or is failing to comply with an obligation under this Part.

(5) In subsection (3)(b) 'condition' includes a condition requiring that the court be satisfied of something.

(6) In the case of an individual who is adjudged bankrupt on a petition under section 264(1)(d) –

(a)   subsections (1) to (5) shall not apply, and
(b)   the bankrupt is discharged from bankruptcy by an order of the court under section 280.

(7) This section is without prejudice to any power of the court to annul a bankruptcy order.

Amendments—Enterprise Act 2002, s 256(1).

280 Discharge by order of the court

(1) An application for an order of the court discharging an individual from bankruptcy in a case falling within section 279(6) may be made by the bankrupt at any time after the end of the period of 5 years beginning with the date on which the bankruptcy commences.

(2) On an application under this section the court may –

    (a)   refuse to discharge the bankrupt from bankruptcy,

    (b)   make an order discharging him absolutely, or

    (c)   make an order discharging him subject to such conditions with respect to any income which may subsequently become due to him, or with respect to property devolving upon him, or acquired by him, after his discharge, as may be specified in the order.

(3) The court may provide for an order falling within subsection (2)(b) or (c) to have immediate effect or to have its effect suspended for such period, or until the fulfilment of such conditions (including a condition requiring the court to be satisfied as to any matter), as may be specified in the order.

Amendments—Enterprise Act 2002, s 269, Sch 23, paras 1, 3(a), 3(b).

281 Effect of discharge

(1) Subject as follows, where a bankrupt is discharged, the discharge releases him from all the bankruptcy debts, but has no effect –

    (a)   on the functions (so far as they remain to be carried out) of the trustee of his estate, or

    (b)   on the operation, for the purposes of the carrying out of those functions, of the provisions of this Part;

and, in particular, discharge does not affect the right of any creditor of the bankrupt to prove in the bankruptcy for any debt from which the bankrupt is released.

(2) Discharge does not affect the right of any secured creditor of the bankrupt to enforce his security for the payment of a debt from which the bankrupt is released.

(3) Discharge does not release the bankrupt from any bankruptcy debt which he incurred in respect of, or forbearance in respect of which was secured by means of, any fraud or fraudulent breach of trust to which he was a party.

(4) Discharge does not release the bankrupt from any liability in respect of a fine imposed for an offence or from any liability under a recognisance except, in the case of a penalty imposed for an offence under an enactment relating to the public revenue or of a recognisance, with the consent of the Treasury.

(4A) In subsection (4) the reference to a fine includes a reference to a confiscation order under Part 2, 3 or 4 of the Proceeds of Crime Act 2002.

(5) Discharge does not, except to such extent and on such conditions as the court may direct, release the bankrupt from any bankruptcy debt which –

(a)   consists in a liability to pay damages for negligence, nuisance or breach of a statutory, contractual or other duty, or to pay damages by virtue of Part I of the Consumer Protection Act 1987, being in either case damages in respect of personal injuries to any person, or
(b)   arises under any order made in family proceedings or under a maintenance calculation made under the Child Support Act 1991.

(6) Discharge does not release the bankrupt from such other bankruptcy debts, not being debts provable in his bankruptcy, as are prescribed.

(7) Discharge does not release any person other than the bankrupt from any liability (whether as partner or co-trustee of the bankrupt or otherwise) from which the bankrupt is released by the discharge, or from any liability as surety for the bankrupt or as a person in the nature of such a surety.

(8) In this section –

'family proceedings' means –
(a)   family proceedings within the meaning of the Magistrates' Courts Act 1980 and any proceedings which would be such proceedings but for section 65(1)(ii) of that Act (proceedings for variation of order for periodical payments); and
(b)   family proceedings within the meaning of Part V of the Matrimonial and Family Proceedings Act 1984.

'fine' means the same as in the Magistrates' Courts Act 1980; and
'personal injuries' includes death and any disease or other impairment of a person's physical or mental condition.

Amendments—Consumer Protection Act 1987; Children Act 1989, ss 92(11), 108(7) Sch 11, Pt II, para 11(1), (2), Sch 15; Child Support Act 1991, s 58(13), Sch 5, para 7; Child Support, Pensions and Social Security Act 2000, s 26, Sch 3, para 6; Proceeds of Crime Act 2002, s 456, Sch 11, paras 1, 16(1), (2).

281A Post-discharge restrictions

Schedule 4A to this Act (bankruptcy restrictions order and bankruptcy restrictions undertaking) shall have effect.

Amendments—Inserted by Enterprise Act 2002, s 257(1).

282 Court's power to annul bankruptcy order

(1) The court may annul a bankruptcy order if it at any time appears to the court –

(a)   that, on the grounds existing at the time the order was made, the order ought not to have been made, or
(b)   that, to the extent required by the rules, the bankruptcy debts and the expenses of the bankruptcy have all, since the making of the order, been either paid or secured for to the satisfaction of the court.

(2) The court may annul a bankruptcy order made against an individual on a petition under paragraph (a), (b) or (c) of section 264(1) if it at any time appears to the court, on an application by the Official Petitioner –

(a)   that the petition was pending at a time when a criminal bankruptcy order was made against the individual or was presented after such an order was so made, and

(b)   no appeal is pending (within the meaning of section 277) against the individual's conviction of any offence by virtue of which the criminal bankruptcy order was made;

and the court shall annul a bankruptcy order made on a petition under section 264(1)(d) if it at any time appears to the court that the criminal bankruptcy order on which the petition was based has been rescinded in consequence of an appeal.

(3) The court may annul a bankruptcy order whether or not the bankrupt has been discharged from the bankruptcy.

(4) Where the court annuls a bankruptcy order (whether under this section or under section 261 or 263D in Part VIII) –

(a)   any sale or other disposition of property, payment made or other thing duly done, under any provision in this Group of Parts, by or under the authority of the official receiver or a trustee of the bankrupt's estate or by the court is valid, but

(b)   if any of the bankrupt's estate is then vested, under any such provision, in such a trustee, it shall vest in such person as the court may appoint or, in default of any such appointment, revert to the bankrupt on such terms (if any) as the court may direct;

and the court may include in its order such supplemental provisions as may be authorised by the rules.

(5) (*repealed*)

Amendments—Enterprise Act 2002, ss 269, 278(2), Sch 23, paras 1, 4(a), (b), Sch 26.

Chapter II
Protection of Bankrupt's Estate and Investigation of His Affairs

283 Definition of bankrupt's estate

(1) Subject as follows, a bankrupt's estate for the purposes of any of this Group of Parts comprises –

(a)   all property belonging to or vested in the bankrupt at the commencement of the bankruptcy, and

(b)   any property which by virtue of any of the following provisions of this Part is comprised in that estate or is treated as falling within the preceding paragraph.

(2) Subsection (1) does not apply to –

(a)   such tools, books, vehicles and other items of equipment as are necessary to the bankrupt for use personally by him in his employment, business or vocation;

(b)   such clothing, bedding, furniture, household equipment and provisions as are necessary for satisfying the basic domestic needs of the bankrupt and his family.

This subsection is subject to section 308 in Chapter IV (certain excluded property reclaimable by trustee).

(3) Subsection (1) does not apply to –

(a)   property held by the bankrupt on trust for any other person, or
(b)   the right of nomination to a vacant ecclesiastical benefice.

(3A) Subject to section 308A in Chapter IV, subsection (1) does not apply to –

(a)   a tenancy which is an assured tenancy or an assured agricultural occupancy, within the meaning of Part I of the Housing Act 1988, and the terms of which inhibit an assignment as mentioned in section 127(5) of the Rent Act 1977, or

(b)   a protected tenancy, within the meaning of the Rent Act 1977, in respect of which, by virtue of any provision of Part IX of that Act, no premium can lawfully be required as a condition of assignment, or

(c)   a tenancy of a dwelling-house by virtue of which the bankrupt is, within the meaning of the Rent (Agriculture) Act 1976, a protected occupier of the dwelling-house, and the terms of which inhibit an assignment as mentioned in section 127(5) of the Rent Act 1977, or

(d)   a secure tenancy, within the meaning of Part IV of the Housing Act 1985, which is not capable of being assigned, except in the cases mentioned in section 91(3) of that Act.

(4) References in any of this Group of Parts to property, in relation to a bankrupt, include references to any power exercisable by him over or in respect of property except in so far as the power is exercisable over or in respect of property not for the time being comprised in the bankrupt's estate and –

(a)   is so exercisable at a time after either the official receiver has had his release in respect of that estate under section 299(2) in Chapter III or a meeting summoned by the trustee of that estate under section 331 in Chapter IV has been held, or

(b)   cannot be so exercised for the benefit of the bankrupt;

and a power exercisable over or in respect of property is deemed for the purposes of any of this Group of Parts to vest in the person entitled to exercise it at the time of the transaction or event by virtue of which it is exercisable by that person (whether or not it becomes so exercisable at that time).

(5) For the purposes of any such provision in this Group of Parts, property comprised in a bankrupt's estate is so comprised subject to the rights of any person other than the bankrupt (whether as a secured creditor of the bankrupt or otherwise) in relation thereto, but disregarding –

(a)   any rights in relation to which a statement such as is required by section 269(1)(a) was made in the petition on which the bankrupt was adjudged bankrupt, and

(b)   any rights which have been otherwise given up in accordance with the rules.

(6) This section has effect subject to the provisions of any enactment not contained in this Act under which any property is to be excluded from a bankrupt's estate.

Amendments—Housing Act 1988, s 117(1).

283A Bankrupt's home ceasing to form part of estate

(1) This section applies where property comprised in the bankrupt's estate consists of an interest in a dwelling-house which at the date of the bankruptcy was the sole or principal residence of –

(a)   the bankrupt,

(b)   the bankrupt's spouse or civil partner, or

(c)   a former spouse or former civil partner of the bankrupt.

(2) At the end of the period of three years beginning with the date of the bankruptcy the interest mentioned in subsection (1) shall –

(a)   cease to be comprised in the bankrupt's estate, and

(b)   vest in the bankrupt (without conveyance, assignment or transfer).

(3) Subsection (2) shall not apply if during the period mentioned in that subsection –

(a)   the trustee realises the interest mentioned in subsection (1),

(b)   the trustee applies for an order for sale in respect of the dwelling-house,

(c)   the trustee applies for an order for possession of the dwelling-house,

(d)   the trustee applies for an order under section 313 in Chapter IV in respect of that interest, or

(e)   the trustee and the bankrupt agree that the bankrupt shall incur a specified liability to his estate (with or without the addition of interest from the date of the agreement) in consideration of which the interest mentioned in subsection (1) shall cease to form part of the estate.

(4) Where an application of a kind described in subsection (3)(b) to (d) is made during the period mentioned in subsection (2) and is dismissed, unless the court orders otherwise the interest to which the application relates shall on the dismissal of the application –

(a)   cease to be comprised in the bankrupt's estate, and

(b)   vest in the bankrupt (without conveyance, assignment or transfer).

(5) If the bankrupt does not inform the trustee or the official receiver of his interest in a property before the end of the period of three months beginning with the date of the bankruptcy, the period of three years mentioned in subsection (2) –

(a)   shall not begin with the date of the bankruptcy, but

(b)   shall begin with the date on which the trustee or official receiver becomes aware of the bankrupt's interest.

(6) The court may substitute for the period of three years mentioned in subsection (2) a longer period –

(a)   in prescribed circumstances, and

(b)   in such other circumstances as the court thinks appropriate.

(7) The rules may make provision for this section to have effect with the substitution of a shorter period for the period of three years mentioned in subsection (2) in specified circumstances (which may be described by reference to action to be taken by a trustee in bankruptcy).

(8) The rules may also, in particular, make provision –

(a)   requiring or enabling the trustee of a bankrupt's estate to give notice that this section applies or does not apply;

(b)   about the effect of a notice under paragraph (a);

(c)   requiring the trustee of a bankrupt's estate to make an application to the Chief Land Registrar.

(9) Rules under subsection (8)(b) may, in particular –

(a)   disapply this section;

(b)   enable a court to disapply this section;

(c)   make provision in consequence of a disapplication of this section;

(d)   enable a court to make provision in consequence of a disapplication of this section;

(e)   make provision (which may include provision conferring jurisdiction on a court or tribunal) about compensation.

Amendments—Inserted by Enterprise Act 2002, s 261(1); amended by Civil Partnership Act 2004, s 261(1), Sch 27, para 113.

284 Restrictions on dispositions of property

(1) Where a person is adjudged bankrupt, any disposition of property made by that person in the period to which this section applies is void except to the extent that it is or was made with the consent of the court, or is or was subsequently ratified by the court.

(2) Subsection (1) applies to a payment (whether in cash or otherwise) as it applies to a disposition of property and, accordingly, where any payment is void by virtue of that subsection, the person paid shall hold the sum paid for the bankrupt as part of his estate.

(3) This section applies to the period beginning with the day of the presentation of the petition for the bankruptcy order and ending with the vesting, under Chapter IV of this Part, of the bankrupt's estate in a trustee.

(4) The preceding provisions of this section do not give a remedy against any person –

(a) in respect of any property or payment which he received before the commencement of the bankruptcy in good faith, for value and without notice that the petition had been presented, or

(b) in respect of any interest in property which derives from an interest in respect of which there is, by virtue of this subsection, no remedy.

(5) Where after the commencement of his bankruptcy the bankrupt has incurred a debt to a banker or other person by reason of the making of a payment which is void under this section, that debt is deemed for the purposes of any of this Group of Parts to have been incurred before the commencement of the bankruptcy unless –

(a) that banker or person had notice of the bankruptcy before the debt was incurred, or

(b) it is not reasonably practicable for the amount of the payment to be recovered from the person to whom it was made.

(6) A disposition of property is void under this section notwithstanding that the property is not or, as the case may be, would not be comprised in the bankrupt's estate; but nothing in this section affects any disposition made by a person of property held by him on trust for any other person.

285 Restriction on proceedings and remedies

(1) At any time when proceedings on a bankruptcy petition are pending or an individual has been adjudged bankrupt the court may stay any action, execution or other legal process against the property or person of the debtor or, as the case may be, of the bankrupt.

(2) Any court in which proceedings are pending against any individual may, on proof that a bankruptcy petition has been presented in respect of that individual or that he is an undischarged bankrupt, either stay the proceedings or allow them to continue on such terms as it thinks fit.

(3) After the making of a bankruptcy order no person who is a creditor of the bankrupt in respect of a debt provable in the bankruptcy shall –

(a) have any remedy against the property or person of the bankrupt in respect of that debt, or

(b) before the discharge of the bankrupt, commence any action or other legal proceedings against the bankrupt except with the leave of the court and on such terms as the court may impose.

This is subject to sections 346 (enforcement procedures) and 347 (limited right to distress).

(4) Subject as follows, subsection (3) does not affect the right of a secured creditor of the bankrupt to enforce his security.

(5) Where any goods of an undischarged bankrupt are held by any person by way of pledge, pawn or other security, the official receiver may, after giving notice in writing of his intention to do so, inspect the goods.

Where such a notice has been given to any person, that person is not entitled, without leave of the court, to realise his security unless he has given the trustee of the bankrupt's estate a reasonable opportunity of inspecting the goods and of exercising the bankrupt's right of redemption.

(6) References in this section to the property or goods of the bankrupt are to any of his property or goods, whether or not comprised in his estate.

286 Power to appoint interim receiver

(1) The court may, if it is shown to be necessary for the protection of the debtor's property, at any time after the presentation of a bankruptcy petition and before making a bankruptcy order, appoint the official receiver to be interim receiver of the debtor's property.

(2) Where the court has, on a debtor's petition, appointed an insolvency practitioner under section 273 and it is shown to the court as mentioned in subsection (1) of this section, the court may, without making a bankruptcy order, appoint that practitioner, instead of the official receiver, to be interim receiver of the debtor's property.

(3) The court may by an order appointing any person to be an interim receiver direct that his powers shall be limited or restricted in any respect; but, save as so directed, an interim receiver has, in relation to the debtor's property, all the rights, powers, duties and immunities of a receiver and manager under the next section.

(4) An order of the court appointing any person to be an interim receiver shall require that person to take immediate possession of the debtor's property or, as the case may be, the part of it to which his powers as interim receiver are limited.

(5) Where an interim receiver has been appointed, the debtor shall give him such inventory of his property and such other information, and shall attend on the interim receiver at such times, as the latter may for the purpose of carrying out his functions under this section reasonably require.

(6) Where an interim receiver is appointed, section 285(3) applies for the period between the appointment and the making of a bankruptcy order on the petition, or the dismissal of the petition, as if the appointment were the making of such an order.

(7) A person ceases to be interim receiver of a debtor's property if the bankruptcy petition relating to the debtor is dismissed, if a bankruptcy order is made on the petition or if the court by order otherwise terminates the appointment.

(8) References in this section to the debtor's property are to all his property, whether or not it would be comprised in his estate if he were adjudged bankrupt.

287 Receivership pending appointment of trustee

(1) Between the making of a bankruptcy order and the time at which the bankrupt's estate vests in a trustee under Chapter IV of this Part, the official receiver is the receiver and (subject to section 370 (special manager)) the manager of the bankrupt's estate and is under a duty to act as such.

(2) The function of the official receiver while acting as receiver or manager of the bankrupt's estate under this section is to protect the estate; and for this purpose –

    (a)   he has the same powers as if he were a receiver or manager appointed by the High Court, and

    (b)   he is entitled to sell or otherwise dispose of any perishable goods comprised in the estate and any other goods so comprised the value of which is likely to diminish if they are not disposed of.

(3) The official receiver while acting as receiver or manager of the estate under this section –

    (a)   shall take all such steps as he thinks fit for protecting any property which may be claimed for the estate by the trustee of that estate,

    (b)   is not, except in pursuance of directions given by the Secretary of State, required to do anything that involves his incurring expenditure,

    (c)   may, if he thinks fit (and shall, if so directed by the court) at any time summon a general meeting of the bankrupt's creditors.

(4) Where –

    (a)   the official receiver acting as receiver or manager of the estate under this section seizes or disposes of any property which is not comprised in the estate, and

    (b)   at the time of the seizure or disposal the official receiver believes, and has reasonable grounds for believing, that he is entitled (whether in pursuance of an order of the court or otherwise) to seize or dispose of that property,

the official receiver is not to be liable to any person in respect of any loss or damage resulting from the seizure or disposal except in so far as that loss or damage is caused by his negligence; and he has a lien on the property, or the proceeds of its sale, for such of the expenses of the bankruptcy as were incurred in connection with the seizure or disposal.

(5) This section does not apply where by virtue of section 297 (appointment of trustee; special cases) the bankrupt's estate vests in a trustee immediately on the making of the bankruptcy order.

288 Statement of affairs

(1) Where a bankruptcy order has been made otherwise than on a debtor's petition, the bankrupt shall submit a statement of his affairs to the official receiver before the end of the period of 21 days beginning with the commencement of the bankruptcy.

(2) The statement of affairs shall contain –

(a) such particulars of the bankrupt's creditors and of his debts and other liabilities and of his assets as may be prescribed, and

(b) such other information as may be prescribed.

(3) The official receiver may, if he thinks fit –

(a) release the bankrupt from his duty under subsection (1), or

(b) extend the period specified in that subsection;

and where the official receiver has refused to exercise a power conferred by this section, the court, if it thinks fit, may exercise it.

(4) A bankrupt who –

(a) without reasonable excuse fails to comply with the obligation imposed by this section, or

(b) without reasonable excuse submits a statement of affairs that does not comply with the prescribed requirements,

is guilty of a contempt of court and liable to be punished accordingly (in addition to any other punishment to which he may be subject).

289 Investigatory duties of official receiver

(1) The official receiver shall –

(a) investigate the conduct and affairs of each bankrupt (including his conduct and affairs before the making of the bankruptcy order), and

(b) make such report (if any) to the court as the official receiver thinks fit.

(2) Subsection (1) shall not apply to a case in which the official receiver thinks an investigation under that subsection unnecessary.

(3) Where a bankrupt makes an application for discharge under section 280 –

(a) the official receiver shall make a report to the court about such matters as may be prescribed, and

(b) the court shall consider the report before determining the application.

(4) A report by the official receiver under this section shall in any proceedings be prima facie evidence of the facts stated in it.

Amendments—Enterprise Act 2002, s 248.

290 Public examination of bankrupt

(1) Where a bankruptcy order has been made, the official receiver may at any time before the discharge of the bankrupt apply to the court for the public examination of the bankrupt.

(2) Unless the court otherwise orders, the official receiver shall make an application under subsection (1) if notice requiring him to do so is given to

him, in accordance with the rules, by one of the bankrupt's creditors with the concurrence of not less than one-half, in value, of those creditors (including the creditor giving notice).

(3) On an application under subsection (1), the court shall direct that a public examination of the bankrupt shall be held on a day appointed by the court; and the bankrupt shall attend on that day and be publicly examined as to his affairs, dealings and property.

(4) The following may take part in the public examination of the bankrupt and may question him concerning his affairs, dealings and property and the causes of his failure, namely –

    (a)   the official receiver and, in the case of an individual adjudged bankrupt on a petition under section 264(1)(d), the Official Petitioner,

    (b)   the trustee of the bankrupt's estate, if his appointment has taken effect,

    (c)   any person who has been appointed as special manager of the bankrupt's estate or business,

    (d)   any creditor of the bankrupt who has tendered a proof in the bankruptcy.

(5) If a bankrupt without reasonable excuse fails at any time to attend his public examination under this section he is guilty of a contempt of court and liable to be punished accordingly (in addition to any other punishment to which he may be subject).

291 Duties of bankrupt in relation to official receiver

(1) Where a bankruptcy order has been made, the bankrupt is under a duty –

    (a)   to deliver possession of his estate to the official receiver, and

    (b)   to deliver up to the official receiver all books, papers and other records of which he has possession or control and which relate to his estate and affairs (including any which would be privileged from disclosure in any proceedings).

(2) In the case of any part of the bankrupt's estate which consists of things possession of which cannot be delivered to the official receiver, and in the case of any property that may be claimed for the bankrupt's estate by the trustee, it is the bankrupt's duty to do all such things as may reasonably be required by the official receiver for the protection of those things or that property.

(3) Subsections (1) and (2) do not apply where by virtue of section 297 below the bankrupt's estate vests in a trustee immediately on the making of the bankruptcy order.

(4) The bankrupt shall give the official receiver such inventory of his estate and such other information, and shall attend on the official receiver at such times, as the official receiver may reasonably require –

    (a)   for a purpose of this Chapter, or

    (b)   in connection with the making of a bankruptcy restrictions order.

(5) Subsection (4) applies to a bankrupt after his discharge.

(6) If the bankrupt without reasonable excuse fails to comply with any obligation imposed by this section, he is guilty of a contempt of court and liable to be punished accordingly (in addition to any other punishment to which he may be subject).

Amendments—Enterprise Act 2002, s 269, Sch 23.

Chapter III
Trustees in Bankruptcy

Tenure of office as trustee

292 Power to make appointments

(1) The power to appoint a person as trustee of a bankrupt's estate (whether the first such trustee or a trustee appointed to fill any vacancy) is exercisable –

(a)   by a general meeting of the bankrupt's creditors;
(b)   under section 295(2), 296(2) or 300(6) below in this Chapter, by the Secretary of State; or
(c)   under section 297, by the court.

(2) No person may be appointed as trustee of a bankrupt's estate unless he is, at the time of the appointment, qualified to act as an insolvency practitioner in relation to the bankrupt.

(3) Any power to appoint a person as trustee of a bankrupt's estate includes power to appoint two or more persons as joint trustees; but such an appointment must make provision as to the circumstances in which the trustees must act together and the circumstances in which one or more of them may act for the others.

(4) The appointment of any person as trustee takes effect only if that person accepts the appointment in accordance with the rules. Subject to this, the appointment of any person as trustee takes effect at the time specified in his certificate of appointment.

(5) This section is without prejudice to the provisions of this Chapter under which the official receiver is, in certain circumstances, to be trustee of the estate.

Amendments—Enterprise Act 2002, ss 269, 278(2), Sch 23, paras 1, 6, Sch 26.

****

303 General control of trustee by the court

(1) If a bankrupt or any of his creditors or any other person is dissatisfied by any act, omission or decision of a trustee of the bankrupt's estate, he may apply to the court; and on such an application the court may confirm, reverse or modify any act or decision of the trustee, may give him directions or may make such other order as it thinks fit.

(2) The trustee of a bankrupt's estate may apply to the court for directions in relation to any particular matter arising under the bankruptcy.

(2A) Where at any time after a bankruptcy petition has been presented to the court against any person, whether under the provisions of the Insolvent Partnerships Order 1994 or not, the attention of the court is drawn to the fact that the person in question is a member of an insolvent partnership, the court may make an order as to the future conduct of the insolvency proceedings and any such order may apply any provisions of that Order with any necessary modifications.

(2B) Where a bankruptcy petition has been presented against more than one individual in the circumstances mentioned in subsection (2A) above, the court may give such directions for consolidating the proceedings, or any of them, as it thinks just.

(2C) Any order or directions under subsection (2A) or (2B) may be made or given on the application of the official receiver, any responsible insolvency practitioner, the trustee of the partnership or any other interested person and may include provisions as to the administration of the joint estate of the partnership, and in particular how it and the separate estate of any member are to be administered.

Amendments—SI 1994/2421.

304 Liability of trustee

(1) Where on an application under this section the court is satisfied –

  (a)   that the trustee of a bankrupt's estate has misapplied or retained, or become accountable for, any money or other property comprised in the bankrupt's estate, or
  (b)   that a bankrupt's estate has suffered any loss in consequence of any misfeasance or breach of fiduciary or other duty by a trustee of the estate in the carrying out of his functions,

the court may order the trustee, for the benefit of the estate, to repay, restore or account for money or other property (together with interest at such rate as the court thinks just) or, as the case may require, to pay such sum by way of compensation in respect of the misfeasance or breach of fiduciary or other duty as the court thinks just.

This is without prejudice to any liability arising apart from this section.

(2) An application under this section may be made by the official receiver, the Secretary of State, a creditor of the bankrupt or (whether or not there is, or is likely to be, a surplus for the purposes of section 330(5) (final distribution)) the bankrupt himself.

But the leave of the court is required for the making of an application if it is to be made by the bankrupt or if it is to be made after the trustee has had his release under section 299.

(3) Where –

(a)   the trustee seizes or disposes of any property which is not comprised in the bankrupt's estate, and

(b)   at the time of the seizure or disposal the trustee believes, and has reasonable grounds for believing, that he is entitled (whether in pursuance of an order of the court or otherwise) to seize or dispose of that property,

the trustee is not liable to any person (whether under this section or otherwise) in respect of any loss or damage resulting from the seizure or disposal except in so far as that loss or damage is caused by the negligence of the trustee; and he has a lien on the property, or the proceeds of its sale, for such of the expenses of the bankruptcy as were incurred in connection with the seizure or disposal.

Chapter IV
Administration by Trustee

Preliminary

305 General functions of trustee

(1) This Chapter applies in relation to any bankruptcy where either –

(a)   the appointment of a person as trustee of a bankrupt's estate takes effect, or

(b)   the official receiver becomes trustee of a bankrupt's estate.

(2) The function of the trustee is to get in, realise and distribute the bankrupt's estate in accordance with the following provisions of this Chapter; and in the carrying out of that function and in the management of the bankrupt's estate the trustee is entitled, subject to those provisions, to use his own discretion.

(3) It is the duty of the trustee, if he is not the official receiver –

(a)   to furnish the official receiver with such information,

(b)   to produce to the official receiver, and permit inspection by the official receiver of, such books, papers and other records, and

(c)   to give the official receiver such other assistance,

as the official receiver may reasonably require for the purpose of enabling him to carry out his functions in relation to the bankruptcy.

(4) The official name of the trustee shall be 'the trustee of the estate of, a bankrupt' (inserting the name of the bankrupt); be he may be referred to as 'the trustee in bankruptcy' of the particular bankrupt.

Acquisition, control and realisation of bankrupt's estate

306 Vesting of bankrupt's estate in trustee

(1) The bankrupt's estate shall vest in the trustee immediately on his appointment taking effect or, in the case of the official receiver, on his becoming trustee.

(2) Where any property which is, or is to be, comprised in the bankrupt's estate vests in the trustee (whether under this section or under any other provision of this Part), it shall so vest without any conveyance, assignment or transfer.

306A Property subject to restraint order

(1) This section applies where –

    (a)   property is excluded from the bankrupt's estate by virtue of section 417(2)(a) of the Proceeds of Crime Act 2002 (property subject to a restraint order),

    (b)   an order under section 50, 128, or 198 of that Act has not been made in respect of the property, and

    (c)   the restraint order is discharged.

(2) On the discharge of the restraint order the property vests in the trustee as part of the bankrupt's estate.

(3) But subsection (2) does not apply to the proceeds of property realised by a management receiver under section 49(2)(d) or 197(2)(d) of that Act (realisation of property to meet receiver's remuneration and expenses).

Amendments—Inserted by Proceeds of Crime Act 2002, s 456, Sch 11, paras 1, 16(1), (3); amended by Serious Crime Act 2007, ss 74(2)(g), 92, Sch 8, Pt 7, para 151, Sch 14.

306B Property in respect of which receivership or administration order made

(1) This section applies where –

    (a)   property is excluded from the bankrupt's estate by virtue of section 417(2)(b), (c) or (d) of the Proceeds of Crime Act 2002 (property in respect of which an order for the appointment of a receiver or administrator under certain provisions of that Act is in force),

    (b)   a confiscation order is made under section 6, 92 or 156 of that Act,

    (c)   the amount payable under the confiscation order is fully paid, and

    (d)   any of the property remains in the hands of the receiver or administrator (as the case may be).

(2) The property vests in the trustee as part of the bankrupt's estate.

Amendments—Inserted by Proceeds of Crime Act 2002, s 456, Sch 11, paras 1, 16(1), (3).

306C Property subject to certain orders where confiscation order discharged or quashed

(1) This section applies where –

    (a)   property is excluded from the bankrupt's estate by virtue of section 417(2)(a), (b), (c) or (d) of the Proceeds of Crime Act 2002 (property in respect of which a restraint order or an order for the appointment of a receiver or administrator under that Act is in force),

    (b)   a confiscation order is made under section 6, 92 or 156 of that Act, and

(c)   the confiscation order is discharged under section 30, 114 or 180 of that Act (as the case may be) or quashed under that Act or in pursuance of any enactment relating to appeals against conviction or sentence.

(2) Any such property in the hands of a receiver appointed under Part 2 or 4 of that Act or an administrator appointed under Part 3 of that Act vests in the trustee as part of the bankrupt's estate.

(3) But subsection (2) does not apply to the proceeds of property realised by a management receiver under section 49(2)(d) or 197(2)(d) of that Act (realisation of property to meet receiver's remuneration and expenses).

Amendments—Inserted by Proceeds of Crime Act 2002, s 456, Sch 11, paras 1, 16(1), (3).

307 After-acquired property

(1) Subject to this section and section 309, the trustee may by notice in writing claim for the bankrupt's estate any property which has been acquired by, or has devolved upon, the bankrupt since the commencement of the bankruptcy.

(2) A notice under this section shall not served in respect of –

(a)   any property falling within subsection (2) or (3) of section 283 in Chapter II,

(aa)   any property vesting in the bankrupt by virtue of section 283A in Chapter II,

(b)   any property which by virtue of any other enactment is excluded from the bankrupt's estate, or

(c)   without prejudice to section 280(2)(c) (order of court on application for discharge), any property which is acquired by or, devolves upon, the bankrupt after his discharge.

(3) Subject to the next subsection, upon the service on the bankrupt of a notice under this section the property to which the notice relates shall vest in the trustee as part of the bankrupt's estate; and the trustee's title to that property has relation back to the time at which the property was acquired by, or devolved upon, the bankrupt.

(4) Where, whether before or after service of a notice under this section –

(a)   a person acquires property in good faith, for value and without notice of the bankruptcy, or

(b)   a banker enters into a transaction in good faith and without such notice,

the trustee is not in respect of that property or transaction entitled by virtue of this section to any remedy against that person or banker, or any person whose title to any property derives from that person or banker.

(5) References in this section to property do not include any property which, as part of the bankrupt's income, may be the subject of an income payments order under section 310.

Amendments—Enterprise Act 2002, s 261(4).

308 Vesting in trustee of certain items of excess value

(1) Subject to section 309, where –

    (a)   property is excluded by virtue of section 283(2) (tools of trade, household effects, etc) from the bankrupt's estate, and

    (b)   it appears to the trustee that the realisable value of the whole or any part of that property exceeds the cost of a reasonable replacement for that property or that part of it,

the trustee may by notice in writing claim that property or, as the case may be, that part of it for the bankrupt's estate.

(2) Upon the service on the bankrupt of a notice under this section, the property to which the notice relates vests in the trustee as part of the bankrupt's estate; and, except against a purchaser in good faith, for value and without notice of the bankruptcy, the trustee's title to that property has relation back to the commencement of the bankruptcy.

(3) The trustee shall apply funds comprised in the estate to the purchase by or on behalf of the bankrupt of a reasonable replacement for any property vested in the trustee under this section; and the duty imposed by this subsection has priority over the obligation of the trustee to distribute the estate.

(4) For the purposes of this section property is a reasonable replacement for other property if it is reasonably adequate for meeting the needs met by the other property.

Amendments—Housing Act 1988, s 140(1), Sch 17, para 73.

308A Vesting in trustee of certain tenancies

Upon the service on the bankrupt by the trustee of a notice in writing under this section, any tenancy –

    (a)   which is excluded by virtue of section 283(3A) from the bankrupt's estate, and

    (b)   to which the notice relates,

vests in the trustee as part of the bankrupt's estate; and, except against a purchaser in good faith, for value and without notice of the bankruptcy, the trustee's title to that tenancy has relation back to the commencement of the bankruptcy.

Amendments—Inserted by Housing Act 1988, s 117(2).

309 Time-limit for notice under s 307 or 308

(1) Except with the leave of the court, a notice shall not be served –

(a)   under section 307, after the end of the period of 42 days beginning with the day on which it first came to the knowledge of the trustee that the property in question had been acquired by, or had devolved upon, the bankrupt;

(b)   under section 308 or section 308A, after the end of the period of 42 days beginning with the day on which the property or tenancy in question first came to the knowledge of the trustee.

(2) For the purposes of this section –

(a)   anything which comes to the knowledge of the trustee is deemed in relation to any successor of his as trustee to have come to the knowledge of the successor at the same time; and

(b)   anything which comes (otherwise than under paragraph (a)) to the knowledge of a person before he is the trustee is deemed to come to his knowledge on his appointment taking effect or, in the case of the official receiver, on his becoming trustee.

Amendments—Housing Act 1988, s 117(3).

310 Income payments orders

(1) The court may make an order ('an income payments order') claiming for the bankrupt's estate so much of the income of the bankrupt during the period for which the order is in force as may be specified in the order.

(1A) An income payments order may be made only on an application instituted –

(a)   by the trustee, and

(b)   before the discharge of the bankrupt.

(2) The court shall not make an income payments order the effect of which would be to reduce the income of the bankrupt when taken together with any payments to which subsection (8) applies below what appears to the court to be necessary for meeting the reasonable domestic needs of the bankrupt and his family.

(3) An income payments order shall, in respect of any payment of income to which it is to apply, either –

(a)   require the bankrupt to pay the trustee an amount equal to so much of that payment as is claimed by the order, or

(b)   require the person making the payment to pay so much of it as is so claimed to the trustee, instead of to the bankrupt.

(4) Where the court makes an income payments order it may, if it thinks fit, discharge or vary any attachment of earnings order that is for the time being in force to secure payments by the bankrupt.

(5) Sums received by the trustee under an income payments order form part of the bankrupt's estate.

(6) An income payments order must specify the period during which it is to have effect; and that period –

(a)   may end after the discharge of the bankrupt, but

(b)   may not end after the period of three years beginning with the date on which the order is made.

(6A) An income payments order may (subject to subsection (6)(b)) be varied on the application of the trustee or the bankrupt (whether before or after discharge).

(7) For the purposes of this section the income of the bankrupt comprises every payment in the nature of income which is from time to time made to him or to which he from time to time becomes entitled, including any payment in respect of the carrying on of any business or in respect of any office or employment and (despite anything in section 11 or 12 of the Welfare Reform and Pensions Act 1999) any payment under a pension scheme but excluding any payment to which subsection (8) applies.

(8) This subsection applies to –

(a)   payments by way of guaranteed minimum pension; and

(b)   payments giving effect to the bankrupt's protected rights as a member of a pension scheme.

(9) In this section, 'guaranteed minimum pension' and 'protected rights' have the same meaning as in the Pension Schemes Act 1993.

Amendments—Pensions Act 1995, s 122, Sch 3, para 15(a), (b); Welfare Reform and Pensions Act 1999, s 18, Sch 2, para 2; Enterprise Act 2002, ss 259(1), (2), (3), (4), 278(2), Sch 26.

310A Income payments agreement

(1) In this section 'income payments agreement' means a written agreement between a bankrupt and his trustee or between a bankrupt and the official receiver which provides –

(a)   that the bankrupt is to pay to the trustee or the official receiver an amount equal to a specified part or proportion of the bankrupt's income for a specified period, or

(b)   that a third person is to pay to the trustee or the official receiver a specified proportion of money due to the bankrupt by way of income for a specified period.

(2) A provision of an income payments agreement of a kind specified in subsection (1)(a) or (b) may be enforced as if it were a provision of an income payments order.

(3) While an income payments agreement is in force the court may, on the application of the bankrupt, his trustee or the official receiver, discharge or vary an attachment of earnings order that is for the time being in force to secure payments by the bankrupt.

(4) The following provisions of section 310 shall apply to an income payments agreement as they apply to an income payments order –

    (a)   subsection (5) (receipts to form part of estate), and
    (b)   subsections (7) to (9) (meaning of income).

(5) An income payments agreement must specify the period during which it is to have effect; and that period –

    (a)   may end after the discharge of the bankrupt, but
    (b)   may not end after the period of three years beginning with the date on which the agreement is made.

(6) An income payments agreement may (subject to subsection (5)(b)) be varied –

    (a)   by written agreement between the parties, or
    (b)   by the court on an application made by the bankrupt, the trustee or the official receiver.

(7) The court –

    (a)   may not vary an income payments agreement so as to include provision of a kind which could not be included in an income payments order, and
    (b)   shall grant an application to vary an income payments agreement if and to the extent that the court thinks variation necessary to avoid the effect mentioned in section 310(2).

Amendments—Inserted by Enterprise Act 2002, s 260.

311 Acquisition by trustee of control

(1) The trustee shall take possession of all books, papers and other records which relate to the bankrupt's estate or affairs and which belong to him or are in his possession or under his control (including any which would be privileged from disclosure in any proceedings).

(2) In relation to, and for the purpose of acquiring or retaining possession of, the bankrupt's estate, the trustee is in the same position as if he were a receiver of property appointed by the High Court; and the court may, on his application, enforce such acquisition or retention accordingly.

(3) Where any part of the bankrupt's estate consists of stock or shares in a company, shares in a ship or any other property transferable in the books of a company, office or person, the trustee may exercise the right to transfer the property to the same extent as the bankrupt might have exercised it if he had not become bankrupt.

(4) Where any part of the estate consists of things in action, they are deemed to have been assigned to the trustee; but notice of the deemed assignment need not be given except in so far as it is necessary, in a case where the deemed assignment is from the bankrupt himself, for protecting the priority of the trustee.

(5) Where any goods comprised in the estate are held by any person by way of pledge, pawn or other security and no notice has been served in respect of those goods by the official receiver under subsection (5) of section 285 (restriction on realising security), the trustee may serve such a notice in respect of the goods; and whether or not a notice has been served under this subsection or that subsection, the trustee may, if he thinks fit, exercise the bankrupt's right of redemption in respect of any such goods.

(6) A notice served by the trustee under subsection (5) has the same effect as a notice served by the official receiver under section 285(5).

312 Obligation to surrender control to trustee

(1) The bankrupt shall deliver up to the trustee possession of any property, books, papers or other records of which he has possession or control and of which the trustee is required to take possession.

This is without prejudice to the general duties of the bankrupt under section 333 in this Chapter.

(2) If any of the following is in possession of any property, books, papers or other records of which the trustee is required to take possession, namely –

   (a)   the official receiver,
   (b)   a person who has ceased to be trustee of the bankrupt's estate, or
   (c)   a person who has been the supervisor of a voluntary arrangement approved in relation to the bankrupt under Part VIII,

the official receiver or, as the case may be, that person shall deliver up possession of the property, books, papers or records to the trustee.

(3) Any banker or agent of the bankrupt or any other person who holds any property to the account of, or for, the bankrupt shall pay or deliver to the trustee all property in his possession or under his control which forms part of the bankrupt's estate and which he is not by law entitled to retain as against the bankrupt or trustee.

(4) If any person without reasonable excuse fails to comply with any obligation imposed by this section, he is guilty of a contempt of court and liable to be punished accordingly (in addition to any other punishment to which he may be subject).

313 Charge on bankrupt's home

(1) Where any property consisting of an interest in a dwelling house which is occupied by the bankrupt or by his spouse or former spouse or by his civil partner or former civil partner is comprised in the bankrupt's estate and the trustee is, for any reason, unable for the time being to realise that property, the trustee may apply to the court for an order imposing a charge on the property for the benefit of the bankrupt's estate.

(2) If on an application under this section the court imposes a charge on any property, the benefit of that charge shall be comprised in the bankrupt's estate

and is enforceable, up to the charged value from time to time, for the payment of any amount which is payable otherwise than to the bankrupt out of the estate and of interest on that amount at the prescribed rate.

(2A) In subsection (2) the charged value means –

  (a) the amount specified in the charging order as the value of the bankrupt's interest in the property at the date of the order, plus
  (b) interest on that amount from the date of the charging order at the prescribed rate.

(2B) In determining the value of an interest for the purposes of this section the court shall disregard any matter which it is required to disregard by the rules.

(3) An order under this section made in respect of property vested in the trustee shall provide, in accordance with the rules, for the property to cease to be comprised in the bankrupt's estate and, subject to the charge (and any prior charge), to vest in the bankrupt.

(4) Subsections (1) and (2) and (4) to (6) of section 3 of the Charging Orders Act 1979 (supplemental provisions with respect to charging orders) have effect in relation to orders under this section as in relation to charging orders under that Act.

(5) But an order under section 3(5) of that Act may not vary a charged value.

Amendments—Enterprise Act 2002, s 261(2)(a), (b), (c); Civil Partnership Act 2004, s 261(1), Sch 27, para 114.

313A Low value home: application for sale, possession or charge

(1) This section applies where –

  (a) property comprised in the bankrupt's estate consists of an interest in a dwelling-house which at the date of the bankruptcy was the sole or principal residence of –
    (i)   the bankrupt,
    (ii) the bankrupt's spouse or civil partner, or
    (iii) a former spouse or former civil partner of the bankrupt, and
  (b) the trustee applies for an order for the sale of the property, for an order for possession of the property or for an order under section 313 in respect of the property.

(2) The court shall dismiss the application if the value of the interest is below the amount prescribed for the purposes of this subsection.

(3) In determining the value of an interest for the purposes of this section the court shall disregard any matter which it is required to disregard by the order which prescribes the amount for the purposes of subsection (2).

Amendments—Inserted by the Enterprise Act 2002, s 261(3); amended by Civil Partnership Act 2004, s 261(1), Sch 27, para 115.

314 Powers of trustee

(1) The trustee may –

    (a)   with the permission of the creditors' committee or the court, exercise any of the powers specified in Part I of Schedule 5 to this Act, and

    (b)   without that permission, exercise any of the general powers specified in Part II of that Schedule.

(2) With the permission of the creditors' committee or the court, the trustee may appoint the bankrupt –

    (a)   to superintend the management of his estate or any part of it,

    (b)   to carry on his business (if any) for the benefit of his creditors, or

    (c)   in any other respect to assist in administering the estate in such manner and on such terms as the trustee may direct.

(3) A permission given for the purposes of subsection (1)(a) or (2) shall not be a general permission but shall relate to a particular proposed exercise of the power in question; and a person dealing with the trustee in good faith and for value is not to be concerned to enquire whether any permission required in either case has been given.

(4) Where the trustee has done anything without the permission required by subsection (1)(a) or (2), the court or the creditors' committee may, for the purpose of enabling him to meet his expenses out of the bankrupt's estate, ratify what the trustee has done.

But the committee shall not do so unless it is satisfied that the trustee has acted in a case of urgency and has sought its ratification without undue delay.

(5) Part III of Schedule 5 to this Act has effect with respect to the things which the trustee is able to do for the purposes of, or in connection with, the exercise of any of his powers under any of this Group of Parts.

(6) Where the trustee (not being the official receiver) in exercise of the powers conferred on him by any provision in this Group of Parts –

    (a)   disposes of any property comprised in the bankrupt's estate to an associate of the bankrupt, or

    (b)   employs a solicitor,

he shall, if there is for the time being a creditors' committee, give notice to the committee of that exercise of his powers.

(7) Without prejudice to the generality of subsection (5) and Part III of Schedule 5, the trustee may, if he thinks fit, at any time summon a general meeting of the bankrupt's creditors.

Subject to the preceding provisions in this Group of Parts, he shall summon such a meeting if he is requested to do so by a creditor of the bankrupt and the request is made with the concurrence of not less than one-tenth, in value, of the bankrupt's creditors (including the creditor making the request).

(8) Nothing in this Act is to be construed as restricting the capacity of the trustee to exercise any of his powers outside England and Wales.

Disclaimer of onerous property

315 Disclaimer (general power)

(1) Subject as follows, the trustee may, by the giving of the prescribed notice, disclaim any onerous property and may do so notwithstanding that he has taken possession of it, endeavoured to sell it or otherwise exercised rights of ownership in relation to it.

(2) The following is onerous property for the purposes of this section, that is to say –

   (a)   any unprofitable contract, and
   (b)   any other property comprised in the bankrupt's estate which is unsaleable or not readily saleable, or is such that it may give rise to a liability to pay money or perform any other onerous act.

(3) A disclaimer under this section –

   (a)   operates so as to determine, as from the date of the disclaimer, the rights, interests and liabilities of the bankrupt and his estate in or in respect of the property disclaimed, and
   (b)   discharges the trustee from all personal liability in respect of that property as from the commencement of his trusteeship,

but does not, except so far as is necessary for the purpose of releasing the bankrupt, the bankrupt's estate and the trustee from any liability, affect the rights or liabilities of any other person.

(4) A notice of disclaimer shall not be given under this section in respect of any property that has been claimed for the estate under section 307 (after-acquired property) or 308 (personal property of bankrupt exceeding reasonable replacement value) or 308A, except with the leave of the court.

(5) Any person sustaining loss or damage in consequence of the operation of a disclaimer under this section is deemed to be a creditor of the bankrupt to the extent of the loss or damage and accordingly may prove for the loss or damage as a bankruptcy debt.

Amendments—Housing Act 1988, s 117(4).

316 Notice requiring trustee's decision

(1) Notice of disclaimer shall not be given under section 315 in respect of any property if –

   (a)   a person interested in the property has applied in writing to the trustee or one of his predecessors as trustee requiring the trustee or that predecessor to decide whether he will disclaim or not, and

(b)   the period of 28 days beginning with the day on which that application was made has expired without a notice of disclaimer having been given under section 315 in respect of that property.

(2) The trustee is deemed to have adopted any contract which by virtue of this section he is not entitled to disclaim.

317 Disclaimer of leaseholds

(1) The disclaimer of any property of a leasehold nature does not take effect unless a copy of the disclaimer has been served (so far as the trustee is aware of their addresses) on every person claiming under the bankrupt as underlessee or mortgagee and either –

(a)   no application under section 320 below is made with respect to the property before the end of the period of 14 days beginning with the day on which the last notice served under this subsection was served, or

(b)   where such an application has been made, the court directs that the disclaimer is to take effect.

(2) Where the court gives a direction under subsection (1)(b) it may also, instead of or in addition to any order it makes under section 320, make such orders with respect to fixtures, tenant's improvements and other matters arising out of the lease as it thinks fit.

318 Disclaimer of dwelling house

Without prejudice to section 317, the disclaimer of any property in a dwelling house does not take effect unless a copy of the disclaimer has been served (so far as the trustee is aware of their addresses) on every person in occupation of or claiming a right to occupy the dwelling house and either –

(a)   no application under section 320 is made with respect to the property before the end of the period of 14 days beginning with the day on which the last notice served under this section was served, or

(b)   where such an application has been made, the court directs that the disclaimer is to take effect.

319 Disclaimer of land subject to rentcharge

(1) The following applies where, in consequence of the disclaimer under section 315 of any land subject to a rentcharge, that land vests by operation of law in the Crown or any other person (referred to in the next subsection as 'the proprietor').

(2) The proprietor, and the successors in title of the proprietor, are not subject to any personal liability in respect of any sums becoming due under the rentcharge, except sums becoming due after the proprietor, or some person claiming under or through the proprietor, has taken possession or control of the land or has entered into occupation of it.

320 Court order vesting disclaimed property

(1) This section and the next apply where the trustee has disclaimed property under section 315.

(2) An application may be made to the court under this section by –

  (a)   any person who claims an interest in the disclaimed property,
  (b)   any person who is under any liability in respect of the disclaimed property, not being a liability discharged by the disclaimer, or
  (c)   where the disclaimed property is property in a dwelling-house, any person who at the time when the bankruptcy petition was presented was in occupation of or entitled to occupy the dwelling house.

(3) Subject as follows in this section and the next, the court may, on an application under this section, make an order on such terms as it thinks fit for the vesting of the disclaimed property in, or for its delivery to –

  (a)   a person entitled to it or a trustee for such a person,
  (b)   a person subject to such a liability as is mentioned in subsection (2)(b) or a trustee for such a person, or
  (c)   where the disclaimed property is property in a dwelling-house, any person who at the time when the bankruptcy petition was presented was in occupation of or entitled to occupy the dwelling house.

(4) The court shall not make an order by virtue of subsection (3)(b) except where it appears to the court that it would be just to do so for the purpose of compensating the person subject to the liability in respect of the disclaimer.

(5) The effect of any order under this section shall be taken into account in assessing for the purposes of section 315(5) the extent of any loss or damage sustained by any person in consequence of the disclaimer.

(6) An order under this section vesting property in any person need not be completed by any conveyance, assignment or transfer.

321 Order under s 320 in respect of leaseholds

(1) The court shall not make an order under section 320 vesting property of a leasehold nature in any person, except on terms making that person –

  (a)   subject to the same liabilities and obligations as the bankrupt was subject to under the lease on the day the bankruptcy petition was presented, or
  (b)   if the court thinks fit, subject to the same liabilities and obligations as that person would be subject to if the lease had been assigned to him on that day.

(2) For the purposes of an order under section 320 relating to only part of any property comprised in a lease, the requirements of subsection (1) apply as if the lease comprised only the property to which the order relates.

(3) Where subsection (1) applies and no person is willing to accept an order under section 320 on the terms required by that subsection, the court may (by

order under section 320) vest the estate or interest of the bankrupt in the property in any person who is liable (whether personally or in a representative capacity and whether alone or jointly with the bankrupt) to perform the lessee's covenants in the lease.

The court may by virtue of this subsection vest that estate and interest in such a person freed and discharged from all estates, incumbrances and interests created by the bankrupt.

(4) Where subsection (1) applies and a person declines to accept any order under section 320, that person shall be excluded from all interest in the property.

****

329 Debts to spouse or civil partner

(1) This section applies to bankruptcy debts owed in respect of credit provided by a person who (whether or not the bankrupt's spouse or civil partner at the time the credit was provided) was the bankrupt's spouse or civil partner at the commencement of the bankruptcy.

(2) Such debts –

(a)   rank in priority after the debts and interest required to be paid in pursuance of section 328(3) and (4), and

(b)   are payable with interest at the rate specified in section 328(5) in respect of the period during which they have been outstanding since the commencement of the bankruptcy;

and the interest payable under paragraph (b) has the same priority as the debts on which it is payable.

Amendments—Civil Partnership Act 2004, s 261(1), Sch 27, para 116.

****

332 Saving for bankrupt's home

(1) This section applies where –

(a)   there is comprised in the bankrupt's estate property consisting of an interest in a dwelling house which is occupied by the bankrupt or by his spouse or former spouse or by his civil partner or former civil partner, and

(b)   the trustee has been unable for any reason to realise that property.

(2) The trustee shall not summon a meeting under section 331 unless either –

(a)   the court has made an order under section 313 imposing a charge on that property for the benefit of the bankrupt's estate, or

(b)   the court has declined, on an application under that section, to make such an order, or

(c)   the Secretary of State has issued a certificate to the trustee stating that it would be inappropriate or inexpedient for such an application to be made in the case in question.

Amendments—Civil Partnership Act 2004, s 261(1), Sch 27, para 117.

Supplemental

333 Duties of bankrupt in relation to trustee

(1) The bankrupt shall –

(a)   give to the trustee such information as to his affairs,
(b)   attend on the trustee at such times, and
(c)   do all such other things,

as the trustee may for the purposes of carrying out his functions under any of this Group of Parts reasonably require.

(2) Where at any time after the commencement of the bankruptcy any property is acquired by, or devolves upon, the bankrupt or there is an increase of the bankrupt's income, the bankrupt shall, within the prescribed period, give the trustee notice of the property or, as the case may be, of the increase.

(3) Subsection (1) applies to a bankrupt after his discharge.

(4) If the bankrupt without reasonable excuse fails to comply with any obligation imposed by this section, he is guilty of a contempt of court and liable to be punished accordingly (in addition to any other punishment to which he may be subject).

334 Stay of distribution in case of second bankruptcy

(1) This section and the next apply where a bankruptcy order is made against an undischarged bankrupt; and in both sections –

(a)   'the later bankruptcy' means the bankruptcy arising from that order,
(b)   'the earlier bankruptcy' means the bankruptcy (or, as the case may be, most recent bankruptcy) from which the bankrupt has not been discharged at the commencement of the later bankruptcy, and
(c)   'the existing trustee' means the trustee (if any) of the bankrupt's estate for the purposes of the earlier bankruptcy.

(2) Where the existing trustee has been given the prescribed notice of the presentation of the petition for the later bankruptcy, any distribution or other disposition by him of anything to which the next subsection applies, if made after the giving of the notice, is void except to the extent that it was made with the consent of the court or is or was subsequently ratified by the court.

This is without prejudice to section 284 (restrictions on dispositions of property following bankruptcy order).

(3) This subsection applies to –

(a) any property which is vested in the existing trustee under section 307(3) (after-acquired property);

(b) any money paid to the existing trustee in pursuance of an income payments order under section 310; and

(c) any property or money which is, or in the hands of the existing trustee represents, the proceeds of sale or application of property or money falling within paragraph (a) or (b) of this subsection.

335 Adjustment between earlier and later bankruptcy estates

(1) With effect from the commencement of the later bankruptcy anything to which section 334(3) applies which, immediately before the commencement of that bankruptcy, is comprised in the bankrupt's estate for the purposes of the earlier bankruptcy is to be treated as comprised in the bankrupt's estate for the purposes of the later bankruptcy and, until there is a trustee of that estate, is to be dealt with by the existing trustee in accordance with the rules.

(2) Any sums which in pursuance of an income payments order under section 310 are payable after the commencement of the later bankruptcy to the existing trustee shall form part of the bankrupt's estate for the purposes of the later bankruptcy; and the court may give such consequential directions for the modification of the order as it thinks fit.

(3) Anything comprised in a bankrupt's estate by virtue of subsection (1) or (2) is so comprised subject to a first charge in favour of the existing trustee for any bankruptcy expenses incurred by him in relation thereto.

(4) Except as provided above and in section 334, property which is, or by virtue of section 308 (personal property of bankrupt exceeding reasonable replacement value) or section 308A (vesting in trustee of certain tenancies) is capable of being, comprised in the bankrupt's estate for the purposes of the earlier bankruptcy, or of any bankruptcy prior to it, shall not be comprised in his estate for the purposes of the later bankruptcy.

(5) The creditors of the bankrupt in the earlier bankruptcy and the creditors of the bankrupt in any bankruptcy prior to the earlier one, are not to be creditors of his in the later bankruptcy in respect of the same debts; but the existing trustee may prove in the later bankruptcy for –

(a) the unsatisfied balance of the debts (including any debt under this subsection) provable against the bankrupt's estate in the earlier bankruptcy;

(b) any interest payable on that balance; and

(c) any unpaid expenses of the earlier bankruptcy.

(6) Any amount provable under subsection (5) ranks in priority after all the other debts provable in the later bankruptcy and after interest on those debts and, accordingly, shall not be paid unless those debts and that interest have first been paid in full.

Amendments—Housing Act 1988, s 140, Sch 17, Part I, para 74.

Chapter V
Effect of Bankruptcy on Certain Rights, Transactions, Etc

Rights under trusts of land

335A Rights under trusts of land

(1) Any application by a trustee of a bankrupt's estate under section 14 of the Trusts of Land and Appointment of Trustees Act 1996 (powers of court in relation to trusts of land) for an order under that section for the sale of land shall be made to the court having jurisdiction in relation to the bankruptcy.

(2) On such an application the court shall make such order as it thinks just and reasonable having regard to –

  (a)   the interests of the bankrupt's creditors;
  (b)   where the application is made in respect of land which includes a dwelling house which is or has been the home of the bankrupt or the bankrupt's spouse or civil partner or former spouse or former civil partner –
    (i)   the conduct of the spouse, civil partner, former spouse or former civil partner, so far as contributing to the bankruptcy,
    (ii)   the needs and financial resources of the spouse, civil partner, former spouse or former civil partner, and
    (iii) the needs of any children; and
  (c)   all the circumstances of the case other than the needs of the bankrupt.

(3) Where such an application is made after the end of the period of one year beginning with the first vesting under Chapter IV of this Part of the bankrupt's estate in a trustee, the court shall assume, unless the circumstances of the case are exceptional, that the interests of the bankrupt's creditors outweigh all other considerations.

(4) The powers conferred on the court by this section are exercisable on an application whether it is made before or after the commencement of this section.

Amendments—Inserted by the Trusts of Land and Appointment of Trustees Act 1996, s 25(1), Sch 3, para 23; amended by Civil Partnership Act 2004, s 261(1), Sch 27, para 118.

Rights of occupation

336 Rights of occupation etc of bankrupt's spouse or civil partner

(1) Nothing occurring in the initial period of the bankruptcy (that is to say, the period beginning with the day of the presentation of the petition for the bankruptcy order and ending with the vesting of the bankrupt's estate in a trustee) is to be taken as having given rise to any home rights under Part IV of the Family Law Act 1996 in relation to a dwelling house comprised in the bankrupt's estate.

(2) Where a spouse's or civil partner's home rights under the Act of 1996 are a charge on the estate or interest of the other spouse or civil partner, or of trustees for the other spouse or civil partner, and the other spouse or civil partner is adjudged bankrupt –

(a) the charge continues to subsist notwithstanding the bankruptcy and, subject to the provisions of that Act, binds the trustee of the bankrupt's estate and persons deriving title under that trustee, and

(b) any application for an order under section 33 of that Act shall be made to the court having jurisdiction in relation to the bankruptcy.

(3) (Repealed)

(4) On such an application as is mentioned in subsection (2) the court shall make such order under section 33 of the Act of 1996 as it thinks just and reasonable having regard to –

(a) the interests of the bankrupt's creditors,

(b) the conduct of the spouse or former spouse or civil partner or former civil partner, so far as contributing to the bankruptcy,

(c) the needs and financial resources of the spouse or former spouse or civil partner or former civil partner,

(d) the needs of any children, and

(e) all the circumstances of the case other than the needs of the bankrupt.

(5) Where such an application is made after the end of the period of one year beginning with the first vesting under Chapter IV of this Part of the bankrupt's estate in a trustee, the court shall assume, unless the circumstances of the case are exceptional, that the interests of the bankrupt's creditors outweigh all other considerations.

Amendments—Family Law Act 1996, s 66(1), Sch 8, para 57(2), (3)(a), (b), (4); Trusts of Land and Appointment of Trustees Act 1996, s 25(2), Sch 4; Civil Partnership Act 2004, s 82, Sch 9.

337 Rights of occupation of bankrupt

(1) This section applies where –

(a) a person who is entitled to occupy a dwelling house by virtue of a beneficial estate or interest is adjudged bankrupt, and

(b) any persons under the age of 18 with whom that person had at some time occupied that dwelling house had their home with that person at the time when the bankruptcy petition was presented and at the commencement of the bankruptcy.

(2) Whether or not the bankrupt's spouse or civil partner (if any) has home rights under Part IV of the Family Law Act 1996 –

(a) the bankrupt has the following rights as against the trustee of his estate –

(i) if in occupation, a right not to be evicted or excluded from the dwelling house or any part of it, except with the leave of the court,

(ii)   if not in occupation, a right with the leave of the court to enter into and occupy the dwelling house, and

(b)   the bankrupt's rights are a charge, having the like priority as an equitable interest created immediately before the commencement of the bankruptcy, on so much of his estate or interest in the dwelling house as vests in the trustee.

(3) The Act of 1996 has effect, with the necessary modifications, as if –

(a)   the rights conferred by paragraph (a) of subsection (2) were home rights under that Act,

(b)   any application for such leave as is mentioned in that paragraph were an application for an order under section 33 of that Act, and

(c)   any charge under paragraph (b) of that subsection on the estate or interest of the trustee were a charge under that Act on the estate or interest of a spouse or civil partner.

(4) Any application for leave such as is mentioned in subsection (2)(a) or otherwise by virtue of this section for an order under section 33 of the Act of 1996 shall be made to the court having jurisdiction in relation to the bankruptcy.

(5) On such an application the court shall make such order under section 33 of the Act of 1996 as it thinks just and reasonable having regard to the interests of the creditors, to the bankrupt's financial resources, to the needs of the children and to all the circumstances of the case other than the needs of the bankrupt.

(6) Where such an application is made after the end of the period of one year beginning with the vesting (under Chapter IV of this Part) of the bankrupt's estate in a trustee, the court shall assume, unless the circumstances of the case are exceptional, that the interests of the bankrupt's creditors outweigh all other considerations.

Amendments—Family Law Act 1996, s 66(1), Sch 8, para 58(2), (3), (4); Civil Partnership Act 2004, s 82, Sch 9.

338 Payments in respect of premises occupied by bankrupt

Where any premises comprised in a bankrupt's estate are occupied by him (whether by virtue of the preceding section or otherwise) on condition that he makes payments towards satisfying any liability arising under a mortgage of the premises or otherwise towards the outgoings of the premises, the bankrupt does not, by virtue of those payments, acquire any interest in the premises.

339 Transactions at an undervalue

(1) Subject as follows in this section and sections 341 and 342, where an individual is adjudged bankrupt and he has at a relevant time (defined in section 341) entered into a transaction with any person at an undervalue, the trustee of the bankrupt's estate may apply to the court for an order under this section.

(2) The court shall, on such an application, make such order as it thinks fit for restoring the position to what it would have been if that individual had not entered into that transaction.

(3) For the purposes of this section and sections 341 and 342, an individual enters into a transaction with a person at an undervalue if –

(a) he makes a gift to that person or he otherwise enters into a transaction with that person on terms that provide for him to receive no consideration,

(b) he enters into a transaction with that person in consideration of marriage or the formation of a civil partnership, or

(c) he enters into a transaction with that person for a consideration the value of which, in money or money's worth, is significantly less than the value, in money or money's worth, of the consideration provided by the individual.

Amendments—Civil Partnership Act 2004, s 261(1), Sch 27, para 119.

340 Preferences

(1) Subject as follows in this and the next two sections, where an individual is adjudged bankrupt and he has at a relevant time (defined in section 341) given a preference to any person, the trustee of the bankrupt's estate may apply to the court for an order under this section.

(2) The court shall, on such an application, make such order as it thinks fit for restoring the position to what it would have been if that individual had not given that preference.

(3) For the purposes of this and the next two sections, an individual gives a preference to a person if –

(a) that person is one of the individual's creditors or a surety or guarantor for any of his debts or other liabilities, and

(b) the individual does anything or suffers anything to be done which (in either case) has the effect of putting that person into a position which, in the event of the individual's bankruptcy, will be better than the position he would have been in if that thing had not been done.

(4) The court shall not make an order under this section in respect of a preference given to any person unless the individual who gave the preference was influenced in deciding to give it by a desire to produce in relation to that person the effect mentioned in subsection (3)(b) above.

(5) An individual who has given a preference to a person who, at the time the preference was given, was an associate of his (otherwise than by reason only of being his employee) is presumed, unless the contrary is shown, to have been influenced in deciding to give it by such a desire as is mentioned in subsection (4).

(6) The fact that something has been done in pursuance of the order of a court does not, without more, prevent the doing or suffering of that thing from constituting the giving of a preference.

341 'Relevant time' under ss 339, 340

(1) Subject as follows, the time at which an individual enters into a transaction at an undervalue or gives a preference is a relevant time if the transaction is entered into or the preference given –

- (a)   in the case of a transaction at an undervalue, at a time in the period of 5 years ending with the day of the presentation of the bankruptcy petition on which the individual is adjudged bankrupt,
- (b)   in the case of a preference which is not a transaction at an undervalue and is given to a person who is an associate of the individual (otherwise than by reason only of being his employee), at a time in the period of 2 years ending with that day, and
- (c)   in any other case of a preference which is not a transaction at an undervalue, at a time in the period of 6 months ending with that day.

(2) Where an individual enters into a transaction at an undervalue or gives a preference at a time mentioned in paragraph (a), (b) or (c) of subsection (1) (not being, in the case of a transaction at an undervalue, a time less than 2 years before the end of the period mentioned in paragraph (a)), that time is not a relevant time for the purposes of sections 339 and 340 unless the individual –

- (a)   is insolvent at that time, or
- (b)   becomes insolvent in consequence of the transaction or preference;

but the requirements of this subsection are presumed to be satisfied, unless the contrary is shown, in relation to any transaction at an undervalue which is entered into by an individual with a person who is an associate of his (otherwise than by reason only of being his employee).

(3) For the purposes of subsection (2), an individual is insolvent if –

- (a)   he is unable to pay his debts as they fall due, or
- (b)   the value of his assets is less than the amount of his liabilities, taking into account his contingent and prospective liabilities.

(4) A transaction entered into or preference given by a person who is subsequently adjudged bankrupt on a petition under section 264(1)(d) (criminal bankruptcy) is to be treated as having been entered into or given at a relevant time for the purposes of sections 339 and 340 if it was entered into or given at any time on or after the date specified for the purposes of this subsection in the criminal bankruptcy order on which the petition was based.

(5) No order shall be made under section 339 or 340 by virtue of subsection (4) of this section where an appeal is pending (within the meaning of section 277) against the individual's conviction of any offence by virtue of which the criminal bankruptcy order was made.

342 Orders under ss 339, 340

(1) Without prejudice to the generality of section 339(2) or 340(2), an order under either of those sections with respect to a transaction or preference entered into or given by an individual who is subsequently adjudged bankrupt may (subject as follows) –

(a) require any property transferred as part of the transaction, or in connection with the giving of the preference, to be vested in the trustee of the bankrupt's estate as part of that estate;

(b) require any property to be so vested if it represents in any person's hands the application either of the proceeds of sale of property so transferred or of money so transferred;

(c) release or discharge (in whole or in part) any security given by the individual;

(d) require any person to pay, in respect of benefits received by him from the individual, such sums to the trustee of his estate as the court may direct;

(e) provide for any surety or guarantor whose obligations to any person were released or discharged (in whole or in part) under the transaction or by the giving of the preference to be under such new or revived obligations to that person as the court thinks appropriate;

(f) provide for security to be provided for the discharge of any obligation imposed by or arising under the order, for such an obligation to be charged on any property and for the security or charge to have the same priority as a security or charge released or discharged (in whole or in part) under the transaction or by the giving of the preference; and

(g) provide for the extent to which any person whose property is vested by the order in the trustee of the bankrupt's estate, or on whom obligations are imposed by the order, is to be able to prove in the bankruptcy for debts or other liabilities which arose from, or were released or discharged (in whole or in part) under or by, the transaction or the giving of the preference.

(2) An order under section 339 or 340 may affect the property of, or impose any obligation on, any person whether or not he is the person with whom the individual in question entered into the transaction or, as the case may be, the person to whom the preference was given; but such an order –

(a) shall not prejudice any interest in property which was acquired from a person other than that individual and was acquired in good faith and for value, or prejudice any interest deriving from such an interest, and

(b) shall not require a person who received a benefit from the transaction or preference in good faith and for value to pay a sum to the trustee of the bankrupt's estate, except where he was a party to the transaction or the payment is to be in respect of a preference given to that person at a time when he was a creditor of that individual.

(2A) Where a person has acquired an interest in property from a person other than the individual in question, or has received a benefit from the transaction or preference, and at the time of that acquisition or receipt –

(a)   he had notice of the relevant surrounding circumstances and of the relevant proceedings, or

(b)   he was an associate of, or was connected with, either the individual in question or the person with whom that individual entered into the transaction or to whom that individual gave the preference,

then, unless the contrary is shown, it shall be presumed for the purposes of paragraph (a) or (as the case may be) paragraph (b) of subsection (2) that the interest was acquired or the benefit was received otherwise than in good faith.

(3) Any sums required to be paid to the trustee in accordance with an order under section 339 or 340 shall be comprised in the bankrupt's estate.

(4) For the purposes of subsection (2A)(a), the relevant surrounding circumstances are (as the case may require) –

(a)   the fact that the individual in question entered into the transaction at an undervalue; or

(b)   the circumstances which amounted to the giving of the preference by the individual in question.

(5) For the purposes of subsection (2A)(a), a person has notice of the relevant proceedings if he has notice –

(a)   of the fact that the petition on which the individual in question is adjudged bankrupt has been presented; or

(b)   of the fact that the individual in question has been adjudged bankrupt.

(6) Section 249 in Part VII of this Act shall apply for the purposes of subsection (2A)(b) as it applies for the purposes of the first Group of Parts.

Amendments—Insolvency (No 2) Act 1994, s 2(1), (2), (3).

342A Recovery of excessive pension contributions

(1) Where an individual who is adjudged bankrupt –

(a)   has rights under an approved pension arrangement, or

(b)   has excluded rights under an unapproved pension arrangement,

the trustee of the bankrupt's estate may apply to the court for an order under this section.

(2) If the court is satisfied –

(a)   that the rights under the arrangement are to any extent, and whether directly or indirectly, the fruits of relevant contributions, and

(b)   that the making of any of the relevant contributions ('the excessive contributions') has unfairly prejudiced the individual's creditors,

the court may make such order as it thinks fit for restoring the position to what it would have been had the excessive contributions not been made.

(3) Subsection (4) applies where the court is satisfied that the value of the rights under the arrangement is, as a result of rights of the individual under the arrangement or any other pension arrangement having at any time become subject to a debit under section 29(1)(a) of the Welfare Reform and Pensions Act 1999 (debits giving effect to pension-sharing), less than it would otherwise have been.

(4) Where this subsection applies –

   (a)   any relevant contributions which were represented by the rights which became subject to the debit shall, for the purposes of subsection (2), be taken to be contributions of which the rights under the arrangement are the fruits, and

   (b)   where the relevant contributions represented by the rights under the arrangement (including those so represented by virtue of paragraph (a)) are not all excessive contributions, relevant contributions which are represented by the rights under the arrangement otherwise than by virtue of paragraph (a) shall be treated as excessive contributions before any which are so represented by virtue of that paragraph.

(5) In subsections (2) to (4) 'relevant contributions' means contributions to the arrangement or any other pension arrangement –

   (a)   which the individual has at any time made on his own behalf, or

   (b)   which have at any time been made on his behalf.

(6) The court shall, in determining whether it is satisfied under subsection (2)(b), consider in particular –

   (a)   whether any of the contributions were made for the purpose of putting assets beyond the reach of the individual's creditors or any of them, and

   (b)   whether the total amount of any contributions –

      (i)   made by or on behalf of the individual to pension arrangements, and

      (ii)   represented (whether directly or indirectly) by rights under approved pension arrangements or excluded rights under unapproved pension arrangements,

   is an amount which is excessive in view of the individual's circumstances when those contributions were made.

(7) For the purposes of this section and sections 342B and 342C ('the recovery provisions'), rights of an individual under an unapproved pension arrangement are excluded rights if they are rights which are excluded from his estate by virtue of regulations under section 12 of the Welfare Reform and Pensions Act 1999.

(8) In the recovery provisions –

   'approved pension arrangement' has the same meaning as in section 11 of the Welfare Reform and Pensions Act 1999;

   'unapproved pension arrangement' has the same meaning as in section 12 of that Act.

Amendments—Welfare Reform and Pensions Act 1999, s 15.

342B Orders under section 342A

(1) Without prejudice to the generality of section 342A(2), an order under section 342A may include provision –

(a)   requiring the person responsible for the arrangement to pay an amount to the individual's trustee in bankruptcy,

(b)   adjusting the liabilities of the arrangement in respect of the individual,

(c)   adjusting any liabilities of the arrangement in respect of any other person that derive, directly or indirectly, from rights of the individual under the arrangement,

(d)   for the recovery by the person responsible for the arrangement (whether by deduction from any amount which that person is ordered to pay or otherwise) of costs incurred by that person in complying in the bankrupt's case with any requirement under section 342C(1) or in giving effect to the order.

(2) In subsection (1), references to adjusting the liabilities of the arrangement in respect of a person include (in particular) reducing the amount of any benefit or future benefit to which that person is entitled under the arrangement.

(3) In subsection (1)(c), the reference to liabilities of the arrangement does not include liabilities in respect of a person which result from giving effect to an order or provision falling within section 28(1) of the Welfare Reform and Pensions Act 1999 (pension sharing orders and agreements).

(4) The maximum amount which the person responsible for an arrangement may be required to pay by an order under section 342A is the lesser of –

(a)   the amount of the excessive contributions, and

(b)   the value of the individual's rights under the arrangement (if the arrangement is an approved pension arrangement) or of his excluded rights under the arrangement (if the arrangement is an unapproved pension arrangement).

(5) An order under section 342A which requires the person responsible for an arrangement to pay an amount ('the restoration amount') to the individual's trustee in bankruptcy must provide for the liabilities of the arrangement to be correspondingly reduced.

(6) For the purposes of subsection (5), liabilities are correspondingly reduced if the difference between –

(a)   the amount of the liabilities immediately before the reduction, and

(b)   the amount of the liabilities immediately after the reduction,

is equal to the restoration amount.

(7) An order under section 342A in respect of an arrangement –

(a)   shall be binding on the person responsible for the arrangement, and

(b)   overrides provisions of the arrangement to the extent that they conflict with the provisions of the order.

Amendments—Welfare Reform and Pensions Act 1999, s 15.

342C Orders under section 342A: supplementary

(1) The person responsible for –

(a)   an approved pension arrangement under which a bankrupt has rights,
(b)   an unapproved pension arrangement under which a bankrupt has excluded rights, or
(c)   a pension arrangement under which a bankrupt has at any time had rights,

shall, on the bankrupt's trustee in bankruptcy making a written request, provide the trustee with such information about the arrangement and rights as the trustee may reasonably require for, or in connection with, the making of applications under section 342A.

(2) Nothing in –

(a)   any provision of section 159 of the Pension Schemes Act 1993 or section 91 of the Pensions Act 1995 (which prevent assignment and the making of orders that restrain a person from receiving anything which he is prevented from assigning),
(b)   any provision of any enactment (whether passed or made before or after the passing of the Welfare Reform and Pensions Act 1999) corresponding to any of the provisions mentioned in paragraph (a), or
(c)   any provision of the arrangement in question corresponding to any of those provisions,

applies to a court exercising its powers under section 342A.

(3) Where any sum is required by an order under section 342A to be paid to the trustee in bankruptcy, that sum shall be comprised in the bankrupt's estate.

(4) Regulations may, for the purposes of the recovery provisions, make provision about the calculation and verification of –

(a)   any such value as is mentioned in section 342B(4)(b);
(b)   any such amounts as are mentioned in section 342B(6)(a) and (b).

(5) The power conferred by subsection (4) includes power to provide for calculation or verification –

(a)   in such manner as may, in the particular case, be approved by a prescribed person; or
(b)   in accordance with guidance from time to time prepared by a prescribed person.

(6) References in the recovery provisions to the person responsible for a pension arrangement are to –

(a)   the trustees, managers or provider of the arrangement, or

(b)   the person having functions in relation to the arrangement corresponding to those of a trustee, manager or provider.

(7) In this section and sections 342A and 342B –

'prescribed' means prescribed by regulations;
'the recovery provisions' means this section and sections 342A and 342B;
'regulations' means regulations made by the Secretary of State.

(8) Regulations under the recovery provisions may –

(a)   make different provision for different cases;
(b)   contain such incidental, supplemental and transitional provisions as appear to the Secretary of State necessary or expedient.

(9) Regulations under the recovery provisions shall be made by statutory instrument subject to annulment in pursuance of a resolution of either House of Parliament.

Amendments—Welfare Reform and Pensions Act 1999, s 15; Pensions Act 2007, s 17, Sch 5, para 3.

342D Recovery of excessive contributions in pension-sharing cases

(1) For the purposes of sections 339, 341 and 342, a pension-sharing transaction shall be taken –

(a)   to be a transaction, entered into by the transferor with the transferee, by which the appropriate amount is transferred by the transferor to the transferee; and
(b)   to be capable of being a transaction entered into at an undervalue only so far as it is a transfer of so much of the appropriate amount as is recoverable.

(2) For the purposes of sections 340 to 342, a pension-sharing transaction shall be taken –

(a)   to be something (namely a transfer of the appropriate amount to the transferee) done by the transferor; and
(b)   to be capable of being a preference given to the transferee only so far as it is a transfer of so much of the appropriate amount as is recoverable.

(3) If on an application under section 339 or 340 any question arises as to whether, or the extent to which, the appropriate amount in the case of a pension-sharing transaction is recoverable, the question shall be determined in accordance with subsections (4) to (8).

(4) The court shall first determine the extent (if any) to which the transferor's rights under the shared arrangement at the time of the transaction appear to have been (whether directly or indirectly) the fruits of contributions ('personal contributions') –

(a)   which the transferor has at any time made on his own behalf, or
(b)   which have at any time been made on the transferor's behalf,

to the shared arrangement or any other pension arrangement.

(5) Where it appears that those rights were to any extent the fruits of personal contributions, the court shall then determine the extent (if any) to which those rights appear to have been the fruits of personal contributions whose making has unfairly prejudiced the transferor's creditors ('the unfair contributions').

(6) If it appears to the court that the extent to which those rights were the fruits of the unfair contributions is such that the transfer of the appropriate amount could have been made out of rights under the shared arrangement which were not the fruits of the unfair contributions, then the appropriate amount is not recoverable.

(7) If it appears to the court that the transfer could not have been wholly so made, then the appropriate amount is recoverable to the extent to which it appears to the court that the transfer could not have been so made.

(8) In making the determination mentioned in subsection (5) the court shall consider in particular –

(a) whether any of the personal contributions were made for the purpose of putting assets beyond the reach of the transferor's creditors or any of them, and

(b) whether the total amount of any personal contributions represented, at the time the pension-sharing transaction was made, by rights under pension arrangements is an amount which is excessive in view of the transferor's circumstances when those contributions were made.

(9) In this section and sections 342E and 342F –

'appropriate amount', in relation to a pension-sharing transaction, means the appropriate amount in relation to that transaction for the purposes of section 29(1) of the Welfare Reform and Pensions Act 1999 (creation of pension credits and debits);

'pension-sharing transaction' means an order or provision falling within section 28(1) of the Welfare Reform and Pensions Act 1999 (orders and agreements which activate pension-sharing);

'shared arrangement', in relation to a pension-sharing transaction, means the pension arrangement to which the transaction relates;

'transferee', in relation to a pension-sharing transaction, means the person for whose benefit the transaction is made;

'transferor', in relation to a pension-sharing transaction, means the person to whose rights the transaction relates

Amendments—Welfare Reform and Pensions Act 1999, s 84(1), Sch 12, Pt II, paras 70, 71.

342E Orders under section 339 or 340 in respect of pension-sharing transactions

(1) This section and section 342F apply if the court is making an order under section 339 or 340 in a case where –

(a)   the transaction or preference is, or is any part of, a pension-sharing transaction, and

(b)   the transferee has rights under a pension arrangement ('the destination arrangement', which may be the shared arrangement or any other pension arrangement) that are derived, directly or indirectly, from the pension-sharing transaction.

(2) Without prejudice to the generality of section 339(2) or 340(2), or of section 342, the order may include provision –

(a)   requiring the person responsible for the destination arrangement to pay an amount to the transferor's trustee in bankruptcy,

(b)   adjusting the liabilities of the destination arrangement in respect of the transferee,

(c)   adjusting any liabilities of the destination arrangement in respect of any other person that derive, directly or indirectly, from rights of the transferee under the destination arrangement,

(d)   for the recovery by the person responsible for the destination arrangement (whether by deduction from any amount which that person is ordered to pay or otherwise) of costs incurred by that person in complying in the transferor's case with any requirement under section 342F(1) or in giving effect to the order,

(e)   for the recovery, from the transferor's trustee in bankruptcy, by the person responsible for a pension arrangement, of costs incurred by that person in complying in the transferor's case with any requirement under section 342F(2) or (3).

(3) In subsection (2), references to adjusting the liabilities of the destination arrangement in respect of a person include (in particular) reducing the amount of any benefit or future benefit to which that person is entitled under the arrangement.

(4) The maximum amount which the person responsible for the destination arrangement may be required to pay by the order is the smallest of –

(a)   so much of the appropriate amount as, in accordance with section 342D, is recoverable,

(b)   so much (if any) of the amount of the unfair contributions (within the meaning given by section 342D(5)) as is not recoverable by way of an order under section 342A containing provision such as is mentioned in section 342B(1)(a), and

(c)   the value of the transferee's rights under the destination arrangement so far as they are derived, directly or indirectly, from the pension-sharing transaction.

(5) If the order requires the person responsible for the destination arrangement to pay an amount ('the restoration amount') to the transferor's trustee in bankruptcy it must provide for the liabilities of the arrangement to be correspondingly reduced.

(6) For the purposes of subsection (5), liabilities are correspondingly reduced if the difference between –

(a) the amount of the liabilities immediately before the reduction, and

(b) the amount of the liabilities immediately after the reduction,

is equal to the restoration amount.

(7) The order –

(a) shall be binding on the person responsible for the destination arrangement, and

(b) overrides provisions of the destination arrangement to the extent that they conflict with the provisions of the order.

Amendments—Welfare Reform and Pensions Act 1999, s 84(1), Sch 12, Pt II, paras 70, 71.

342F Orders under section 339 or 340 in pension-sharing cases: supplementary

(1) On the transferor's trustee in bankruptcy making a written request to the person responsible for the destination arrangement, that person shall provide the trustee with such information about –

(a) the arrangement,

(b) the transferee's rights under it, and

(c) where the destination arrangement is the shared arrangement, the transferor's rights under it,

as the trustee may reasonably require for, or in connection with, the making of applications under sections 339 and 340.

(2) Where the shared arrangement is not the destination arrangement, the person responsible for the shared arrangement shall, on the transferor's trustee in bankruptcy making a written request to that person, provide the trustee with such information about –

(a) the arrangement, and

(b) the transferor's rights under it,

as the trustee may reasonably require for, or in connection with, the making of applications under sections 339 and 340.

(3) On the transferor's trustee in bankruptcy making a written request to the person responsible for any intermediate arrangement, that person shall provide the trustee with such information about –

(a) the arrangement, and

(b) the transferee's rights under it,

as the trustee may reasonably require for, or in connection with, the making of applications under sections 339 and 340.

(4) In subsection (3) 'intermediate arrangement' means a pension arrangement, other than the shared arrangement or the destination arrangement, in relation to which the following conditions are fulfilled –

(a) there was a time when the transferee had rights under the arrangement that were derived (directly or indirectly) from the pension-sharing transaction, and

(b) the transferee's rights under the destination arrangement (so far as derived from the pension-sharing transaction) are to any extent derived (directly or indirectly) from the rights mentioned in paragraph (a).

(5) Nothing in –

(a) any provision of section 159 of the Pension Schemes Act 1993 or section 91 of the Pensions Act 1995 (which prevent assignment and the making of orders which restrain a person from receiving anything which he is prevented from assigning),

(b) any provision of any enactment (whether passed or made before or after the passing of the Welfare Reform and Pensions Act 1999) corresponding to any of the provisions mentioned in paragraph (a), or

(c) any provision of the destination arrangement corresponding to any of those provisions,

applies to a court exercising its powers under section 339 or 340.

(6) Regulations may, for the purposes of sections 339 to 342, sections 342D and 342E and this section, make provision about the calculation and verification of –

(a) any such value as is mentioned in section 342E(4)(c);

(b) any such amounts as are mentioned in section 342E(6)(a) and (b).

(7) The power conferred by subsection (6) includes power to provide for calculation or verification –

(a) in such manner as may, in the particular case, be approved by a prescribed person; or

(b) in accordance with guidance from time to time prepared by a prescribed person .

(8) In section 342E and this section, references to the person responsible for a pension arrangement are to –

(a) the trustees, managers or provider of the arrangement, or

(b) the person having functions in relation to the arrangement corresponding to those of a trustee, manager or provider.

(9) In this section –

'prescribed' means prescribed by regulations;
'regulations' means regulations made by the Secretary of State.

(10) Regulations under this section may –

(a) make different provision for different cases;

(b) contain such incidental, supplemental and transitional provisions as appear to the Secretary of State necessary or expedient.

(11) Regulations under this section shall be made by statutory instrument subject to annulment in pursuance of a resolution of either House of Parliament.

Amendments—Welfare Reform and Pensions Act 1999, s 84(1), Sch 12, Pt II, paras 70, 71; Pensions Act 2007,s 17, Sch 5, para 4.

****

345 Contracts to which bankrupt is a party

(1) The following applies where a contract has been made with a person who is subsequently adjudged bankrupt.

(2) The court may, on the application of any other party to the contract, make an order discharging obligations under the contract on such terms as to payment by the applicant or the bankrupt of damages for non-performance or otherwise as appear to the court to be equitable.

(3) Any damages payable by the bankrupt by virtue of an order of the court under this section are provable as a bankruptcy debt.

(4) Where an undischarged bankrupt is a contractor in respect of any contract jointly with any person, that person may sue or be sued in respect of the contract without the joinder of the bankrupt.

****

350 Scheme of this Chapter

(1) Subject to section 360(3) below, this Chapter applies where the court has made a bankruptcy order on a bankruptcy petition.

(2) This Chapter applies whether or not the bankruptcy order is annulled, but proceedings for an offence under this Chapter shall not be instituted after the annulment.

(3) Without prejudice to his liability in respect of a subsequent bankruptcy, the bankrupt is not guilty of an offence under this Chapter in respect of anything done after his discharge; but nothing in this Group of Parts prevents the institution of proceedings against a discharged bankrupt for an offence committed before his discharge.

(3A) Subsection (3) is without prejudice to any provision of this Chapter which applies to a person in respect of whom a bankruptcy restrictions order is in force.

(4) It is not a defence in proceedings for an offence under this Chapter that anything relied on, in whole or in part, as constituting that offence was done outside England and Wales.

(5) Proceedings for an offence under this Chapter or under the rules shall not be instituted except by the Secretary of State or by or with the consent of the Director of Public Prosecutions.

(6) A person guilty of an offence under this Chapter is liable to imprisonment or a fine, or both.

Amendments—Enterprise Act 2002, s 257(3), Sch 21, para 2.

****

366 Inquiry into bankrupt's dealings and property

(1) At any time after a bankruptcy order has been made the court may, on the application of the official receiver or the trustee of the bankrupt's estate, summon to appear before it –

(a)   the bankrupt or the bankrupt's spouse or former spouse or civil partner or former civil partner,

(b)   any person known or believed to have any property comprised in the bankrupt's estate in his possession or to be indebted to the bankrupt,

(c)   any person appearing to the court to be able to give information concerning the bankrupt or the bankrupt's dealings, affairs or property.

The court may require any such person as is mentioned in paragraph (b) or (c) to submit an affidavit to the court containing an account of his dealings with the bankrupt or to produce any documents in his possession or under his control relating to the bankrupt or the bankrupt's dealings, affairs or property.

(2) Without prejudice to section 364, the following applies in a case where –

(a)   a person without reasonable excuse fails to appear before the court when he is summoned to do so under this section, or

(b)   there are reasonable grounds for believing that a person has absconded, or is about to abscond, with a view to avoiding his appearance before the court under this section.

(3) The court may, for the purpose of bringing that person and anything in his possession before the court, cause a warrant to be issued to a constable or prescribed officer of the court –

(a)   for the arrest of that person, and

(b)   for the seizure of any books, papers, records, money or goods in that person's possession.

(4) The court may authorise a person arrested under such a warrant to be kept in custody, and anything seized under such a warrant to be held, in accordance with the rules, until that person is brought before the court under the warrant or until such other time as the court may order.

Amendments—Civil Partnership Act 2004, s 261(1), Sch 27, para 120.

****

375 Appeals etc from courts exercising insolvency jurisdiction

(1) Every court having jurisdiction for the purposes of the Parts in this Group may review, rescind or vary any order made by it in the exercise of that jurisdiction.

(2) An appeal from a decision made in the exercise of jurisdiction for the purposes of those Parts by a county court or by a registrar in bankruptcy of

the High Court lies to a single judge of the High Court; and an appeal from a decision of that judge on such an appeal lies to the Court of Appeal.

(3) A county court is not, in the exercise of its jurisdiction for the purposes of those Parts, to be subject to be restrained by the order of any other court, and no appeal lies from its decision in the exercise of that jurisdiction except as provided by this section.

Amendments—Access to Justice Act 1999, s 106, Sch 15, Pt III.

****

382 'Bankruptcy debt', etc

(1) 'Bankruptcy debt', in relation to a bankrupt, means (subject to the next subsection) any of the following –

(a) any debt or liability to which he is subject at the commencement of the bankruptcy,

(b) any debt or liability to which he may become subject after the commencement of the bankruptcy (including after his discharge from bankruptcy) by reason of any obligation incurred before the commencement of the bankruptcy,

(c) any amount specified in pursuance of section 39(3)(c) of the Powers of Criminal Courts Act 1973 in any criminal bankruptcy order made against him before the commencement of the bankruptcy, and

(d) any interest provable as mentioned in section 322(2) in Chapter IV of Part IX.

(2) In determining for the purposes of any provision in this Group of Parts whether any liability in tort is a bankruptcy debt, the bankrupt is deemed to become subject to that liability by reason of an obligation incurred at the time when the cause of action accrued.

(3) For the purposes of references in this Group of Parts to a debt or liability, it is immaterial whether the debt or liability is present or future, whether it is certain or contingent or whether its amount is fixed or liquidated, or is capable of being ascertained by fixed rules or as a matter of opinion; and references in this Group of Parts to owing a debt are to be read accordingly.

(4) In this Group of Parts, except in so far as the context otherwise requires, 'liability' means (subject to subsection (3) above) a liability to pay money or money's worth, including any liability under an enactment, any liability for breach of trust, any liability in contract, tort or bailment and any liability arising out of an obligation to make restitution.

****

385 Miscellaneous definitions

(1) The following definitions have effect –

'the court', in relation to any matter, means the court to which, in accordance with section 373 in Part X and the rules, proceedings with respect to that matter are allocated or transferred;

'creditor's petition' means a bankruptcy petition under section 264(1)(a);

'criminal bankruptcy order' means an order under section 39(1) of the Powers of Criminal Courts Act 1973;

'debt' is to be construed in accordance with section 382(3);

'the debtor' –

    (za) in relation to a debt relief order or an application for such an order, has the same meaning as in Part 7A,

    (a) in relation to a proposal for the purposes of Part VIII, means the individual making or intending to make that proposal, and

    (b) in relation to a bankruptcy petition, means the individual to whom the petition relates;

'debtor's petition' means a bankruptcy petition presented by the debtor himself under section 264(1)(b);

'debt relief order' means an order made by the official receiver under Part 7A

'dwelling house' includes any building or part of a building which is occupied as a dwelling and any yard, garden, garage or outhouse belonging to the dwelling house and occupied with it;

'estate', in relation to a bankrupt is to be construed in accordance with section 283 in Chapter II of Part IX;

'family', in relation to a bankrupt, means the persons (if any) who are living with him and are dependent on him;

'insolvency administration order' means an order for the administration in bankruptcy of the insolvent estate of a deceased debtor (being an individual at the date of his death);

'insolvency administration petition' means a petition for an insolvency administration order;

'the Rules' means the Insolvency Rules 1986.

'secured' and related expressions are to be construed in accordance with section 383; and

'the trustee', in relation to a bankruptcy and the bankrupt, means the trustee of the bankrupt's estate.

(2) References in this Group of Parts to a person's affairs include his business, if any.

Amendments—Criminal Justice Act 1988, s 170(2), Sch 16; Tribunals, Courts and Enforcement Act 2007, s 108(3), Sch 20, Pt 1, paras 1, 5.

****

389A Authorisation of nominees and supervisors

(1) Section 389 does not apply to a person acting, in relation to a voluntary arrangement proposed or approved under Part I or Part VIII, as nominee or supervisor if he is authorised so to act.

(2) For the purposes of subsection (1) and those Parts, an individual to whom subsection (3) does not apply is authorised to act as nominee or supervisor in relation to such an arrangement if –

(a) he is a member of a body recognised for the purpose by the Secretary of State or of a body recognised for the purpose of Article 348A(2)(a) of the Insolvency (Northern Ireland) Order 1989 by the Department of Enterprise, Trade and Investment for Northern Ireland, and

(b) there is in force security (in Scotland, caution) for the proper performance of his functions and that security or caution meets the prescribed requirements with respect to his so acting in relation to the arrangement.

(3) This subsection applies to a person if –

(a) he has been adjudged bankrupt or sequestration of his estate has been awarded and (in either case) he has not been discharged,

(b) he is subject to a disqualification order made or a disqualification undertaking accepted under the Company Directors Disqualification Act 1986 or the Company Directors Disqualification (Northern Ireland) Order 2002,

(c) he is a patient within the meaning of section 329(1) of the Mental Health (Care and Treatment) (Scotland) Act 2003, or

(d) he lacks capacity (withing the meaning of the Mental Health Capacity Act 2005) to act as nominee of supervisor.

(4) The Secretary of State may by order declare a body which appears to him to fall within subsection (5) to be a recognised body for the purposes of subsection (2)(a).

(5) A body may be recognised if it maintains and enforces rules for securing that its members –

(a) are fit and proper persons to act as nominees or supervisors, and

(b) meet acceptable requirements as to education and practical training and experience.

(6) For the purposes of this section, a person is a member of a body only if he is subject to its rules when acting as nominee or supervisor (whether or not he is in fact a member of the body).

(7) An order made under subsection (4) in relation to a body may be revoked by a further order if it appears to the Secretary of State that the body no longer falls within subsection (5).

(8) An order of the Secretary of State under this section has effect from such date as is specified in the order; and any such order revoking a previous order may make provision for members of the body in question to continue to be treated as members of a recognised body for a specified period after the revocation takes effect.

Amendments—Inserted by Insolvency Act 2000, s 4(1), (4); amended by SI 2004/1941; SI 2005/2078; Mental Capacity Act 2005, s 67 (1), (2), Sch 6; SI 2009/1941; SI 2009/3081.

****

PART XVI
PROVISIONS AGAINST DEBT AVOIDANCE (ENGLAND AND WALES ONLY)

423 Transactions defrauding creditors

(1) This section relates to transactions entered into at an undervalue; and a person enters into such a transaction with another person if –

(a)   he makes a gift to the other person or he otherwise enters into a transaction with the other on terms that provide for him to receive no consideration;

(b)   he enters into a transaction with the other in consideration of marriage or the formation of a civil partnership; or

(c)   he enters into a transaction with the other for a consideration the value of which, in money or money's worth, is significantly less than the value, in money or money's worth, of the consideration provided by himself.

(2) Where a person has entered into such a transaction, the court may, if satisfied under the next subsection, make such order as it thinks fit for –

(a)   restoring the position to what it would have been if the transaction had not been entered into, and

(b)   protecting the interests of persons who are victims of the transaction.

(3) In the case of a person entering into such a transaction, an order shall only be made if the court is satisfied that it was entered into by him for the purpose –

(a)   of putting assets beyond the reach of a person who is making, or may at some time make, a claim against him, or

(b)   of otherwise prejudicing the interests of such a person in relation to the claim which he is making or may make.

(4) In this section 'the court' means the High Court or –

(a)   if the person entering into the transaction is an individual, any other court which would have jurisdiction in relation to a bankruptcy petition relating to him;

(b)   if that person is a body capable of being wound up under Part IV or V of this Act, any other court having jurisdiction to wind it up.

(5) In relation to a transaction at an undervalue, references here and below to a victim of the transaction are to a person who is, or is capable of being, prejudiced by it; and in the following two sections the person entering into the transaction is referred to as 'the debtor'.

Amendments—Civil Partnership Act 2004, s 261(1), Sch 27, para 121.

424 Those who may apply for an order under s 423

(1) An application for an order under section 423 shall not be made in relation to a transaction except –

(a) in a case where the debtor has been adjudged bankrupt or is a body corporate which is being wound up or is in administration, by the official receiver, by the trustee of the bankrupt's estate or the liquidator or administrator of the body corporate or (with the leave of the court) by a victim of the transaction;

(b) in a case where a victim of the transaction is bound by a voluntary arrangement approved under Part I or Part VIII of this Act, by the supervisor of the voluntary arrangement or by any person who (whether or not so bound) is such a victim; or

(c) in any other case, by a victim of the transaction.

(2) An application made under any of the paragraphs of subsection (1) is to be treated as made on behalf of every victim of the transaction.

Amendments—Enterprise Act 2002, s 248(3), Sch 17, paras 9, 36.

425 Provision which may be made by order under s 423

(1) Without prejudice to the generality of section 423, an order made under that section with respect to a transaction may (subject as follows) –

(a) require any property transferred as part of the transaction to be vested in any person, either absolutely or for the benefit of all the persons on whose behalf the application for the order is treated as made;

(b) require any property to be so vested if it represents, in any person's hands, the application either of the proceeds of sale of property so transferred or of money so transferred;

(c) release or discharge (in whole or in part) any security given by the debtor;

(d) require any person to pay to any other person in respect of benefits received from the debtor such sums as the court may direct;

(e) provide for any surety or guarantor whose obligations to any person were released or discharged (in whole or in part) under the transaction to be under such new or revived obligations as the court thinks appropriate;

(f) provide for security to be provided for the discharge of any obligation imposed by or arising under the order, for such an obligation to be charged on any property and for such security or charge to have the same priority as a security or charge released or discharged (in whole or in part) under the transaction.

(2) An order under section 423 may affect the property of, or impose any obligation on, any person whether or not he is the person with whom the debtor entered into the transaction; but such an order –

(a) shall not prejudice any interest in property which was acquired from a person other than the debtor and was acquired in good faith, for value and without notice of the relevant circumstances, or prejudice any interest deriving from such an interest, and

(b)   shall not require a person who received a benefit from the transaction in good faith, for value and without notice of the relevant circumstances to pay any sum unless he was a party to the transaction.

(3) For the purposes of this section the relevant circumstances in relation to a transaction are the circumstances by virtue of which an order under section 423 may be made in respect of the transaction.

(4) In this section 'security' means any mortgage, charge, lien or other security.

****

435 Meaning of 'associate'

(1) For the purposes of this Act any question whether a person is an associate of another person is to be determined in accordance with the following provisions of this section (any provision that a person is an associate of another person being taken to mean that they are associates of each other).

(2) A person is an associate of an individual if that person is –

(a)   the individual's husband or wife or civil partner,
(b)   a relative of –
    (i)   the individual, or
    (ii)   the individual's husband or wife or civil partner, or
(c)   the husband or wife or civil partner of a relative of –
    (i)   the individual, or
    (ii)   the individual's husband or wife or civil partner.

(3) A person is an associate of any person with whom he is in partnership, and of the husband or wife or civil partner or a relative of any individual with whom he is in partnership; and a Scottish firm is an associate of any person who is a member of the firm.

(4) A person is an associate of any person whom he employs or by whom he is employed.

(5) A person in his capacity as trustee of a trust other than –

(a)   a trust arising under any of the second Group of Parts or the Bankruptcy (Scotland) Act 1985, or
(b)   a pension scheme or an employees' share scheme,

is an associate of another person if the beneficiaries of the trust include, or the terms of the trust confer a power that may be exercised for the benefit of, that other person or an associate of that other person.

(6) A company is an associate of another company –

(a)   if the same person has control of both, or a person has control of one and persons who are his associates, or he and persons who are his associates, have control of the other, or

(b)   if a group of two or more persons has control of each company, and the groups either consist of the same persons or could be regarded as consisting of the same persons by treating (in one or more cases) a member of either group as replaced by a person of whom he is an associate.

(7) A company is an associate of another person if that person has control of it or if that person and persons who are his associates together have control of it.

(8) For the purposes of this section a person is a relative of an individual if he is that individual's brother, sister, uncle, aunt, nephew, niece, lineal ancestor or lineal descendant, treating –

(a)   any relationship of the half blood as a relationship of the whole blood and the stepchild or adopted child of any person as his child, and
(b)   an illegitimate child as the legitimate child of his mother and reputed father;

and references in this section to a husband or wife include a former husband or wife and a reputed husband or wife and references to a civil partner include a former civil partner and a reputed civil partner.

(9) For the purposes of this section any director or other officer of a company is to be treated as employed by that company.

(10) For the purposes of this section a person is to be taken as having control of a company if –

(a)   the directors of the company or of another company which has control of it (or any of them) are accustomed to act in accordance with his directions or instructions, or
(b)   he is entitled to exercise, or control the exercise of, one third or more of the voting power at any general meeting of the company or of another company which has control of it;

and where two or more persons together satisfy either of the above conditions, they are to be taken as having control of the company.

(11) In this section 'company' includes any body corporate (whether incorporated in Great Britain or elsewhere); and references to directors and other officers of a company and to voting power at any general meeting of a company have effect with any necessary modifications.

Amendments—Civil Partnership Act 2004, s 261(1), Sch 27, para 122; SI 2005/3129; SI 2009/1941.

436 Expressions used generally

(1) In this Act, except in so far as the context otherwise requires (and subject to Parts VII and XI) –

'the appointed day' means the day on which this Act comes into force under section 443;
'associate' has the meaning given by section 435;

'body corporate' includes a body incorporated outside Great Britain, but does not include –

(a)   a corporation sole, or

(b)   a partnership that, whether or not a legal person, is not regarded as a body corporate under the law by which it is governed;

'business' includes a trade or profession;

(repealed)' the Companies Act' means the Companies Act (as defined in section 2 of the Companies Act 2006) as they have effect in Great Britain;

'conditional sale agreement' and 'hire-purchase agreement' have the same meanings as in the Consumer Credit Act 1974;

'the EC Regulation' means Council Regulation (EC) No 1346/2000;

'EEA State' means a state that is a Contracting Party to the Agreement on the European Economic Area signed at Oporto on 2nd May 1992 as adjusted by the Protocol signed at Brussels on 17th March 1993;

'employees' share scheme' means a scheme for encouraging or facilitating the holding of shares in or debentures of a company by or for the benefit of –

(a) the bona fide employees or former employees of –

(i)   the company,

(ii)   any subsidiary of the company, or

(iii)   the company's holding company or any subsidiary of the company's holding company, or

(b) the spouses, civil partners, surviving spouses, surviving civil partners, or minor children or step-children of such employees or former employees;

'modifications' includes additions, alterations and omissions and cognate expressions shall be construed accordingly;

'property' includes money, goods, things in action, land and every description of property wherever situated and also obligations and every description of interest, whether present or future or vested or contingent, arising out of, or incidental to, property;

'records' includes computer records and other non-documentary records;

'subordinate legislation' has the same meaning as in the Interpretation Act 1978; and

'transaction' includes a gift, agreement or arrangement, and references to entering into a transaction shall be construed accordingly.

(2) The following expressions have the same meaning in this Act as in the Companies Acts –

'articles', in relation to a company (see section 18 of the Companies Act 2006);

'debenture' (see section 738 of that Act);

'holding company' (see sections 1159 and 1160 of, and Schedule 6 to, that Act);

'the Joint Stock Companies Acts' (see section 1171 of that Act);

'overseas company' (see section 1044 of that Act);

'paid up' (see section 583 of that Act);

'private company' and 'public company' (see section 4 of that Act);

'registrar of companies' (see section 1060 of that Act);

'share' (see section 540 of that Act);
'subsidiary' (see sections 1159 and 1160 of, and Schedule 6 to, that Act).

Amendments—SI 2002/1037; SI 2005/879; SI 2007/2194; SI 2009/1941.

****

MATRIMONIAL CAUSES ACT 1973

****

39 Settlement etc made in compliance with a property adjustment order may be avoided on bankruptcy of settlor

The fact that a settlement or transfer of property had to be made in order to comply with a property adjustment order shall not prevent that settlement or transfer from being a transaction in respect of which an order may be made under section 339 or 340 of the Insolvency Act 1986 (transfers at an undervalue and preferences).

Amendments—Insolvency Act 1986, s 235(1), Sch 8, para 23, s 439(2), Sch 14.

****

Appendix 5

INSOLVENCY RULES 1986

SI 1986/1925

ARRANGEMENT OF SECTIONS

PART 5

INDIVIDUAL VOLUNTARY ARRANGEMENTS

Chapter 1

Preliminary

****

PART 5
INDIVIDUAL VOLUNTARY ARRANGEMENTS

Chapter 1
Preliminary

5.1 Introductory

(1) The Rules in this Part apply in relation to a voluntary arrangement under Part VIII of the Act, except in relation to voluntary arrangements under section 263A, in relation to which only Chapters 7, 10, 11 and 12 of this Part shall apply.

(2) In this Part, in respect of voluntary arrangements other than voluntary arrangements under section 263A –

    (a)   Chapter 2 applies in all cases;
    (b)   Chapter 3 applies in cases where an application for an interim order is made;
    (c)   Chapter 4 applies in cases where no application for an interim order is or is to be made;
    (d)   except where otherwise stated, Chapters 5 and 6 apply in all cases;

(e)   Chapter 8 applies where a bankrupt makes an application under section 261(2)(a); and
(f)   Chapter 9 applies where the official receiver makes an application under section 261(2)(b).

(3) In this Part, in respect of voluntary arrangements under section 263A –

(a)   Chapter 7 applies in all cases; and
(b)   Chapter 10 applies where the official receiver makes an application under section 263D(3).

(4) In this Part, Chapters 11 and 12 apply in all cases.

Amendments—SI 2002/2712; SI 2003/1730.

Chapter 2
Preparation of the Debtor's Proposal

5.2 Preparation of proposal

The debtor shall prepare for the intended nominee a proposal on which (with or without amendments to be made under Rule 5.3(3) below) to make his report to the court under section 256 or section 256A.

Amendments—SI 2002/2712.

5.3 Contents of proposal

(1) The debtor's proposal shall provide a short explanation why, in his opinion, a voluntary arrangement under Part VIII is desirable, and give reasons why his creditors may be expected to concur with such an arrangement.

(2) The following matters shall be stated, or otherwise dealt with, in the proposal –

(a)   the following matters, so far as within the debtor's immediate knowledge –
   (i)   his assets, with an estimate of their respective values,
   (ii)   the extent (if any) to which the assets are charged in favour of creditors,
   (iii) the extent (if any) to which particular assets are to be excluded from the voluntary arrangement;
(b)   particulars of any property, other than assets of the debtor himself, which is proposed to be included in the arrangement, the source of such property and the terms on which it is to be made available for inclusion;
(c)   the nature and amount of the debtor's liabilities (so far as within his immediate knowledge), the manner in which they are proposed to be met, modified, postponed or otherwise dealt with by means of the arrangement and (in particular) –
   (i)   how it is proposed to deal with preferential creditors (defined in section 258(7)) and creditors who are, or claim to be, secured,

(ii) how associates of the debtor (being creditors of his) are proposed to be treated under the arrangement, and

(iii) in any case where the debtor is an undischarged bankrupt, whether, to the debtor's knowledge, claims have been made under section 339 (transactions at an undervalue), section 340 (preferences) or section 343 (extortionate credit transactions), or where the debtor is not an undischarged bankrupt, whether there are circumstances which would give rise to the possibility of such claims in the event that he should be adjudged bankrupt,

and, where any such circumstances are present, whether, and if so how, it is proposed under the voluntary arrangement to make provision for wholly or partly indemnifying the insolvent estate in respect of such claims;

(d) whether any, and if so what, guarantees have been given of the debtor's debts by other persons, specifying which (if any) of the guarantors are associates of his;

(e) the proposed duration of the voluntary arrangement;

(f) the proposed dates of distributions to creditors, with estimates of their amounts;

(g) how it is proposed to deal with the claims of any person who is bound by the arrangement by virtue of section 260(2)(b)(ii);

(h) the amount proposed to be paid to the nominee (as such) by way of remuneration and expenses;

(j) the manner in which it is proposed that the supervisor of the arrangement should be remunerated, and his expenses defrayed;

(k) whether, for the purposes of the arrangement, any guarantees are to be offered by any persons other than the debtor, and whether (if so) any security is to be given or sought;

(l) the manner in which funds held for the purposes of the arrangement are to be banked, invested or otherwise dealt with pending distribution to creditors;

(m) the manner in which funds held for the purpose of payment to creditors, and not so paid on the termination of the arrangement, are to be dealt with;

(n) if the debtor has any business, the manner in which it is proposed to be conducted during the course of the arrangement;

(o) details of any further credit facilities which it is intended to arrange for the debtor, and how the debts so arising are to be paid;

(p) the functions which are to be undertaken by the supervisor of the arrangement;

(q) the name, address and qualification of the person proposed as supervisor of the voluntary arrangement, and confirmation that he is, so far as the debtor is aware, qualified to act as an insolvency practitioner in relation to him or is an authorised person in relation to him; and

(r) whether the EC Regulation will apply and, if so, whether the proceedings will be main proceedings or territorial proceedings.

(3) With the agreement in writing of the nominee, the debtor's proposal may be amended at any time up to the delivery of the former's report to the court under section 256 or section 256A.

Amendments—SI 2002/2712.

5.4 Notice to the intended nominee

(1) The debtor shall give to the intended nominee written notice of his proposal.

(2) The notice, accompanied by a copy of the proposal, shall be delivered either to the nominee himself, or to a person authorised to take delivery of documents on his behalf.

(3) If the intended nominee agrees to act, he shall cause a copy of the notice to be endorsed to the effect that it has been received by him on a specified date.

(4) The copy of the notice so endorsed shall be returned by the nominee as soon as reasonably practicable to the debtor at an address specified by him in the notice for that purpose.

(5) Where the debtor is an undischarged bankrupt and he gives notice of his proposal to the official receiver and (if any) the trustee, the notice must contain the name and address of the insolvency practitioner or (as the case may be) authorised person who has agreed to act as nominee.

Amendments—SI 2002/2712; SI 2009/642.

5.5 Statement of Affairs

(1) Subject to paragraph (2), the debtor shall, within 7 days after his proposal is delivered to the nominee, or such longer time as the latter may allow, deliver to the nominee a statement of his (the debtor's) affairs.

(2) Paragraph (1) shall not apply where the debtor is an undischarged bankrupt and he has already delivered a statement of affairs under section 272 (debtor's petition) or 288 (creditor's petition) but the nominee may require the debtor to submit a further statement supplementing or amplifying the statement of affairs already submitted.

(3) The statement of affairs shall comprise the following particulars (supplementing or amplifying, so far as is necessary for clarifying the state of the debtor's affairs, those already given in his proposal) –

(a)   a list of his assets, divided into such categories as are appropriate for easy identification, with estimated values assigned to each category;

(b)   in the case of any property on which a claim against the debtor is wholly or partly secured, particulars of the claim and its amount, and of how and when the security was created;

(c)   the names and addresses of the debtor's preferential creditors (defined in section 258(7)), with the amounts of their respective claims;

(d)   the names and addresses of the debtor's unsecured creditors, with the amounts of their respective claims;

(e)   particulars of any debts owed by or to the debtor to or by persons who are associates of his;

(f)   such other particulars (if any) as the nominee may in writing require to be furnished for the purposes of making his report to the court on the debtor's proposal.

(4) The statement of affairs shall be made up to a date not earlier than 2 weeks before the date of the notice to the nominee under Rule 5.4.

However, the nominee may allow an extension of that period to the nearest practicable date (not earlier than 2 months before the date of the notice under Rule 5.4); and if he does so, he shall give his reasons in his report to the court on the debtor's proposal.

(5) The statement shall be certified by the debtor as correct, to the best of his knowledge and belief.

Amendments—SI 2002/2712.

5.6 Additional disclosure for assistance of nominee

(1) If it appears to the nominee that he cannot properly prepare his report on the basis of information in the debtor's proposal and statement of affairs, he may call on the debtor to provide him with –

(a)   further and better particulars as to the circumstances in which, and the reasons why, he is insolvent or (as the case may be) threatened with insolvency;

(b)   particulars of any previous proposals which have been made by him under Part VIII of the Act;

(c)   any further information with respect to his affairs which the nominee thinks necessary for the purposes of his report.

(2) The nominee may call on the debtor to inform him whether and in what circumstances he has at any time –

(a)   been concerned in the affairs of any company (whether or not incorporated in England and Wales) which has become insolvent, or

(b)   been adjudged bankrupt, or entered into an arrangement with his creditors.

(3) For the purpose of enabling the nominee to consider the debtor's proposal and prepare his report on it, the latter must give him access to his accounts and records.

Amendments—SI 2002/2712.

Chapter 3
Cases in which an Application for an Interim Order is made

5.7 Application for interim order

(1) An application to the court for an interim order under Part VIII of the Act shall be accompanied by an affidavit of the following matters –

(a)   the reasons for making the application;

(b)   particulars of any execution or other legal process or levying of any distress which, to the debtor's knowledge, has been commenced against him;

(c)   that he is an undischarged bankrupt or (as the case may be) that he is able to petition for his own bankruptcy;

(d)   that no previous application for an interim order has been made by or in respect of the debtor in the period of 12 months ending with the date of the affidavit;

(e)   that the nominee under the proposal (naming him) is willing to act in relation to the proposal and is a person who is either qualified to act as an insolvency practitioner in relation to the debtor or is authorised to act as nominee in relation to him; and

(f)   that the debtor has not submitted to the official receiver either the document referred to at section 263B(1)(a) or the statement referred to at section 263B(1)(b).

(2) A copy of the notice to the intended nominee under Rule 5.4, endorsed to the effect that he agrees so to act, and a copy of the debtor's proposal given to the nominee under that Rule, shall be exhibited to the affidavit.

(3) On receiving the application and affidavit, the court shall fix a venue for the hearing of the application.

(4) The applicant shall give at least 2 days' notice of the hearing –

(a)   where the debtor is an undischarged bankrupt, to the bankrupt, the official receiver and the trustee (whichever of those three is not himself the applicant),

(b)   where the debtor is not an undischarged bankrupt, to any creditor who (to the debtor's knowledge) has presented a bankruptcy petition against him, and

(c)   in either case, to the nominee who has agreed to act in relation to the debtor's proposal.

Amendments—SI 2002/2712; SI 2003/1730.

5.8 Court in which application to be made

(1) Except in the case of an undischarged bankrupt, an application to the court under Part VIII of the Act shall be made to a court in which the debtor would be entitled to present his own petition in bankruptcy under Rule 6.40.

(2) The application shall contain sufficient information to establish that it is brought in the appropriate court.

(3) In the case of an undischarged bankrupt, such an application shall be made to the court having the conduct of his bankruptcy and shall be filed with the bankruptcy proceedings.

Amendments—SI 2002/2712.

5.9 Hearing of the application

(1) Any of the persons who have been given notice under Rule 5.7(4) may appear or be represented at the hearing of the application.

(2) The court, in deciding whether to make an interim order on the application, shall take into account any representations made by or on behalf of any of those persons (in particular, whether an order should be made containing such provision as is referred to in section 255(3) and (4)).

(3) If the court makes an interim order, it shall fix a venue for consideration of the nominee's report. Subject to the following paragraph, the date for that consideration shall be not later than that on which the interim order ceases to have effect under section 255(6).

(4) If under section 256(4) an extension of time is granted for filing the nominee's report, the court shall, unless there appear to be good reasons against it, correspondingly extend the period for which the interim order has effect.

Amendments—SI 2002/2712.

5.10 Action to follow making of order

(1) Where an interim order is made, at least 2 sealed copies of the order shall be sent by the court to the person who applied for it; and that person shall serve one of the copies on the nominee under the debtor's proposal.

(2) The applicant shall also as soon as reasonably practicable give notice of the making of the order to any person who was given notice of the hearing pursuant to Rule 5.7(4) and was not present or represented at it.

Amendments—SI 2002/2712; SI 2009/642.

5.11 Nominee's report on the proposal

(1) Where the nominee makes his report to the court under section 256, he shall deliver 2 copies of it to the court not less than 2 days before the interim order ceases to have effect.

(2) With his report the nominee shall deliver –

    (a)   a copy of the debtor's proposal (with amendments, if any, authorised under Rule 5.3(3)); and

    (b)   a copy or summary of any statement of affairs provided by the debtor.

(3) If the nominee makes known his opinion that the debtor's proposal has a reasonable prospect of being approved and implemented, and that a meeting of the debtor's creditors should be summoned under section 257, his report shall have annexed to it his comments on the debtor's proposal.

If his opinion is otherwise, he shall give his reasons for that opinion.

(4) The court shall upon receipt of the report cause one copy of the report to be endorsed with the date of its filing in court and returned to the nominee.

(5) Any creditor of the debtor is entitled, at all reasonable times on any business day, to inspect the file.

(6) Where the debtor is an undischarged bankrupt, the nominee shall send to the official receiver and (if any) the trustee –

    (a)   a copy of the debtor's proposal,

    (b)   a copy of his (the nominee's) report and his comments accompanying it (if any), and

    (c)   a copy or summary of the debtor's statement of affairs.

(7) Where the debtor is not an undischarged bankrupt, the nominee shall send a copy of each of the documents referred to in paragraph (6) to any person who has presented a bankruptcy petition against the debtor.

Amendments—SI 2002/2712.

5.12 Replacement of nominee

(1) Where the debtor intends to apply to the court under section 256(3) for the nominee to be replaced, he shall give to the nominee at least 7 days' notice of his application.

(2) No appointment of a replacement nominee shall be made by the court unless there is filed in court a statement by the replacement nominee indicating his consent to act.

Amendments—SI 2002/2712.

5.13 Consideration of nominee's report

(1) At the hearing by the court to consider the nominee's report, any of the persons who have been given notice under Rule 5.7(4) may appear or be represented.

(2) Rule 5.10 applies to any order made by the court at the hearing.

Amendments—SI 2002/2712.

Chapter 4
Cases where no Interim Order is to be Obtained

5.14 Nominee's report to the court

(1) The nominee shall deliver 2 copies of his report to the court (as defined in Rule 5.15) under section 256A within 14 days (or such longer period as the court may allow) after receiving from the debtor the document and statement mentioned in section 256A(2) but the court shall not consider the report unless an application is made under the Act or these Rules in relation to the debtor's proposal.

(2) With his report the nominee shall deliver –

    (a)   a copy of the debtor's proposal (with amendments, if any, authorised under Rule 5.3(3));

   (b)   a copy or summary of any statement of affairs provided by the debtor; and

   (c)   a copy of the notice referred to in Rule 5.4(3),

together with 2 copies of Form 5.5 listing the documents referred to in (a) to (c) above and containing a statement that no application for an interim order under section 252 is to be made.

(3) If the nominee makes known his opinion that the debtor's proposal has a reasonable prospect of being approved and implemented, and that a meeting of the debtor's creditors should be summoned under section 257, his report shall have annexed to it his comments on the debtor's proposal.

If his opinion is otherwise, he shall give his reasons for that opinion.

(4) The court shall upon receipt of the report and Form 5.5 cause one copy of the form to be endorsed with the date of its filing in court and returned to the nominee.

(5) Any creditor of the debtor is entitled, at all reasonable times on any business day, to inspect the file.

(6) Where the debtor is an undischarged bankrupt, the nominee shall send to the official receiver and (if any) the trustee –

   (a)   a copy of the debtor's proposal,

   (b)   a copy of his (the nominee's) report and his comments accompanying it (if any), and

   (c)   a copy or summary of the debtor's statement of affairs.

(7) Where the debtor is not an undischarged bankrupt, the nominee shall send a copy of each of the documents referred to in paragraph (6) to any person who has presented a bankruptcy petition against the debtor.

(8) The filing in court of the report under section 256A shall constitute an insolvency proceeding for the purpose of Rule 7.27 and Rule 7.30.

Amendments—SI 2002/2712.

5.15 Filing of reports made under section 256A – appropriate court

(1) Except where the debtor is an undischarged bankrupt, the court in which the nominee's report under section 256A is to be filed is the court in which the debtor would be entitled to present his own petition in bankruptcy under Rule 6.40.

(2) The report shall contain sufficient information to establish that it is filed in the appropriate court.

(3) Where the debtor is an undischarged bankrupt, such report shall be filed in the court having the conduct of his bankruptcy and shall be filed with the bankruptcy proceedings.

Amendments—SI 2002/2712.

5.16 Applications to the court

(1) Any application to court in relation to any matter relating to a voluntary arrangement or a proposal for a voluntary arrangement shall be made in the court in which the nominee's report was filed.

(2) Where the debtor intends to apply to the court under section 256A(4)(a) or (b) for the nominee to be replaced, he shall give to the nominee at least 7 days' notice of the application.

(3) Where the nominee intends to apply to the court under section 256A(4)(b) for his replacement as nominee, he shall give to the debtor at least 7 days' notice of the application.

(4) No appointment of a replacement nominee shall be made by the court unless there is filed in court a statement by the replacement nominee indicating his consent to act.

Amendments—SI 2002/2712.

Chapter 5
Creditors' Meetings

5.17 Summoning of creditors' meeting

(1) If in his report the nominee states that in his opinion a meeting of creditors should be summoned to consider the debtor's proposal, the date on which the meeting is to be held shall be –

- (a) in a case where an interim order has not been obtained, not less than 14 days and not more than 28 days from that on which the nominee's report is filed in court under Rule 5.14; and
- (b) in a case where an interim order is in force, not less than 14 days from the date on which the nominee's report is filed in court nor more than 28 days from that on which the report is considered by the court.

(2) Notices calling the meeting shall be sent by the nominee, at least 14 days before the day fixed for it to be held, to all the creditors specified in the debtor's statement of affairs, and any other creditors of whom the nominee is otherwise aware.(3) Each notice sent under this Rule shall specify the court to which the nominee's report on the debtor's proposal has been delivered and shall state the effect of Rule 5.23(1), (3) and (4) (requisite majorities); and with it there shall be sent –

- (a) a copy of the proposal,
- (b) a copy of the statement of affairs or, if the nominee thinks fit, a summary of it (the summary to include a list of the creditors and the amounts of their debts), and
- (c) the nominee's comments on the proposal.

Amendments—SI 2002/2712.

5.18 Creditors' meeting: supplementary

(1) Subject as follows, in fixing the venue for the creditors' meeting, the nominee shall have regard to the convenience of creditors.

(2) The meeting shall be summoned for commencement between 10.00 and 16.00 hours on a business day.

(3) With every notice summoning the meeting there shall be sent out forms of proxy.

Amendments—SI 2002/2712.

5.19 The chairman at the meeting

(1) Subject as follows, the nominee shall be chairman of the creditors' meeting.

(2) If for any reason the nominee is unable to attend, he may nominate another person to act as chairman in his place; but a person so nominated must be –

- (a) a person qualified to act as an insolvency practitioner in relation to the debtor;
- (b) an authorised person in relation to the debtor; or
- (c) an employee of the nominee or his firm who is experienced in insolvency matters.

Amendments—SI 2002/2712.

5.20 The chairman as proxy-holder

The chairman shall not by virtue of any proxy held by him vote to increase or reduce the amount of the remuneration or expenses of the nominee or the supervisor of the proposed arrangement, unless the proxy specifically directs him to vote in that way.

Amendments—SI 2002/2712.

5.21 Entitlement to vote

(1) Subject as follows, every creditor who has notice of the creditors' meeting is entitled to vote at the meeting or any adjournment of it.

(2) A creditor's entitlement to vote is calculated as follows –

- (a) where the debtor is not an undischarged bankrupt and an interim order is in force, by reference to the amount of the debt owed to him as at the date of the interim order;
- (b) where the debtor is not an undischarged bankrupt and an interim order is not in force, by reference to the amount of the debt owed to him at the date of the meeting; and
- (c) where the debtor is an undischarged bankrupt, by reference to the amount of the debt owed to him as at the date of the bankruptcy order.

(3) A creditor may vote in respect of a debt for an unliquidated amount or any debt whose value is not ascertained, and for the purposes of voting (but not otherwise) his debt shall be valued at £1 unless the chairman agrees to put a higher value on it.

Amendments—SI 2002/2712.

5.22 Procedure for admission of creditors' claims for voting purposes

(1) Subject as follows, at the creditors' meeting the chairman shall ascertain the entitlement of persons wishing to vote and shall admit or reject their claims accordingly.

(2) The chairman may admit or reject a claim in whole or in part.

(3) The chairman's decision on any matter under this Rule or under paragraph (3) of Rule 5.21 is subject to appeal to the court by any creditor or by the debtor.

(4) If the chairman is in doubt whether a claim should be admitted or rejected, he shall mark it as objected to and allow votes to be cast in respect of it, subject to such votes being subsequently declared invalid if the objection to the claim is sustained.

(5) If on an appeal the chairman's decision is reversed or varied, or votes are declared invalid, the court may order another meeting to be summoned, or make such order as it thinks just.

The court's power to make an order under this paragraph is exercisable only if it considers that the circumstances giving rise to the appeal are such as give rise to unfair prejudice or material irregularity.

(6) An application to the court by way of appeal against the chairman's decision shall not be made after the end of the period of 28 days beginning with the first day on which the report required by section 259 is made to the court.

(7) The chairman is not personally liable for any costs incurred by any person in respect of an appeal under this Rule.

Amendments—SI 2002/2712.

5.23 Requisite majorities

(1) Subject as follows, at the creditors' meeting for any resolution to pass approving any proposal or modification there must be a majority in excess of three-quarters in value of the creditors present in person or by proxy and voting on the resolution.

(2) The same applies in respect of any other resolution proposed at the meeting, but substituting one-half for three-quarters.

(3) In the following cases there is to be left out of account a creditor's vote in respect of any claim or part of a claim –

(a) where written notice of the claim was not given, either at the meeting or before it, to the chairman or the nominee;

(b) where the claim or part is secured;

(c) where the claim is in respect of a debt wholly or partly on, or secured by, a current bill of exchange or promissory note, unless the creditor is willing –

    (i) to treat the liability to him on the bill or note of every person who is liable on it antecedently to the debtor, and against whom a bankruptcy order has not been made (or, in the case of a company, which has not gone into liquidation), as a security in his hands, and

    (ii) to estimate the value of the security and (for the purpose of entitlement to vote, but not of any distribution under the arrangement) to deduct it from his claim.

(4) Any resolution is invalid if those voting against it include more than half in value of the creditors, counting in these latter only those –

(a) who have notice of the meeting;

(b) whose votes are not to be left out of account under paragraph (3); and

(c) who are not, to the best of the chairman's belief, associates of the debtor.

(5) It is for the chairman of the meeting to decide whether under this Rule –

(a) a vote is to be left out of account in accordance with the paragraph (3), or

(b) a person is an associate of the debtor for the purposes of paragraph (4)(c);

and in relation to the second of these cases the chairman is entitled to rely on the information provided by the debtor's statement of affairs or otherwise in accordance with this Part of the Rules.

(6) If the chairman uses a proxy contrary to Rule 5.20, his vote with that proxy does not count towards any majority under this Rule.

(7) The chairman's decision on any matter under this Rule is subject to appeal to the court by any creditor or by the debtor and paragraphs (5) to (7) of Rule 5.22 apply as regards such an appeal.

Amendments—SI 2002/2712.

5.24 Proceedings to obtain agreement on the proposal

(1) On the day on which the creditors' meeting is held, it may from time to time be adjourned.

(2) If on that day the requisite majority for the approval of the voluntary arrangement (with or without modifications) has not been obtained, the chairman may, and shall if it is so resolved, adjourn the meeting for not more than 14 days.

(3) If there are subsequently further adjournments, the final adjournment shall not be to a day later than 14 days after that on which the meeting was originally held.

(4) If the meeting is adjourned under paragraph (2), notice of the fact shall be given by the chairman as soon as reasonably practicable to the court.

(5) If following any final adjournment of the meeting the proposal (with or without modifications) is not agreed to, it is deemed rejected.

Amendments—SI 2002/2712; SI 2009/642.

Chapter 6
Implementation of the Arrangement

5.25 Resolutions to follow approval

(1) If the voluntary arrangement is approved (with or without modifications), a resolution may be taken by the creditors, where two or more individuals are appointed to act as supervisor, on the question whether acts to be done in connection with the arrangement may be done by any one of them, or must be done by both or all.

(2) If at the creditors' meeting a resolution is moved for the appointment of some person other than the nominee to be supervisor of the arrangement, there must be produced to the chairman, at or before the meeting –

    (a)   that person's written consent to act (unless he is present and then and there signifies his consent), and

    (b)   his written confirmation that he is qualified to act as an insolvency practitioner in relation to the debtor or is an authorised person in relation to the debtor.

Amendments—SI 2002/2712.

5.26 Hand-over of property, etc to supervisor

(1) As soon as reasonably practicable after the approval of the voluntary arrangement, the debtor or, where the debtor is an undischarged bankrupt, the official receiver or the debtor's trustee, shall do all that is required for putting the supervisor into possession of the assets included in the arrangement.

(2) On taking possession of the assets in any case where the debtor is an undischarged bankrupt, the supervisor shall discharge any balance due to the official receiver and (if other) the trustee by way of remuneration or on account of –

    (a)   fees, costs, charges and expenses properly incurred and payable under the Act or the Rules, and

    (b)   any advances made in respect of the insolvent estate, together with interest on such advances at the rate specified in section 17 of the Judgments Act 1838 at the date of the bankruptcy order.

(3) Alternatively where the debtor is an undischarged bankrupt, the supervisor must, before taking possession, give the official receiver or the trustee a written undertaking to discharge any such balance out of the first realisation of assets.

(4) Where the debtor is an undischarged bankrupt, the official receiver and (if other) the trustee has a charge on the assets included in the voluntary arrangement in respect of any sums due as above until they have been discharged, subject only to the deduction from realisations by the supervisor of the proper costs and expenses of realisation.

Any sums due to the official receiver take priority over those due to a trustee.

(5) The supervisor shall from time to time out of the realisation of assets discharge all guarantees properly given by the official receiver or the trustee for the benefit of the estate, and shall pay all their expenses.

Amendments—SI 2002/2712; SI 2009/642.

5.27 Report of creditors' meeting

(1) A report of the creditors' meeting shall be prepared by the chairman of the meeting.

(2) The report shall –

    (a)   state whether the proposal for a voluntary arrangement was approved or rejected and, if approved, with what (if any) modifications;

    (b)   set out the resolutions which were taken at the meeting, and the decision on each one;

    (c)   list the creditors (with their respective values) who were present or represented at the meeting, and how they voted on each resolution;

    (d)   whether in the opinion of the supervisor,

        (i)   the EC Regulation applies to the voluntary arrangement, and

        (ii)   if so, whether the proceedings are main proceedings or territorial proceedings; and

    (e)   include such further information (if any) as the chairman thinks it appropriate to make known to the court.

(3) A copy of the chairman's report shall, within 4 days of the meeting being held, be filed in court; and the court shall cause that copy to be endorsed with the date of filing.

(4) The persons to whom notice of the result is to be given, under section 259(1), are all those who were sent notice of the meeting under this Part of the Rules and any other creditor of whom the chairman is aware, and where the debtor is an undischarged bankrupt, the official receiver and (if any) the trustee.

The notice shall be sent immediately after a copy of the chairman's report is filed in court under paragraph (3).

(5) In a case where no interim order has been obtained the court shall not consider the chairman's report unless an application is made to the court under the Act or the Rules in relation to it.

Amendments—SI 2002/2712.

****

5.29 Reports to Secretary of State

(1) Immediately after the chairman of the creditors' meeting has filed in court a report that the meeting has approved the voluntary arrangement, he shall report to the Secretary of State the following details of the arrangement –

    (a)   the name and address of the debtor;
    (b)   the date on which the arrangement was approved by the creditors;
    (c)   the name and address of the supervisor; and
    (d)   the court in which the chairman's report has been filed.

(2) A person who is appointed to act as supervisor of an individual voluntary arrangement (whether in the first instance or by way of replacement of another person previously appointed) shall as soon as reasonably practicable give written notice to the Secretary of State of his appointment.

If he vacates office as supervisor, he shall as soon as reasonably practicable give written notice of that fact also to the Secretary of State.

Amendments—SI 2002/2712; SI 2009/642.

5.30 Revocation or suspension of the arrangement

(1) This Rule applies where the court makes an order of revocation or suspension under section 262.

(2) The person who applied for the order shall serve sealed copies of it –

    (a)   in a case where the debtor is an undischarged bankrupt, on the debtor, the official receiver and the trustee;
    (b)   in any other case, on the debtor; and
    (c)   in either case, on the supervisor of the voluntary arrangement.

(3) If the order includes a direction by the court under section 262(4)(b) for any further creditors' meeting to be summoned, notice shall also be given (by the person who applied for the order) to whoever is, in accordance with the direction, required to summon the meeting.

(4) The debtor or (where the debtor is an undischarged bankrupt) the trustee or (if there is no trustee) the official receiver shall –

    (a)   as soon as reasonably practicable after receiving a copy of the court's order, give notice of it to all persons who were sent notice of the creditors' meeting which approved the voluntary arrangement or who, not having been sent that notice, are affected by the order;
    (b)   within 7 days of their receiving a copy of the order (or within such longer period as the court may allow), give notice to the court whether it is intended to make a revised proposal to creditors, or to invite reconsideration of the original proposal.

(5) The person on whose application the order of revocation or suspension was made shall, within 7 days after the making of the order, give written notice of it to the Secretary of State and shall, in the case of an order of suspension, within 7 days of the expiry of any suspension order, given written notice of such expiry to the Secretary of State.

Amendments—SI 2002/2712; SI 2009/642.

5.31 Supervisor's accounts and reports

(1) Where the voluntary arrangement authorises or requires the supervisor –

(a)   to carry on the debtor's business or to trade on his behalf or in his name, or

(b)   to realise assets of the debtor or (in a case where the debtor is an undischarged bankrupt) belonging to the estate, or

(c)   otherwise to administer or dispose of any funds of the debtor or the estate,

he shall keep accounts and records of his acts and dealings in and in connection with the arrangement, including in particular records of all receipts and payments of money.

(2) The supervisor shall, not less often than once in every 12 months beginning with the date of his appointment, prepare an abstract of such receipts and payments, and send copies of it, accompanied by his comments on the progress and efficacy of the arrangement, to –

(a)   the court,

(b)   the debtor, and

(c)   all those of the debtor's creditors who are bound by the arrangement.

If in any period of 12 months he has made no payments and had no receipts, he shall at the end of that period send a statement to that effect to all who are specified in sub-paragraphs (a) to (c) above.

(3) An abstract provided under paragraph (2) shall relate to a period beginning with the date of the supervisor's appointment or (as the case may be) the day following the end of the last period for which an abstract was prepared under this Rule; and copies of the abstract shall be sent out, as required by paragraph (2), within the 2 months following the end of the period to which the abstract relates.

(4) If the supervisor is not authorised as mentioned in paragraph (1), he shall, not less often than once in every 12 months beginning with the date of his appointment, send to all those specified in paragraph 2(a) to (c) a report on the progress and efficacy of the voluntary arrangement.

(5) The court may, on application by the supervisor, vary the dates on which the obligation to send abstracts or reports arises.

Amendments—SI 2002/2712.

5.32 Production of accounts and records to Secretary of State

(1) The Secretary of State may at any time during the course of the voluntary arrangement or after its completion require the supervisor to produce for inspection –

(a)   his records and accounts in respect of the arrangement, and
(b)   copies of abstracts and reports prepared in compliance with Rule 5.31.

(2) The Secretary of State may require production either at the premises of the supervisor or elsewhere; and it is the duty of the supervisor to comply with any requirement imposed on him under this Rule.

(3) The Secretary of State may cause any accounts and records produced to him under this Rule to be audited; and the supervisor shall give to the Secretary of State such further information and assistance as he needs for the purposes of his audit.

Amendments—SI 2002/2712.

5.33 Fees, costs, charges and expenses

The fees, costs, charges and expenses that may be incurred for any purposes of the voluntary arrangement are –

(a)   any disbursements made by the nominee prior to the approval of the arrangement, and any remuneration for his services as such agreed between himself and the debtor, the official receiver or the trustee;
(b)   any fees, costs, charges or expenses which –
    (i)   are sanctioned by the terms of the arrangement, or
    (ii)   would be payable, or correspond to those which would be payable, in the debtor's bankruptcy.

Amendments—SI 2002/2712.

5.34 Completion or termination of the arrangement

(1) Not more than 28 days after the final completion or termination of the voluntary arrangement, the supervisor shall send to all creditors of the debtor who are bound by the arrangement, and to the debtor, a notice that the arrangement has been fully implemented or (as the case may be) terminated.

(2) With the notice there shall be sent to each of those persons a copy of a report by the supervisor summarising all receipts and payments made by him in pursuance of the arrangement, and explaining any difference in the actual implementation of it as compared with the proposal as approved by the creditors' meeting or (in the case of termination of the arrangement) explaining the reasons why the arrangement has not been implemented in accordance with the proposal as approved by the creditors' meeting.

(3) The supervisor shall, within the 28 days mentioned above, send to the Secretary of State and to the court a copy of the notice under paragraph (1), together with a copy of the report under paragraph (2), and he shall not vacate office until after such copies have been sent.

(4) The court may, on application by the supervisor, extend the period of 28 days under paragraphs (1) and (3).

Amendments—SI 2002/2712.

****

PART 6
BANKRUPTCY

Chapter 1
The Statutory Demand

6.1 Form and content of statutory demand

(1) A statutory demand under section 268 must be dated, and be signed either by the creditor himself or by a person stating himself to be authorised to make the demand on the creditor's behalf.

(2) The statutory demand must specify whether it is made under section 268(1) (debt payable immediately) or section 268(2) (debt not so payable).

(3) The demand must state the amount of the debt, and the consideration for it (or, if there is no consideration, the way in which it arises) and –

  (a)   if made under section 268(1) and founded on a judgment or order of a court, it must give details of the judgment or order, and
  (b)   if made under section 268(2), it must state the grounds on which it is alleged that the debtor appears to have no reasonable prospect of paying the debt.

(4) If the amount claimed in the demand includes –

  (a)   any charge by way of interest not previously notified to the debtor as a liability of his, or
  (b)   any other charge accruing from time to time,

the amount or rate of the charge must be separately identified, and the grounds on which payment of it is claimed must be stated.

In either case the amount claimed must be limited to that which has accrued due at the date of the demand.

(5) If the creditor holds any security in respect of the debt, the full amount of the debt shall be specified, but –

  (a)   there shall in the demand be specified the nature of the security, and the value which the creditor puts upon it as at the date of the demand, and
  (b)   the amount of which payment is claimed by the demand shall be the full amount of the debt, less the amount specified as the value of the security.

6.2 Information to be given in statutory demand

(1) The statutory demand must include an explanation to the debtor of the following matters –

(a)   the purpose of the demand, and the fact that, if the debtor does not comply with the demand, bankruptcy proceedings may be commenced against him;

(b)   the time within which the demand must be complied with, if that consequence is to be avoided;

(c)   the methods of compliance which are open to the debtor; and

(d)   his right to apply to the court for the statutory demand to be set aside.

(2) The demand must specify one or more named individuals with whom the debtor may, if he wishes, enter into communication with a view to securing or compounding for the debt to the satisfaction of the creditor or (as the case may be) establishing to the creditor's satisfaction that there is a reasonable prospect that the debt will be paid when it falls due.

In the case of any individual so named in the demand, his address and telephone number (if any) must be given.

6.3 Requirements as to service

(1) Rule 6.11 in Chapter 2 below has effect as regards service of the statutory demand, and proof of that service by affidavit to be filed with a bankruptcy petition.

(2) The creditor is, by virtue of the Rules, under an obligation to do all that is reasonable for the purpose of bringing the statutory demand to the debtor's attention and, if practicable in the particular circumstances, to cause personal service of the demand to be effected.

(3) Where the statutory demand is for payment of a sum due under a judgment or order of any court and the creditor knows, or believes with reasonable cause –

(a)   that the debtor has absconded or is keeping out of the way with a view to avoiding service, and

(b)   there is no real prospect of the sum due being recovered by execution or other process,

the creditor may advertise the demand in such manner as the creditor thinks fit; and the time limited for compliance with the demand runs from the date of the advertisement's appearance or (as the case may be) its first appearance.

Amendments—SI 2009/642.

6.4 Application to set aside statutory demand

(1) The debtor may, within the period allowed by this Rule, apply to the appropriate court for an order setting the statutory demand aside.

That period is 18 days from the date of the service on him of the statutory demand or, where the demand is advertised pursuant to Rule 6.3, from the date of the advertisement's appearance or (as the case may be) its first appearance.

(2) Where the creditor issuing the statutory demand is a Minister of the Crown or a Government Department, and –

    (a)   the debt in respect of which the demand is made, or a part of it equal to or exceeding the bankruptcy level (within the meaning of section 267), is the subject of a judgment or order of any court, and

    (b)   the statutory demand specifies the date of the judgment or order and the court in which it was obtained, but indicates the creditor's intention to present a bankruptcy petition against the debtor in the High Court,

the appropriate court under this Rule is the High Court; and in any other case it is that to which the debtor would, in accordance with paragraphs (1) and (2) of Rule 6.40 in Chapter 3 below, present his own bankruptcy petition.

(3) As from (inclusive) the date on which the application is filed in court, the time limited for compliance with the statutory demand ceases to run, subject to any order of the court under Rule 6.5(6).

(4) The debtor's application shall be supported by an affidavit –

    (a)   specifying the date on which the statutory demand came into his hands, and

    (b)   stating the grounds on which he claims that it should be set aside.

The affidavit shall have exhibited to it a copy of the statutory demand.

Amendments—SI 2009/642.

6.5 Hearing of application to set aside

(1) On receipt of an application under Rule 6.4, the court may, if satisfied that no sufficient cause is shown for it, dismiss it without giving notice to the creditor. As from (inclusive) the date on which the application is dismissed, the time limited for compliance with the statutory demand runs again.

(2) If the application is not dismissed under paragraph (1), the court shall fix a venue for it to be heard, and shall give at least 7 days' notice of it to –

    (a)   the debtor or, if the debtor's application was made by a solicitor acting for him, to the solicitor,

    (b)   the creditor, and

    (c)   whoever is named in the statutory demand as the person with whom the debtor may enter into communication with reference to the demand (or, if more than one person is so named, the first of them).

(3) On the hearing of the application, the court shall consider the evidence then available to it, and may either summarily determine the application or adjourn it, giving such directions as it thinks appropriate.

(4) The court may grant the application if –

(a)   the debtor appears to have a counterclaim, set-off or cross demand which equals or exceeds the amount of the debt or debts specified in the statutory demand; or

(b)   the debt is disputed on grounds which appear to the court to be substantial; or

(c)   it appears that the creditor holds some security in respect of the debt claimed by the demand, and either Rule 6.1(5) is not complied with in respect of it, or the court is satisfied that the value of the security equals or exceeds the full amount of the debt; or

(d)   the court is satisfied, on other grounds, that the demand ought to be set aside.

(5) Where the creditor holds some security in respect of his debt, and Rule 6.1(5) is complied with in respect of it but the court is satisfied that the security is under-valued in the statutory demand, the creditor may be required to amend the demand accordingly (but without prejudice to his right to present a bankruptcy petition by reference to the original demand).

(6) If the court dismisses the application, it shall make an order authorising the creditor to present a bankruptcy petition either as soon as reasonably practicable, or on or after a date specified in the order.

A copy of the order shall be sent by the court as soon as reasonably practicable to the creditor.

Amendments—SI 2009/642.

Chapter 2
Bankruptcy Petition (Creditor's)

6.6 Preliminary

The Rules in this Chapter relate to a creditor's petition, and the making of a bankruptcy order thereon; and in those Rules "the debt" means, except where the context otherwise requires, the debt (or debts) in respect of which the petition is presented.

Those Rules also apply to a petition under section 264(1)(c) (supervisor of, or person bound by, voluntary arrangement), with any necessary modifications.

6.7 Identification of debtor

(1) The petition shall state the following matters with respect to the debtor, so far as they are within the petitioner's knowledge –

(a)   his name, place of residence and occupation (if any);

(b)   the name or names in which he carries on business, if other than his true name, and whether, in the case of any business of a specified nature, he carries it on alone or with others;

(c)   the nature of his business, and the address or addresses at which he carries it on;

(d) any name or names, other than his true name, in which he has carried on business at or after the time when the debt was incurred, and whether he has done so alone or with others;

(e) any address or addresses at which he has resided or carried on business at or after that time, and the nature of that business;

(f) whether the debtor has his centre of main interests or an establishment in another member State.

(2) The particulars of the debtor given under this Rule determine the full title of the proceedings.

(3) If to the petitioner's personal knowledge the debtor has used any name other than the one specified under paragraph (1)(a), that fact shall be stated in the petition.

Amendments—SI 2002/1307.

6.8 Identification of debt

(1) There shall be stated in the petition, with reference to every debt in respect of which it is presented –

(a) the amount of the debt, the consideration for it (or, if there is no consideration, the way in which it arises) and the fact that it is owed to the petitioner;

(b) when the debt was incurred or became due;

(c) if the amount of the debt includes –

(i) any charge by way of interest not previously notified to the debtor as a liability of his, or

(ii) any other charge accruing from time to time,

the amount or rate of the charge (separately identified) and the grounds on which it is claimed to form part of the debt, provided that such amount or rate must, in the case of a petition based on a statutory demand, be limited to that claimed in that demand;

(d) either –

(i) that the debt is for a liquidated sum payable immediately, and the debtor appears to be unable to pay it, or

(ii) that the debt is for a liquidated sum payable at some certain, future time (that time to be specified), and the debtor appears to have no reasonable prospect of being able to pay it,

and, in either case (subject to section 269) that the debt is unsecured.

(2) Where the debt is one for which, under section 268, a statutory demand must have been served on the debtor –

(a) there shall be specified the date and manner of service of the statutory demand, and

(b) it shall be stated that, to the best of the creditor's knowledge and belief –

(i) the demand has been neither complied with nor set aside in accordance with the Rules, and

(ii) no application to set it aside is outstanding.

(3) If the case is within section 268(1)(b) (debt arising under judgment or order of court; execution returned unsatisfied), the court from which the execution or other process issued shall be specified, and particulars shall be given relating to the return.

Amendments—SI 1987/1919.

6.9 Court in which petition to be presented

(1) In the following cases, the petition shall be presented to the High Court –

    (a)   if the petition is presented by a Minister of the Crown or a Government Department, and either in any statutory demand on which the petition is based the creditor has indicated the intention to present a bankruptcy petition to that Court, or the petition is presented under section 268(1)(b), or

    (b)   if the debtor has resided or carried on business within the London insolvency district for the greater part of the 6 months immediately preceding the presentation of the petition, or for a longer period in those 6 months than in any other insolvency district, or

    (c)   if the debtor is not resident in England and Wales, or

    (d)   if the petitioner is unable to ascertain the residence of the debtor, or his place of business.

(2) In any other case the petition shall be presented to the county court for the insolvency district in which the debtor has resided or carried on business for the longest period during those 6 months.

(3) If the debtor has for the greater part of those 6 months carried on business in one insolvency district and resided in another, the petition shall be presented to the court for the insolvency district in which he has carried on business.

(4) If the debtor has during those 6 months carried on business in more than one insolvency district, the petition shall be presented to the court for the insolvency district in which is, or has been for the longest period in those 6 months, his principal place of business.

(4A) Notwithstanding any other provision of this Rule, where there is in force for the debtor a voluntary arrangement under Part VIII of the Act, the petition shall be presented to the court to which the nominee's report under section 256 or section 256A or 263C was submitted.

(5) The petition shall contain sufficient information to establish that it is brought in the appropriate court.

Amendments—SI 1987/1919; SI 2003/1730.

6.10 Procedure for presentation and filing

(1) The petition, verified by affidavit in accordance with Rule 6.12(1) below, shall be filed in court.

(2) No petition shall be filed unless there is produced on presentation of the petition a receipt for the deposit payable or paragraph (2A) applies.

(2A) This paragraph applies in any case where the Secretary of State has given written notice to the court that the petitioner has made suitable alternative arrangements for the payment of the deposit to the official receiver and such notice has not been revoked in relation to the petitioner in accordance with paragraph (2B).

(2B) A notice of the kind referred to in paragraph (2A) may be revoked in relation to the petitioner in whose favour it is given by a further notice in writing to the court stating that the earlier notice is revoked in relation to the petitioner.

(3) The following copies of the petition shall also be delivered to the court with the petition –

(a) one for service on the debtor,

(b) one to be exhibited to the affidavit verifying that service , and

(c) if there is in force for the debtor a voluntary arrangement under Part VIII of the Act, and the petitioner is not the supervisor of the arrangement, one copy for him.

Each of these copies shall have applied to it the seal of the court, and shall be issued to the petitioner.

(4) The date and time of filing the petition shall be endorsed on the petition and on any copy issued under paragraph (3).

(5) The court shall fix a venue for hearing the petition, and this also shall be endorsed on the petition and on any copy so issued.

(6) Where a petition contains a request for the appointment of a person as trustee in accordance with section 297(5) (appointment of former supervisor as trustee) the person whose appointment is sought shall, not less than 2 days before the day appointed for hearing the petition, file in court a report including particulars of –

(a) a date on which he gave written notification to creditors bound by the arrangement of the intention to seek his appointment as trustee, such date to be at least 10 days before the day on which the report under this paragraph is filed, and

(b) details of any response from creditors to that notice, including any objections to his appointment.

Amendments—SI 1987/1919; SI 2004/584.

6.11 Proof of service of statutory demand

(1) Where under section 268 the petition must have been preceded by a statutory demand, there must be filed in court, with the petition, an affidavit or affidavits proving service of the demand.

(2) Every affidavit must have exhibited to it a copy of the demand as served.

(3) Subject to the next paragraph, if the demand has been served personally on the debtor, the affidavit must be made by the person who effected that service.

(4) If service of the demand (however effected) has been acknowledged in writing either by the debtor himself, or by some person stating himself in the acknowledgement to be authorised to accept service on the debtor's behalf, the affidavit must be made either by the creditor or by a person acting on his behalf, and the acknowledgement of service must be exhibited to the affidavit.

(5) If neither paragraph (3) nor paragraph (4) applies, the affidavit or affidavits must be made by a person or persons having direct personal knowledge of the means adopted for serving the statutory demand, and must –

(a)   give particulars of the steps which have been taken with a view to serving the demand personally, and

(b)   state the means whereby (those steps having been ineffective) it was sought to bring the demand to the debtor's attention, and

(c)   specify a date by which, to the best of the knowledge, information and belief of the person making the affidavit, the demand will have come to the debtor's attention.

(6) The steps of which particulars are given for the purposes of paragraph (5)(a) must be such as would have sufficed to justify an order for substituted service of a petition.

(7) If the affidavit specifies a date for the purposes of compliance with paragraph (5)(c), then unless the court otherwise orders, that date is deemed for the purposes of the Rules to have been the date on which the statutory demand was served on the debtor.

(8) Where the creditor has taken advantage of Rule 6.3(3) (advertisement), the affidavit must be made either by the creditor himself or by a person having direct personal knowledge of the circumstances; and there must be specified in the affidavit –

(a)   the means of the creditor's knowledge or (as the case may be) belief required for the purposes of that Rule, and

(b)   the method by which, and the date or dates on which the statutory demand was advertised under that rule;

and there shall be exhibited to the affidavit either a copy of any advertisement of the statutory demand or, where this is not reasonably practicable, the affidavit shall contain or exhibit a description of the contents of any such advertisement of the statutory demand.

(9) The court may decline to file the petition if not satisfied that the creditor has discharged the obligation imposed on him by Rule 6.3(2).

Amendments—SI 1987/1919; SI 2009/642.

6.12 Verification of petition

(1) The petition shall be verified by an affidavit that the statements in the petition are true, or are true to the best of the deponent's knowledge, information and belief.

(2) If the petition is in respect of debts to different creditors, the debts to each creditor must be separately verified.

(3) The petition shall be exhibited to the affidavit verifying it.

(4) The affidavit shall be made –

(a) by the petitioner (or if there are two or more petitioners, any one of them), or

(b) by some person such as a director, company secretary or similar company officer, or a solicitor, who has been concerned in the matters giving rise to the presentation of the petition, or

(c) by some responsible person who is duly authorised to make the affidavit and has the requisite knowledge of those matters.

(5) Where the maker of the affidavit is not the petitioner himself, or one of the petitioners, he must in the affidavit identify himself and state –

(a) the capacity in which, and the authority by which, he makes it, and

(b) the means of his knowledge of the matters sworn to in the affidavit.

(6) The affidavit is prima facie evidence of the truth of the statements in the petition to which it relates.

(7) If the petition is based upon a statutory demand, and more than 4 months have elapsed between the service of the demand and the presentation of the petition, the affidavit must also state the reasons for the delay.

6.13 Notice to Chief Land Registrar

When the petition is filed, the court shall as soon as reasonably practicable send to the Chief Land Registrar notice of the petition together with a request that it may be registered in the register of pending actions.

Amendments—SI 2009/642.

6.14 Service of petition

(1) Subject as follows, the petition shall be served personally on the debtor by an officer of the court, or by the petitioning creditor or his solicitor, or by a person instructed by the creditor or his solicitor for that purpose; and service shall be effected by delivering to him a sealed copy of the petition.

(2) If the court is satisfied by affidavit or other evidence on oath that prompt personal service cannot be effected because the debtor is keeping out of the way to avoid service of the petition or other legal process, or for any other cause, it may order substituted service to be effected in such manner as it thinks fit.

(3) Where an order for substituted service has been carried out, the petition is deemed duly served on the debtor.

(4) If to the petitioner's knowledge there is in force for the debtor a voluntary arrangement under Part VIII of the Act, and the petitioner is not himself the supervisor of the arrangement, a copy of the petition shall be sent by him to the supervisor.

(5) If to the petitioner's knowledge, there is a member State liquidator appointed in main proceedings in relation to the bankrupt, a copy of the petition shall be sent by him to the member State liquidator.

Amendments—SI 1987/1919; SI 2002/1307.

6.15 Proof of service

(1) Service of the petition shall be proved by affidavit.

(2) The affidavit shall have exhibited to it –

   (a)   a sealed copy of the petition, and
   (b)   if substituted service has been ordered, a sealed copy of the order;

and it shall be filed in court immediately after service.

6.16 Death of debtor before service

If the debtor dies before service of the petition, the court may order service to be effected on his personal representatives, or on such other persons as it thinks fit.

6.17 Security for costs (s 268(2) only)

(1) This Rule applies where the debt in respect of which the petition is presented is for a liquidated sum payable at some future time, it being claimed in the petition that the debtor appears to have no reasonable prospect of being able to pay it.

(2) The petitioning creditor may, on the debtor's application, be ordered to give security for the debtor's costs.

(3) The nature and amount of the security to be ordered is in the court's discretion.

(4) If an order is made under this Rule, there shall be no hearing of the petition until the whole amount of the security has been given.

6.18 Hearing of petition

(1) Subject as follows, the petition shall not be heard until at least 14 days have elapsed since it was served on the debtor.

(2) The court may, on such terms as it thinks fit, hear the petition at an earlier date, if it appears that the debtor has absconded, or the court is satisfied that it is a proper case for an expedited hearing, or the debtor consents to a hearing within the 14 days.

(3) Any of the following may appear and be heard, that is to say, the petitioning creditor, the debtor , the supervisor of any voluntary arrangement under Part VIII of the Act in force for the debtor and any creditor who has given notice under Rule 6.23 below.

Amendments—SI 1987/1919.

6.20 Petition by moneylender

A petition in respect of a moneylending transaction made before 27th January 1980 of a creditor who at the time of the transaction was a licensed moneylender shall at the hearing of the petition be supported by an affidavit incorporating a statement setting out in detail the particulars mentioned in section 9(2) of the Moneylenders Act 1927.

6.21 Petition opposed by debtor

Where the debtor intends to oppose the petition, he shall not later than 7 days before the day fixed for the hearing –

(a)   file in court a notice specifying the grounds on which he will object to the making of a bankruptcy order, and

(b)   send a copy of the notice to the petitioning creditor or his solicitor.

6.22 Amendment of petition

With the leave of the court (given on such terms, if any, as the court thinks fit to impose), the petition may be amended at any time after presentation by the omission of any creditor or any debt.

6.23 Notice by persons intending to appear

(1) Every creditor who intends to appear on the hearing of the petition shall give to the petitioning creditor notice of his intention in accordance with this Rule.

(2) The notice shall specify –

(a)   the name and address of the person giving it, and any telephone number and reference which may be required for communication with him or with any other person (to be also specified in the notice) authorised to speak or act on his behalf;

(b)   whether his intention is to support or oppose the petition; and

(c)   the amount and nature of his debt.

(3) The notice shall be sent so as to reach the addressee not later than 16.00 hours on the business day before that which is appointed for the hearing (or, where the hearing has been adjourned, for the adjourned hearing).

(4) A person failing to comply with this Rule may appear on the hearing of the petition only with the leave of the court.

6.24 List of appearances

(1) The petitioning creditor shall prepare for the court a list of the creditors (if any) who have given notice under Rule 6.23, specifying their names and addresses and (if known to him) their respective solicitors.

(2) Against the name of each creditor in the list it shall be stated whether his intention is to support the petition, or to oppose it.

(3) On the day appointed for the hearing of the petition, a copy of the list shall be handed to the court before the commencement of the hearing.

(4) If any leave is given under Rule 6.23(4), the petitioner shall add to the list the same particulars in respect of the person to whom leave has been given.

6.25 Decision on the hearing

(1) On the hearing of the petition, the court may make a bankruptcy order if satisfied that the statements in the petition are true, and that the debt on which it is founded has not been paid, or secured or compounded for.

(2) If the petition is brought in respect of a judgment debt, or a sum ordered by any court to be paid, the court may stay or dismiss the petition on the ground that an appeal is pending from the judgment or order, or that execution of the judgment has been stayed.

(3) A petition preceded by a statutory demand shall not be dismissed on the ground only that the amount of the debt was over-stated in the demand, unless the debtor, within the time allowed for complying with the demand, gave notice to the creditor disputing the validity of the demand on that ground; but, in the absence of such notice, the debtor is deemed to have complied with the demand if he has, within the time allowed, paid the correct amount.

6.26 Non-appearance of creditor

If the petitioning creditor fails to appear on the hearing of the petition, no subsequent petition against the same debtor, either alone or jointly with any other person, shall be presented by the same creditor in respect of the same debt, without the leave of the court to which the previous petition was presented.

6.27 Vacating registration on dismissal of petition

If the petition is dismissed or withdrawn by leave of the court, an order shall be made at the same time permitting vacation of the registration of the petition as a pending action; and the court shall send to the debtor two sealed copies of the order.

6.28 Extension of time for hearing

(1) The petitioning creditor may, if the petition has not been served, apply to the court to appoint another venue for the hearing.

(2) The application shall state the reasons why the petition has not been served.

(3) No costs occasioned by the application shall be allowed in the proceedings except by order of the court.

(4) If the court appoints another day for the hearing, the petitioning creditor shall as soon as reasonably practicable notify any creditor who has given notice under Rule 6.23.

Amendments—SI 2009/642.

6.29 Adjournment

(1) If the court adjourns the hearing of the petition, the following applies.

(2) Unless the court otherwise directs, the petitioning creditor shall as soon as reasonably practicable send –

(a) to the debtor, and
(b) where any creditor has given notice under Rule 6.23 but was not present at the hearing, to him,

notice of the making of the order of adjournment. The notice shall state the venue for the adjourned hearing.

Amendments—SI 2009/642.

6.30 Substitution of petitioner

(1) This Rule applies where a creditor petitions and is subsequently found not entitled to do so, or where the petitioner –

(a) consents to withdraw his petition or to allow it to be dismissed, or consents to an adjournment, or fails to appear in support of his petition when it is called on in court on the day originally fixed for the hearing, or on a day to which it is adjourned, or
(b) appears, but does not apply for an order in the terms of the prayer of his petition.

(2) The court may, on such terms as it thinks just, order that there be substituted as petitioner any creditor who –

(a) has under Rule 6.23 given notice of his intention to appear at the hearing,
(b) is desirous of prosecuting the petition, and
(c) was, at the date on which the petition was presented, in such a position in relation to the debtor as would have enabled him (the creditor) on that date to present a bankruptcy petition in respect of a debt or debts owed to him by the debtor (or in the case of the member State liquidator, owed to creditors in proceedings in relation to which he holds office), paragraphs (a) to (d) of section 267(2) being satisfied in respect of that debt or those debts.

Amendments—SI 2002/1307.

6.31 Change of carriage of petition

(1) On the hearing of the petition, any person who claims to be a creditor of the debtor, and who has given notice under Rule 6.23 of his intention to appear at the hearing, may apply to the court for an order giving him carriage of the petition in place of the petitioning creditor, but without requiring any amendment of the petition.

(2) The court may, on such terms as it thinks just, make a change of carriage order if satisfied that –

(a)   the applicant is an unpaid and unsecured creditor of the debtor, and

(b)   the petitioning creditor either –

   (i)   intends by any means to secure the postponement, adjournment or withdrawal of the petition, or

   (ii)   does not intend to prosecute the petition, either diligently or at all.

(3) The court shall not make the order if satisfied that the petitioning creditor's debt has been paid, secured or compounded for by means of –

(a)   a disposition of property made by some person other than the debtor, or

(b)   a disposition of the debtor's own property made with the approval of, or ratified by, the court.

(4) A change of carriage order may be made whether or not the petitioning creditor appears at the hearing.

(5) If the order is made, the person given the carriage of the petition is entitled to rely on all evidence previously adduced in the proceedings (whether by affidavit or otherwise).

6.32 Petitioner seeking dismissal or leave to withdraw

(1) Where the petitioner applies to the court for the petition to be dismissed, or for leave to withdraw it, he must, unless the court otherwise orders, file in court an affidavit specifying the grounds of the application and the circumstances in which it is made.

(2) If, since the petition was filed, any payment has been made to the petitioner by way of settlement (in whole or in part) of the debt or debts in respect of which the petition was brought, or any arrangement has been entered into for securing or compounding it or them, the affidavit must state –

(a)   what dispositions of property have been made for the purposes of the settlement or arrangement, and

(b)   whether, in the case of any disposition, it was property of the debtor himself, or of some other person, and

(c)   whether, if it was property of the debtor, the disposition was made with the approval of, or has been ratified by, the court (if so, specifying the relevant court order).

(3) No order giving leave to withdraw a petition shall be given before the petition is heard.

****

Chapter 3
Bankruptcy Petition (Debtor's)

6.37 Preliminary

The Rules in this Chapter relate to a debtor's petition, and the making of a bankruptcy order thereon.

6.38 Identification of debtor

(1) The petition shall state the following matters with respect to the debtor –

(a) his name, place of residence and occupation (if any);

(b) the name or names in which he carries on business, if other than his true name, and whether, in the case of any business of a specified nature, he carries it on alone or with others;

(c) the nature of his business, and the address or addresses at which he carries it on;

(d) any name or names, other than his true name, in which he has carried on business in the period in which any of his bankruptcy debts were incurred and, in the case of any such business, whether he has carried it on alone or with others; and

(e) any address or addresses at which he has resided or carried on business during that period, and the nature of that business.

(2) The particulars of the debtor given under this Rule determine the full title of the proceedings.

(3) If the debtor has at any time used a name other than the one given under paragraph (1)(a), that fact shall be stated in the petition.

6.39 Admission of insolvency

(1) The petition shall contain the statement that the petitioner is unable to pay his debts, and a request that a bankruptcy order be made against him.

(2) If within the period of 5 years ending with the date of the petition the petitioner has been adjudged bankrupt, or has made a composition with his creditors in satisfaction of his debts or a scheme of arrangement of his affairs, or he has entered into any voluntary arrangement or been subject to an administration order under Part VI of the County Courts Act 1984, particulars of these matters shall be given in the petition.

(3) If there is at the date of the petition in force for the debtor a voluntary arrangement under Part VIII of the Act, the particulars required by paragraph (2) above shall contain a statement to that effect and the name and address of the supervisor of the arrangement.

Amendments—SI 1987/1919.

6.40 Court in which petition to be filed

(1) In the following cases, the petition shall be presented to the High Court –

(a) if the debtor has resided or carried on business in the London insolvency district for the greater part of the 6 months immediately preceding the presentation of the petition, or for a longer period in those 6 months than in any other insolvency district, or

(b) if the debtor is not resident in England and Wales.

(2) In any other case, the petition shall (subject to paragraph (3) below), be presented to the debtor's own county court, which is –

(a)   the county court for the insolvency district in which he has resided or carried on business for the longest period in those 6 months, or

(b)   if he has for the greater part of those 6 months carried on business in one insolvency district and resided in another, the county court for that in which he has carried on business, or

(c)   if he has during those 6 months carried on business in more than one insolvency district, the county court for that in which is, or has been for the longest period in those 6 months, his principal place of business.

(3) If, in a case not falling within paragraph (1), it is more expedient for the debtor with a view to expediting his petition –

(a)   it may in any case be presented to whichever court is specified by Schedule 2 to the Rules as being, in relation to the debtor's own court, the nearest full-time court, and

(b)   it may alternatively, in a case falling within paragraph (2)(b), be presented to the court for the insolvency district in which he has resided for the greater part of the 6 months there referred to.

(3A) Notwithstanding any other provision of this Rule, where there is in force for the debtor a voluntary arrangement under Part VIII of the Act the petition shall be presented to the court to which the nominee's report under section 256 or section 256A or 263C was submitted.

(4) The petition shall contain sufficient information to establish that it is brought in the appropriate court.

Amendments—SI 1987/1919; SI 2003/1730.

6.41 Statement of affairs

(1) The petition shall be accompanied by a statement of the debtor's affairs, verified by affidavit.

(2) Section B of Chapter 5 below applies with respect to the statement of affairs.

6.42 Procedure for presentation and filing

(1) The petition and the statement of affairs shall be filed in court, together with three copies of the petition, and one copy of the statement. No petition shall be filed unless there is produced with it the receipt for the deposit payable on presentation.

(2) Subject to paragraph (2A), the court may hear the petition as soon as reasonably practicable. If it does not do so, it shall fix a venue for the hearing.

(2A) If the petition contains particulars of a voluntary arrangement under Part VIII of the Act in force for the debtor, the court shall fix a venue for the hearing and give at least 14 days' notice of it to the supervisor of the arrangement; the supervisor may appear and be heard on the petition.

(3) Of the three copies of the petition delivered –

(a)   one shall be returned to the petitioner, endorsed with any venue fixed;

(b)   another, so endorsed, shall be sent by the court to the official receiver; and

(c)   the remaining copy shall be retained by the court, to be sent to an insolvency practitioner (if appointed under section 273(2)).

(4) The copy of the statement of affairs shall be sent by the court to the official receiver.

(5) The affidavit verifying the debtor's statement of affairs may be sworn before an officer of the court duly authorised in that behalf.

(6) Where the court hears a petition as soon as reasonably practicable, or it will in the opinion of the court otherwise expedite the delivery of any document to the official receiver, the court may, instead of sending that document to the official receiver, direct the bankrupt as soon as reasonably practicable to deliver it to him.

(7) Where a petition contains a request for the appointment of a person as trustee in accordance with section 297(5) (appointment of former supervisor as trustee) the person whose appointment is sought shall, not less than 2 days before the day appointed for hearing the petition, file in court a report including particulars of –

(a)   a date on which he gave written notification to creditors bound by the arrangement of the intention to seek his appointment as trustee, such date to be at least 10 days before the day on which the report under this paragraph is filed, and

(b)   details of any response from creditors to that notice, including any objections to his appointment.

Amendments—SI 1987/1919; SI 2005/527; SI 2009/642.

6.43 Notice to Chief Land Registrar

When the petition is filed, the court shall as soon as reasonably practicable send to the Chief Land Registrar notice of the petition, for registration in the register of pending actions.

Amendments—SI 2009/642.

****

6.96 Meaning of 'prove'

(1) A person claiming to be a creditor of the bankrupt and wishing to recover his debt in whole or in part must (subject to any order of the court under Rule 6.93(2)) submit his claim in writing to the official receiver, where acting as receiver and manager, or to the trustee.

(2) The creditor is referred to as 'proving' for his debt; and the document by which he seeks to establish his claim is his 'proof'.

(3) Subject to the next two paragraphs, the proof must be in the form known as 'proof of debt' (whether the form prescribed by the Rules, or a substantially similar form), which shall be made out by or under the directions of the creditor, and signed by him or a person authorised in that behalf.

(4) Where a debt is due to a Minister of the Crown or a Government Department, the proof need not be in that form, provided that there are shown all such particulars of the debt as are required in the form used by other creditors, and as are relevant in the circumstances.

(5) Where an existing trustee proves in a later bankruptcy under section 335(5), the proof must be in Form 6.38.

(6) In certain circumstances, specified below in this Chapter, the proof must be in the form of an affidavit.

****

6.98 Contents of proof

(1) Subject to Rule 6.96(4), the following matters shall be stated in a creditor's proof of debt –

    (a)   the creditor's name and address, and, if a company, its company registration number;

    (b)   the total amount of his claim (including any Value Added Tax) as at the date of the bankruptcy order;

    (c)   whether or not that amount includes outstanding uncapitalised interest;

    (d)   particulars of how and when the debt was incurred by the debtor;

    (e)   particulars of any security held, the date when it was given and the value which the creditor puts upon it

    (f)   details of any reservation of title in respect of goods to which the debt refers; and

    (g)   the name, and address and authority of the person signing the proof (if other than the creditor himself).

(2) There shall be specified in the proof any documents by reference to which the debt can be substantiated; but (subject as follows) it is not essential that such documents be attached to the proof or submitted with it.

(3) The trustee, the official receiver, acting as receiver and manager or the convener or chairman of any meeting, may call for any document or other evidence to be produced to him, where he thinks it necessary for the purpose of substantiating the whole or any part of the claim made in the proof.

Amendments—SI 2004/584; SI 2004/1070.

****

6.109 Secured creditors

(1) If a secured creditor realises his security, he may prove for the balance of his debt, after deducting the amount realised.

(2) If a secured creditor voluntarily surrenders his security for the general benefit of creditors, he may prove for his whole debt, as if it were unsecured.

****

Chapter 9
Secured Creditors

6.115 Value of security

(1) A secured creditor may, with the agreement of the trustee or the leave of the court, at any time alter the value which he has, in his proof of debt, put upon his security.

(2) However, if a secured creditor –

    (a)   being the petitioner, has in the petition put a value on his security, or
    (b)   has voted in respect of the unsecured balance of his debt,

he may re-value his security only with leave of the court.

****

Chapter 15
Replacement of Exempt Property

6.188 Money provided in lieu of sale

(1) The following applies where a third party proposes to the trustee that he (the former) should provide the estate with a sum of money enabling the bankrupt to be left in possession of property which would otherwise be made to vest in the trustee under section 308.

(2) The trustee may accept that proposal, if satisfied that it is a reasonable one, and that the estate will benefit to the extent of the value of the property in question less the cost of a reasonable replacement.

Chapter 16
Income Payments Orders

6.189 Application for order

(1) Where the trustee applies for an income payments order under section 310, the court shall fix a venue for the hearing of the application.

(2) Notice of the application, and of the venue, shall be sent by the trustee to the bankrupt at least 28 days before the day fixed for the hearing, together with a copy of the trustee's application and a short statement of the grounds on which it is made.

(3) The notice shall inform the bankrupt that –

    (a)   unless at least 7 days before the date fixed for the hearing he sends to the court and to the trustee written consent to an order being made in the terms of the application, he is required to attend the hearing, and

(b) if he attends, he will be given an opportunity to show cause why the order should not be made, or an order should be made otherwise than as applied for by the trustee.

****

Chapter 19
After-Acquired Property

6.200 Duties of bankrupt in respect of after-acquired property

(1) The notice to be given by the bankrupt to the trustee, under section 333(2), of property acquired by, or devolving upon, him, or of any increase of his income, shall be given within 21 days of his becoming aware of the relevant facts.

(2) Having served notice in respect of property acquired by or devolving upon him, the bankrupt shall not, without the trustee's consent in writing, dispose of it within the period of 42 days beginning with the date of the notice.

(3) If the bankrupt disposes of property before giving the notice required by this Rule or in contravention of paragraph (2), it is the duty as soon as reasonably practicable to disclose to the trustee the name and address of the disponee, and to provide any other information which may be necessary to enable the trustee to trace the property and recover it for the estate.

(4) Subject as follows, paragraphs (1) to (3) do not apply to property acquired by the bankrupt in the ordinary course of a business carried on by him.

(5) If the bankrupt carries on a business, he shall, not less often than 6-monthly, furnish to the trustee information with respect to it, showing the total of goods bought and sold (or, as the case may be, services supplied) and the profit or loss arising from the business.

The trustee may require the bankrupt to furnish fuller details (including accounts) of the business carried on by him.

Amendments—SI 2009/642.

****

6.220 Certificate of discharge

(1) Where it appears to the court that a bankrupt is discharged, whether by expiration of time or otherwise, the court shall, on his application, issue to him a certificate of his discharge, and the date from which it is effective.

(2) The discharged bankrupt may require the Secretary of State to give notice of the discharge. As soon as reasonably practicable such notice shall be –

(a) gazetted; and
(b) advertised in such manner as the bankruptcy order to which it relates was advertised.

(3) Any requirement by the former bankrupt under paragraph (2) shall be addressed to the Secretary of State in writing. The Secretary of State shall notify him as soon as reasonably practicable as to the cost of the advertisement, and is under no obligation to advertise until that sum has been paid.

(4) Where the former bankrupt has died, or is a person incapable of managing his affairs (within the meaning of Chapter 7 in Part 7 of the Rules), the references to him in paragraphs (2) and (3) are to be read as referring to his personal representative or, as the case may be, a person appointed by the court to represent or act for him.

Amendments—SI 2009/642.

****

PART 12
MISCELLANEOUS AND GENERAL

12.3 Provable debts

(1) Subject as follows, in administration, winding up and bankruptcy, all claims by creditors are provable as debts against the company or, as the case may be, the bankrupt, whether they are present or future, certain or contingent, ascertained or sounding only in damages.

(2) The following are not provable –

    (a)   in bankruptcy, any fine imposed for an offence, and any obligation (other than an obligation to pay a lump sum or to pay costs) arising under an order made in family proceedings or any obligation arising under a maintenance assessment made under the Child Support Act 1991;

    (b)   in administration, winding up or bankruptcy, any obligation arising under a confiscation order made under section 1 of the Drug Trafficking Offences Act 1986 or section 1 of the Criminal Justice (Scotland) Act 1987 or section 71 of the Criminal Justice Act 1988 or under Parts 2, 3 or 4 of the Proceeds of Crime Act 2002.

'Fine' and 'family proceedings' have the meanings given by section 281(8) of the Act (which applies the Magistrates' Courts Act 1980 and the Matrimonial and Family Proceedings Act 1984).

(2A) The following are not provable except at a time when all other claims of creditors in the insolvency proceedings (other than any of a kind mentioned in this paragraph) have been paid in full with interest under section 189(2), Rule 2.88 or, as the case may be, section 328(4) –

    (a)   in an administration, a winding up or a bankruptcy, any claim arising by virtue of section 382(1)(a) of the Financial Services and Markets Act 2000, not being a claim also arising by virtue of section 382(1)(b) of that Act;

    (c)   in an administration or a winding up, any claim which by virtue of the Act or any other enactment is a claim the payment of which in a bankruptcy, an administration or a winding up is to be postponed.

(3) Nothing in this Rule prejudices any enactment or rule of law under which a particular kind of debt is not provable, whether on grounds of public policy or otherwise.

Amendments—SI 1987/1919; SI 1989/397; SI 1993/602; SI 2001/3649; SI 2003/1730; SI 2005/527.

Appendix 6

INSOLVENCY SERVICE OFFICES

Birmingham

4th Floor
Cannon House
18 Priory Queensway
Birmingham B4 6FD
DX 713901 Birmingham 37DX
Tel: 0121 698 4000

Blackpool

Seneca House
Links Point
Amy Johnson Way
Blackpool
Lancashire FY4 2FF
DX 719794 Blackpool 4
Tel: 01253 830700

Bournemouth

3rd Floor
Richmond House
Richmond Hill
Bournemouth BH2 6EZ
DX 149540 Bournemouth 22
Tel: 01202 203900

Brighton

69 Middle Street
Brighton BN1 1BE
DX 36687 Brighton 2DX
Tel: 01273 861300

Bristol

First Floor
Tower Wharf
Cheese Lane
Bristol BS2 0JJ
DX200557 Bristol (Temple Meads)
Tel: 0117 9279515

Cambridge

2nd Floor
Abbeygate House
164-167 East Road
Cambridge CB1 1DB
DX 742320, Cambridge 17DX
Tel: 01223 324480

Canterbury

1st and 2nd Floor
Marlowe House
Chaucer Business Park
Thanet Way
Whitstable
Kent CT5 3FE
DX 154300, Whitstable 3
Tel: 01227 284350

Cardiff

3rd Floor
Companies House
Crown Way
Cardiff CF14 3ZA
DX33052 Cardiff 1DX
Tel: 029 2038 1300

Chester

Suite 5
Third Floor
Windsor House
Pepper Street
Chester CH1 1DF
DX 20025 Chester 14DX
Tel: 01244 402750

Croydon

6th Floor
Sunley House
Bedford Park
Croydon CR9 1TX
DX 154520 Croydon 38
Tel: 020 86815166

Exeter

3rd Floor
Senate Court
Southernhay Gardens
Exeter EX1 1UG
DX 8356 Exeter 1DX
Tel: 01392 889 650

Gloucester

1st Floor
Southgate House
Southgate Street
Gloucester GL1 1UB
DX 98662 Gloucester 5
Tel: 01452 338000

Hull

Suite J
Anchor House
The Maltings
Silvester Street
Hull HU1 3HA
DX 724660 Hull 17
Tel: 01482 323729

Ipswich

8th Floor
St Clare House
Princes Street
Ipswich IP1 1LX
DX 3242 Ipswich 1 DX
Tel: 01473 217565

Leeds

3rd Floor
1 City Walk
Leeds LS11 9DA
DX 14079, Leeds Park Square DX
Tel: 0113 200 6000

Leicester

4th Floor
Wellington House
Wellington Street
Leicester LE1 6HL
DX 10813 Leicester DX
Tel: 0116 2795800

Liverpool

2nd Floor
Cunard Building
Pier Head
Liverpool L3 1DS
DX 715712 Liverpool 14DX
Tel: 0151 236 9131

London

5th Floor
Zone B
21 Bloomsbury Street
London WC1B 3SS
DX 120875 Bloomsbury 6DX
Tel: 020 7637 1110

Manchester

2nd Floor
3 Piccadilly Place
London Road
Manchester M1 3BN
DX 744150 Manchester 70
Tel: 0161 234 8500

Medway

1st Floor
Prince Regent House
Quayside
Chatham Maritime
Kent ME4 4QZ
DX 131395 Rochester 2
Tel: 01634 895700

National Dividend Unit

1st Floor
Sunley House
Bedford Park
Croydon CR9 1TX
DX 154521 Croydon 38
Tel: 020 8667 8044

Newcastle upon Tyne

1st Floor
Melbourne House
Pandon Bank
Newcastle upon Tyne NE1 2JQ
DX 61095 Newcastle-upon-Tyne DX
Tel: 0191 260 4600

Northampton

SOL House
1st Floor
29 St Katherine's Street
Northampton NN1 2QZ
DX 702888 Northampton 7DX
Tel: 01604 542400

Norwich

Emmanuel House
2 Convent Road
Norwich NR2 1PA
DX 133137 Norwich 12DX
Tel: 01603 628983

Nottingham

4th Floor
The Frontage
Queen Street
Nottingham NG1 2BL
DX 15487 Nottingham 2
Tel: 0115 852 5000

Plymouth

1st Floor
Cobourg House
Mayflower Street
Plymouth PL1 1DJ
DX 8239 Plymouth 1DX
Tel: 01752 635200

Public Interest Unit (London)

Room 206
21 Bloomsbury Street
London WC1B 3SS
DX 120875 Bloomsbury 6DX
Tel: 020 7637 1110

Public Interest Unit (Manchester)

2nd Floor
3 Piccadilly Place
London Road
Manchester M1 3BN
DX 744150 Manchester 70
Tel: 0161 234 8531

Reading

3D Apex Plaza
Forbury Road
Reading RG1 1AX
DX 117881 Reading (Apex Plaza)
Tel: 0118 958 1931

Sheffield

5th Floor
City Plaza South
Pinfold Street, Sheffield S1 2GU
DX 714500, Sheffield DX
Tel: 0114 221 2700

Southampton

Suite A
Waterside House
Town Quay
Southampton SO14 2AQ
DX154660 Southampton 50
Tel: 023 8083 1600

Southend

4th Floor
Central House
8 Clifftown Road
Southend on Sea SS1 1AB
DX 97783 Southend-on-Sea 2 DX
Tel: 01702 602570

St Albans

1st Floor
Trident House
42-48 Victoria Street
St Albans AL1 3HR
DX 6150 St Albans 1 DX
Tel: 01727 832233

Stockton

2nd Floor
St Marks House
St Marks Court
Teesdale
Thornaby
Stockton-on-Tees TS17 6QT
DX 723014 Stockton-on-Tees 10
Tel: 01642 617720

Stoke-on-Trent

Ground Floor
Copthall House King Street
Newcastle under Lyme ST5 1UE
DX 20992 Newcastle under Lyme DX
Tel: 01782 664100

Swansea

Unit 6
Langdon House
Langdon Road
Swansea Waterfront
Swansea SA1 8QY
DX 744282 Swansea 23
Tel: 01792 642861

INDEX

References are to paragraph numbers.